MW00424736

21 DEBATED

Issues in American Politics

EDITORS

Gregory M. Scott
Loren Gatch

University of Central Oklahoma

Prentice Hall, Upper Saddle River, New Jersey 07458

Library of Congress Cataloging-in-Publication Data

21 debated : issues in American politics / Gregory M. Scott, Loren Gatch, editors.
  p. cm.
  Includes bibliographical references.
  ISBN 0–13–021991–6
    1. Political planning—United States. 2. United States—Politics and government—1993–
  I. Title: Twenty-one debated. II. Scott, Gregory M. III. Gatch, Loren.

JK468.P64 A155 2000
320′.6′0973—dc21

99–050138

Editorial Director: *Charlyce Jones Owens*
Editor in Chief: *Nancy Roberts*
Senior Acquisitions Editor: *Beth Gillett Mejia*
Editorial Assistant: *Brian Prybella*
Managing Editor: *Ann Marie McCarthy*
Production Liaison: *Fran Russello*
Project Manager: *Marianne Hutchinson (Pine Tree Composition)*
Prepress and Manufacturing Buyer: *Ben Smith*
Cover Director: *Jayne Conte*
Cover Illustration: Two-Sided Head, Paul J. Fisch/Stock Illustration Source, Inc.
Marketing Manager: *Christopher DeJohn*

The book was set in 10/12 Trump Medieval by Pine Tree Composition
and was printed and bound by Courier Companies, Inc.
The cover was printed by Phoenix Color Corp.

© 2000 by Prentice-Hall, Inc.
Upper Saddle River, New Jersey 07458

All rights reserved. No part of this book may be
reproduced, in any form or by any means,
without permission in writing from the publisher.

Printed in the United States of America

10 9 8 7 6 5 4 3 2 1

ISBN 0-13-021991-6

Prentice-Hall International (UK) Limited, *London*
Prentice-Hall of Australia Pty, Limited, *Sydney*
Prentice-Hall Canada Inc., *Toronto*
Prentice-Hall Hispanoamericana, S.A., *Mexico*
Prentice-Hall of India Private Limited, *New Delhi*
Prentice-Hall of Japan, Inc., *Tokyo*
Pearson Education Asia Pte. Ltd., *Singapore*
Editora Prentice-Hall do Brasil, Ltda., *Rio de Janeiro*

Contents

Introduction

If you are reading this preface, you are probably a college student taking a course in American politics. You may already know a good deal about politics in America, or you may not have paid too much attention thus far. In either case, this book can be more than just a course requirement. Many important issues are currently shaping America's future, and, as today's citizen and perhaps tomorrow's leader, you will have a role in determining how these issues are resolved in your community. In order to grasp the importance of some of these issues, imagine what would happen if the following headlines should appear in the years to come:

- January 1, 2110: "Last Republican Dies at Age 95; Survives Last Living Democrat by Ten Days"
- February 10, 2045: "FBI Reports All Firearms Now in Hands of the Federal Government"
- March 13, 2015: "Court Reverses *Roe:* Alabama Applies Death Penalty to Abortion Providers"
- April 17, 2020 "Xiang Xio Wan, Black Chinese-American, Elected President"
- May 1, 2066: "New Constitutional Convention Rewrites Constitution; Right to Private Property Eliminated"
- June 3, 2025: "President Leno Removed from Office for Sexual Harassment"

Perhaps these headlines are preposterous, and the events they suggest are beyond possibility. You may want to consider, however, that groups of citizens are actively using the democratic process with the goal of bringing these hypothetical events about. Whether or not these headlines appear in the future is up to you and your fellow citizens. In an increasingly information-driven age, those who are informed will determine the future; therefore, this book can help you.

Realize first what this book does not do. It does not cover all the issues. America hosts more than eighty-thousand separate units of national, state, and local government in which hundreds of thousands of issues are addressed. Furthermore, this book does not address all aspects or sides of any particular issue. Although each issue is presented in a debate format with one author on each side of each issue, in reality every major social and political issue is complex, and many sides may develop in the process of an issue's resolution.

This book does, however, get you started in the right direction. It introduces you to twenty-one of the most controversial and important issues facing America today, which are discussed by some of the nation's most thoughtful commentators. It is unlikely that any single article will allow you to resolve conclusively for yourself any particular issue, but that is not our purpose. As editors, from the start we have had in mind three objectives. The first objective is to pique your interest in the issues themselves. You may have already heard so much discussion on some of the issues that you think nothing of interest can be said. If this is the case, we hope to surprise you with some creative thought and good writing.

Our second objective is to provide you with some of the basic information needed to begin to develop an informed opinion. The articles here include a great many facts and findings, as well as interpretations. Our third objective is to raise questions in your mind. Good analysis often raises more questions than it answers. We hope that after you have read these articles, you will have a wide array of new questions and that you will be more eager to begin a lifelong search for the insights that will make your contribution meaningful. We wish you all the best.

Greg Scott and Loren Gatch
Edmond, Oklahoma

PART I
Democracy and the Constitution

Issue 1
The Constitution

INTRODUCTION

Even more than for their commitment to democracy, Americans are distinctive for venerating their Constitution. Indeed, as both Jonathan Schell and Sebastian Mallaby suggest in the following articles, America's worship of its founding document—its constitutionalism—amounts to a veritable "civil religion." Yet like any other great historical founding, our Constitution is rooted in facts but sustained by myth. The historical facts include economic disputes between the American colonies and their English homeland, tensions between commercial and slave owning elites, and a distrust common to both sets of elites of the political abilities of the common people. In short, it was a document crafted by men with a distinctively dim view of human nature, and not forged by gods. Human conflicts have indelibly stamped the features of our Constitution. At the same time, however, the genius of these features inheres in their capacity for reaching out beyond their original historical circumstances to give continuity and meaning to the ongoing American experiment in self-governance. Our Constitution leaves its grubby origins and takes on a mythic status to the extent that we do regard it as a timeless repository of political wisdom. In this sense, it is the power of myth that gives the Constitution its present-day reality.

In formal terms, the Constitution is simply a set of rules about making rules. As much as this country has moved away from its agrarian and English origins, it is remarkable that the document itself has changed so little in over two hundred years. Even with twenty-seven amendments, it amounts to hardly a dozen pages; compare this with the hundreds of volumes that comprise the Federal Register's labyrinth of regulations. More so than in other democracies, the American Constitution has remained an expression of political principles such as the separation of powers, checks and balances, and federalism. Otherwise, the Constitution sketches only the barest outlines of the nation's governing structures and political processes. Deriving these structures and processes from political principle has been the continuing task of government. What, for example, is the Supreme Court's power of judicial review, if it is not defined in the Constitution? What is the extent of the U.S. Congress's implied powers that are "necessary and proper" to meet its explicit responsibilities? And finally, how does the president see to it that the laws are "faithfully executed" if not by carving out his or her own sphere of discretion?

Our belief in constitutionalism provides ballast to the ship of state as it sails far from its origin. Even if both the Constitution and the American nation itself remain works in progress, Americans are nonetheless emboldened by the thought that certain outcomes simply are not possible. If our Constitution will not produce a political dictatorship, it is not because Americans are incapable of oppressing each other. Rather, it is because our faith in the binding conditions of our origins shields us from our own worst tendencies. In its most self-serving form, constitutionalism confirms our own political conceits. Thus, Jonathan Schell, who opposed the impeachment of President Clinton, sees the wisdom of the Constitution in the barriers that it places against the easy use of Congress's impeachment powers. Like that of many other observers who celebrate the genius of the founders, this judgment may be correct, but it is also convenient. Sebastian Mallaby, an Englishman who is a sympathetic critic of the American scene, is far more willing to suggest drawbacks to constitutionalism. Far from representing ballast, the Constitution to Mallaby is as much an anchor that keeps the American ship of state from sailing where it ought to go. Too often, according to Mallaby, Americans render their political choices unnecessarily difficult by transposing questions of political technique, practicality, or self-interest into strife over the interpretation of principles. Referring continually to the meaning of its origins may prevent a people from facing its future with the flexibility to deal with new problems. Myths are powerful, but they can also be blinding. Ultimately, our constitutional faith may keep us politically immature by preventing us from seeing the most uncomfortable possibility of all: namely, that in some instances, the insights of the founders may have become outdated or may have simply always been wrong.

As you read the articles, consider the following questions.

Discussion Questions

1. Jonathan Schell applauds the Constitution for assuring an outcome—President Clinton's survival of the Monica Lewinsky scandal—that Schell might well have desired for ideological reasons. Would Schell have made the same argument about the Constitution if Clinton had been removed from office, instead? Can you imagine circumstances under which a person might support the Constitution, even though it produced a result that he or she disagreed with?

2. Sebastian Malaby comes from England, a country which, though democratic, has no written Constitution. What might be the advantages and disadvantages of not having a written Constitution? What would have to be different about the United States that would allow us to get along without one?
3. Opinions about the value of our Constitution are often related to how we understand the role of the Supreme Court in public life. What views of the Constitution are implied by the alternatives of activism and restraint?
4. The rules for amending the Constitution are part of the Constitution itself. As you know, these rules make it difficult to alter its wording. Should it be easier to amend the Constitution? What would be the consequences, good or bad?

   For more information on this topic, visit the following websites:

   http://www.nara.gov
   National Archives and Records Administration

   http://supct.law.cornell.edu
   Cornell University's Legal Information Institute

   http://lcweb.loc.gov/global/judiciary/html
   The Library of Congress's Judicial Internet Resources

What Works: The Constitution

JONATHAN SCHELL

In most respects, the impeachment of President Bill Clinton—now destined to go on for yet more weeks—is different from the proceedings against President Richard Nixon a quarter-century ago. Nixon was accused of abuses of the power of his office. You had to be President to bomb Cambodia secretly, to use the IRS to harass your political enemies or to ask the CIA to squelch an investigation by the FBI. Clinton, on the other hand, is accused of violations of law in his individual capacity. It is within the power of almost anyone to fool around at the office, to invite a colleague to dissemble about the affair in court or to ask a friend to do the lover in question a favor.

The historical circumstances were different, too. In the immediate background was the cold war, in whose name the presidency had accumulated powers that Nixon used to break the law. The question before the country was whether to embrace this "imperial" presidency or to restore the constitutional balance, and it chose the latter. Today, by contrast, one would be hard put to name any large public controversy that is going to be settled one way or the other by the impeachment trial. If anything, the trial has created fresh issues (mostly regarding abuse of the impeachment power itself) rather than resolved existing ones.

In at least one respect, however, the two impeachment proceedings are similar. Both, in their different ways, illumine the wisdom, shrewdness and almost uncanny prescience of the Framers of the Constitution of the United States. In recent years this magazine has run a series of articles titled "What Works." The Constitution is the prince of things that have worked—in its case for 210 years. To sing the praises of the Constitution at this moment is, I know, no startling thing to do. Those accusing the President in the Senate chamber as well as those defending him have been doing likewise for several weeks now. One side wants Clinton out, and the other side wants him to stay, but both want what they want in the name of the Constitution. In fact, this general reverence for the document—sometimes called America's civil religion—may in truth be as important as its particular provisions. Agreement about any code of conduct, whether this is the US Constitution, Islamic Sharia, Confucian odes or last week's astrological charts, can be a boon to a country. A king who's respected is worth more than a splendid constitution that's

Jonathan Schell is editor of *The Nation* and the author of "The Gift of Time," Metropolitan Books, 1999.

Reprinted by permission. *Nation*, Feb. 15,1999. Vol. 268, Issue 6, p. 8.

ignored. (Stalin's Constitution of 1936—an exemplary document, guaranteeing every imaginable human right—comes to mind.)

In the events at hand, though, it is also undeniably the provisions of the document that shine. In The Federalist Papers and other writings of that day, the abstract thoughts of the writers often read like descriptions of the events unfolding before our eyes. For example, we instantly recognize today's Republican Party in Alexander Hamilton's warning that "the most conspicuous characters" in impeachment will "be too often the leaders, or the tools of the most cunning or the most numerous faction; and on this account can hardly be expected to possess the requisite neutrality towards those, whose conduct may be the subject of scrutiny."

Therefore the Constitution established certain breakwaters against the tide. One was the provision that two political bodies had to be involved—the House as accuser, the Senate as court. In our case, though, both bodies are under the control of one party. Not to worry, though—the Framers placed one final obstacle in the way of the President's removal: the requirement of a two-thirds majority in the Senate. "The division . . . between the two branches of the legislature," Hamilton wrote in The Federalist Papers, "assigning to one the right of accusing, to the other the right of judging; avoids the inconvenience of making the same persons both accusers and judges; and guards against the danger of persecution from the prevalency of a factious spirit in either of those branches. As the concurrence of two-thirds of the senate will be requisite to a condemnation, the security to innocence, from this additional circumstance, will be as complete as itself can desire." And this provision today stands in the way of a purely partisan removal of the President, just as Hamilton had anticipated.

Such prophetic refinement is especially striking in the impeachment clause, which is probably the loosest cannon on the constitutional deck. It is the final, desperate remedy when the normal, everyday operations of the Constitution have all failed and the Republic is on the edge of catastrophe. Not surprisingly, then, it runs counter to other principles on which the Constitution is based. The separation of powers, for example, is one of the Constitution's very foundations; yet impeachment clearly breaks it down. The separation of jury and judge is basic to our judicial system, but in the persons of the senators at the trial it is erased. The scene before us every day in the Senate chamber—in which the President is in the dock; Congressmen have trooped over from their own House to the Senate; the senators have been rebaptized as hybrid juror-judges; and the Chief Justice of the United States has left his co-equal lair across from the Capitol to preside—is a sort of monstrosity from the separation-of-powers point of view. Here, owing to a contemplated great national emergency (missing in today's case), the separated powers seem, as in time of war, to have fused primitively into one.

Yet this crude power, too, has been tempered and regulated. In effect, a separation of powers was re-created by assigning impeachment to the two bodies and requiring the two-thirds vote. For some months, a majority of the public, according to most observers, has been paying little attention to the spectacle in Washington. The government is in uproar, but they are calm. They go about their daily lives, which they find more important than impeachment. Let us imagine, though, that in some lax moment at the Constitutional Convention the Framers had omitted to require the two-thirds majority. Today, the President would be in clear danger of removal. Immediately, we must suppose, public indifference would end and people would angrily take sides in a battle whose stakes are huge and menacing. But none of this is happening. The two-thirds rule—a great shield held out by the Framers across a gulf of two centuries to shelter us—is in place, and we are undisturbed.

Stop the Celebration:

The Case against the Fourth of July

SEBASTIAN MALLABY

Independence Day is a time for barbecues and beaches. But it is also a good time to reflect upon a paradox, a paradox so simple that perhaps only a foreigner like me would pause to point it out. Americans revere their Founding Fathers: they teach school children about them; they name streets after them; they cite the Declaration of Independence and the Constitution as holy writ. And yet, at the same time, Americans have mixed feelings about the political system that the Founders have created. They feel that the government erected in the name of the people actually ignores the problems of ordinary people; they are fed up with the endless argument that the separation of powers has wrought.

This paradox is not temporary. Veneration for the founding stretches back into the nineteenth century, while antipathy toward gov-

Sebastian Mallaby is Washington bureau chief for *The Economist* and author of the magazine's "Lexington" column.

Reprinted by permission. *New Republic*, July 20–July 27, 1998. Vol. 219, Issue 3/4, p. 19.

ernment has fueled political careers from Thomas Jefferson to Newt Gingrich. Nor is this paradox superficial. The statesmen and the documents of the founding are revered by all kinds of Americans, from new immigrants to descendants of the Pilgrims, while the mistrust of government is documented by a host of opinion polls. Most importantly, this paradox is not without its implications. Americans' veneration for the founding not only contrasts oddly with their unease about its consequences; it actually contributes to modern disillusionment. As long as Americans hanker after the imagined perfection of the early republic, they will never be content with the current state of politics.

This claim, if accepted, turns much talk about American politics on its head. The standard view takes the wisdom of the founding for granted and then blames contemporary discontents on the modern additions to American democracy. Opinion polls, multimillion-dollar advertising campaigns, and spin doctors are thus cast as villains, intruding upon and ruining the Eden created by Washington and Hamilton, Madison and Jefferson. And yet the key to rebuilding Americans' trust in government may lie not in greater fealty to the Founders but rather in greater willingness to break the spell of their memory. In almost all areas, Americans have done well by welcoming modern innovations, not by gazing backwards. They should apply the same habit to politics.

It is never tactful for a visiting foreigner to attack his hosts' patriotism; and attacking America's devotion to the Founders may seem especially unwise (and especially unwise for an Englishman). Lacking a common religion, ethnicity, or anything much else to hold it together, America feels a pressing need for unifying myths and symbols, and it has found these in the Declaration of Independence, the Constitution, the flag. You are Japanese or French if you are born that way. But being American is a matter less of descent than of consent. You must consent to the ideas and freedoms that the founding represents. When the first Americans declared independence from my country, they asserted no cultural or ethnic differences with England. They asserted their right to life, liberty, and the pursuit of happiness.

Based on ideas, and ideas only, America is at once noble and fragile. The Founders themselves understood this fragility, and so they infused their precious ideas with the aura of scripture, hoping this would protect them from the wear and tear of everyday debate. George Washington pleaded that "the Constitution be sacredly maintained," while James Madison described the founding documents as "political scriptures," hoping that they would acquire "that veneration, which time bestows on every thing, and without which perhaps the wisest and freest governments would not possess the requisite stability." And so Americans established a civil religion in place of a spiritual one. Their Protestant reverence for the Bible was transferred to the founding texts.

The Founders' civil religion has been preached enthusiastically by their successors. In 1837, on the fiftieth anniversary of the Constitution's drafting, John Quincy Adams, paraphrasing from the instruction to the Israelites in Deuteronomy, urged his countrymen to "Teach the [Constitution's] principles, teach them to your children, speak of them when sitting in your home, speak of them when walking by the way, when lying down and when rising up, write them upon the doorplate of your home and upon your gates." A generation later, Lincoln advocated "reverence for the laws" as the "political religion of the nation."

Which is precisely what exists today. Each September, the National Constitution Center, an organization created by an act of Congress in the wake of the bicentennial, celebrates Constitution Week. It reminds Americans that their Constitution is the oldest written national charter still in force anywhere; that its opening declaration of "We the People" has been imitated in constitutions all around the world. Over the past six years, more than 1.5 million Americans have added their own names to copies of the Constitution at signing ceremonies in schools, libraries, museums, and national parks. The Constitution Center runs a Constitution website, which invites visitors to click on "The Blessings of Liberty" or "Created Equal." There are plans to build a $130 million constitutional museum on Independence Mall in Philadelphia. Last year, a survey commissioned by the center found that 89 percent of Americans feel proud of their Constitution, while 91 percent regard it as important to them.

It may seem futile, then, for a foreigner to question America's devotion to the founding. And yet I shall persist. Though America's civil religion may indeed serve at times to unite the country, it also has its dangers. When America's leaders declare that the Founding Fathers were divinely inspired, or when celebrations describe the Constitutional Convention as a "miracle," each fuels Americans' belief that their country is "chosen," that it has a "manifest destiny," that it is, or should be, pure. These notions are not sustainable. And so, when Americans discover that their government sometimes lies, cheats, or panders to special interests, the result is bitter disillusionment.

Many thoughtful people acknowledge this danger and defend America's civil religion nonetheless. They contend that national myths not only unify the country but also inspire it—and that these advantages more than outweigh the risk of disillusionment. It would be nice to believe this and to return, relieved, to barbecues. But the unifying power of America's civil religion is not as great as most people suppose it is. Its power to inspire is not always constructive, and the debilitating effects of disillusionment are larger than they seem.

Consider, first, the civil religion's power to unify Americans. At times this power does indeed seem vivid. To unite themselves for war, Americans cast each conflict as a defense of the Founders' ideals of freedom and democracy. To overcome domestic crises, Americans turn to the Founders as well. Lincoln warned that a house divided against itself cannot stand and called upon his countrymen to unite around the promise of equality in the Declaration of Independence. Martin Luther King appealed to all Americans by harking back to the Founders' unifying ideals. His reliance on the Founders is reflected in the civil rights museum in Memphis, where an introductory film emphasizes the importance of the Constitution. In these celebrated cases, it is true, divided Americans have found new unity and purpose in their civil religion.

But America's national myths create forces for disunity as well as unity. In nearly every war America has fought, a minority—inspired by the supposedly unifying civil religion—has argued that the conflict does not serve America's founding ideals, and so has opposed it. In the same way, when Lincoln tried to use America's founding ideals to unite his countrymen, Southerners invoking those same Founders opposed him, citing the Constitution's protections of slavery. A century later, civil rights leaders appealed to a Constitution now rendered more sympathetic to their cause by amendments passed after the Civil War; but they, too, faced segregationist opponents who couched their arguments in terms of loyalty to the Founders, who had, after all, created a Constitution that safeguarded states' autonomy.

At a minimum, then, it is too simple to assert that the venerated documents of America's founding necessarily unify the country. Sanford Levinson, a law professor at the University of Texas, observes that congregations that unite around sacred texts tend to split over their interpretation. This is true for Jews, for Muslims, for Christians, and no less for Americans. In the nineteenth century, America's venerated Constitution did not prevent an uncivil war that cost 620,000 lives and nearly destroyed the Union. As they butchered one another, both sides invoked the Constitution, just as during the 1980s Sunni Iraqis and Shiite Iranians both claimed to be fighting a holy Muslim war. In the twentieth century, America has avoided such extreme calamity. But, on issues ranging from school prayer to abortion to civil rights, both sides in political arguments regularly cite the Constitution.

And, in some ways, the veneration of these documents—the civil religion built on top of them—actually prolongs many arguments. Because of the veneration of the founding, Americans have been taught to identify personally with their Constitution, and so to interpret it personally: you cannot spend long in America without encountering someone who carries a dog-eared copy of the document in his pocket; you cannot get through a political campaign without a candidate reading out some clause or other on the stump. This has a disunifying effect upon America. Because all Americans feel it is their birthright to engage in amateur constitutional exegesis, they think nothing of second-guessing interpretations handed down by the Supreme Court. And this weakens the main technique that text-based congregations use to avoid schism, which is to give interpretational authority to an institution like the Vatican or the Supreme Court.

Fortified by a civil religion that is, in this sense, Protestant, fringe groups in America feel entitled to assert almost anything, provided some clause or other of the Constitution can be construed as sympathetic to their cause. The gun lobby is strident, because it is fortified by a tendentious reading of the Second Amendment. The opponents of campaign finance reform are strident, because the First Amendment has in the past been construed to prohibit some attempts at overhauling political money. In fact, it is a rule of thumb in America that the more marginal and extreme an opinion, the more constitutional arguments are likely to be wheeled in as support. The right-wing militias enjoy sympathy from almost nobody; to make up for this, they can recite large hunks of the Constitution by heart.

None of this is to attack America's Constitution or to disparage its safeguards against majoritarian tyranny. It is merely to question the assumption that America's civil religion promotes national unity. By encouraging personal interpretations of the Constitution, the civil religion exposes the Constitution to an anarchy of conflicting interpretations. As a result, fringe views enjoy a patina of respectability that they do not deserve. And the supposed foundation for American politics, the document that is meant to hold a vast and diverse country together, turns out to be the subject of discord instead.

So the first claim for America's civil religion—that it promotes national cohesion—appears to be exaggerated. Now consider the second claim: that it inspires America to become a better place. Again, the examples of Lincoln and King are useful here, for both men invoked the religion in order to vanquish racial oppression. The project of America, in Lincoln's view and in that of many reformers after him, is to narrow the gap between the founding ideals and its imperfect reality. If people are disillusioned by politics, then disillusionment will inspire them to demand change. The idealization of the founding, on this view, is a source of eternal political vitality.

It is certainly true that Americans demand improvements to their political system at a prodigious rate. At any given time, there is at least one debate raging about America's political machinery: about the ethics rules in Congress, about the president's invocation of executive privilege, about the legality of using a government telephone to dial for campaign dollars. At any given time, too, one of the three branches of the federal government is reckoned to have overreached itself. Over the past 25 years or so, there have been books criticizing the "imperial presidency," the "imperial Congress," and the "imperial judiciary." Americans constantly wonder whether experts have supplanted ordinary citizens; or whether, on the contrary, popular democracy has supplanted the experts. Americans constantly propose amendments to the Constitution—further belying the contention, incidentally, that veneration of the Constitution fosters unifying consensus. This constant clamor for reform gives rise to a peculiar feature of America: The subject of politics is often politics itself.

The question is whether this clamor is really healthy. When the reform at issue is the abolition of slavery, or the entrenchment of black voting rights, reformism seems beyond reproach. But many reforms are less obviously desirable. America's yearning to perfect democracy has stoked support for populist devices, such as citizen ballot initiatives and term limits; and these have often had the perverse effect of making democracy worse. America's yearning to perfect the Declaration's promise of freedom and equality has stoked a gradual extension of rights over the past half-century and so has laid the basis for this decade's culture wars.

Meanwhile, the main drawback of America's civil religion—that it promotes excessive idealism—tends to be underplayed. This is no doubt because it is hard to dislike idealism; if the alternative is cynicism, idealism wins any day. But the seeming choice between idealism and cynicism is a false one. It is precisely because of their idealistic expectations that Americans have fallen into cynicism. Because they are idealistic, Americans are constantly proposing ways of improving their political system. When these proposals fail, cynicism prevails.

This puts the claim that America's civil religion exercises an invigorating influence over American politics in a rather different light: It makes glorious rejuvenation seem like an inglorious perpetuation of adolescence. America stands out for the fact that in no other mature democracy is democracy so immature—in the sense that, rather than settling comfortably into worn routines and patterns, it is forever staying up late to agonize over a possible life change and fret over its most basic goals. America might stop fretting if it let go of its veneration for its Founders and stopped seeing its government in idealized terms. And, by tempering its idealism, America would increase its chances of passing some of the reforms that might actually increase satisfaction with government. For excessive idealism not only causes the disease of cynicism. It blocks the cure as well.

Consider, for example, proposals to make representative government work better, essentially by limiting popular pressures that distort decision-making by lawmakers. At various times, there have been suggestions that senators face the polls every eight years, rather than every six years; that House terms should be four years rather than two. It's a plausible idea: Longer terms of office might reduce the political class's obsession with polls and partisanship. But, because of America's idealism about democracy, these practical proposals turn out to be impractical. There is much more popular enthusiasm for imposing term limits on members of Congress than for extending congressmen's tenure. Idealism not only fosters some naive reformism; it also suffocates the more sober sort.

And so, on Independence Day, it is worth taking a second look at the parades and the patriotism. As a foreigner in America, I have to say that I love living among idealists; I admire the aspiration and the striving and the hope. But I cannot honestly believe that idealism is always healthy. If Americans seemed happy with their political system, I would keep my mouth shut. But Americans say they are not happy. So, nervously, I put aside my English reticence.

Issue 2
Direct Democracy

INTRODUCTION

Democracy is not only hard to define but is also hard to justify in a way that silences its critics. In a vague way, we sense that democracy entails average people having some real say in how public affairs are conducted. We also sense that democracy is a good thing because the alternatives to democracy are clearly worse. Indeed, the more precisely we try to define democracy or the more vigorously to defend its value, the more we realize that the problems of defining and justifying democracy are actually intertwined.

Defining democracy is, first and foremost, a problem of large numbers. A single king who rules over an entire population cannot be democratic, and neither can rule by a small, hereditary elite. Beyond those extremes, though, the existence of democracy seems to be a matter of degree. The most basic question has always been who is to be considered a full citizen. Ancient Athens had a democratic government, even though its free male citizenry comprised only a small part of the population. Indeed, the achievements of Athenian democracy rested squarely on slave labor. In the United States, democracy once excluded blacks and women from public life, and even now it does not automatically confer citizenship upon all who wish it.

Assuming that we know who democratic citizens are, the next question concerns the rights and duties of citizenship. At the extreme, if every citizen took equal part in public life, deliberating and voting on legislation as if the entire nation were one big assembly, then democracy would be entirely participatory and direct in its operation. Short of that, if each citizen took part in public life by voting for public officials who would in turn take up the duties of public decision-making, democracy would be representative and indirect in its operation. In practice, democracy operates with a mixture of participatory and representative elements. Participatory democracy works best on a small scale, where small groups of citizens come together to make decisions regarding the welfare of their communities. On this scale, citizens are more likely to understand the issues at stake, to know each other's needs, and to accept the consequences of their decisions. In contrast, representative democracy works best on a large scale, where many citizens come together merely to vote for representatives who will in turn take up the duties of public life. On this scale, citizens need not be fully informed about the issues. They may, for example, be ignorant of the needs of distant fellow citizens. Also, their particular sense of responsibility for the representatives they choose may be diluted by the sheer vastness of voter turnout and by the complexity of public policy. In short, in a representative democracy, citizens do not experience the same consequences of voting as they would in a participatory democracy.

However democracy may be defined, clearly its healthy operation depends on some degree of civic virtue among the citizenry. The essence of this virtue is the ability of citizens to look beyond their self-interest and to take into account the good of the community. Indeed, one influential view of democracy holds that, as citizens engage in the competitive pursuit of their own interests, the good of the polity is thereby achieved indirectly. At the very least, the good citizen fulfills his or her civic responsibilities by pursuing personal interests in a long term or in an "enlightened" way that respects the social logic of the Golden Rule: Do unto others as you would have them do unto you.

Given this bulwark of civic virtue, the problem of democratic governance appears as a trade-off between the strengths and weaknesses of both forms of democracy. Direct democracy values participation as an end in itself. Yet its greater public legitimacy is offset by its inefficiency and the high demands that it places on citizens to avoid the temptations of selfishness or majoritarian tyranny. Representative democracy achieves efficiencies that erode its legitimacy and diminish its potential for civic renewal. At its worst, representative democracy devolves public decision-making onto an elite of experts who specialize in governance while the mass of citizens sinks into apathy.

On the one hand, modern life with all its complex problems of scale and scope seems to favor rule by experts. On the other hand, new technologies of communication such as the Internet may herald a rejuvenation of citizen participation. The interactive potential of such technologies may restore the conditions for face-to-face public life, albeit on the ghostly terrain of cyberspace. The following article from *The Economist* professes to have seen the technological future and found it democratically empowering. The dangers of direct democracy in the information age are far outweighed by the implied message of democracy's doubters. According to Brian Beedham, however, criticisms of direct democracy are really criticisms of democracy itself. Indeed, the idea that democracy requires specialists in governance undermines the very rationale for democratic life.

As you read the articles, consider the following questions.

Discussion Questions

1. Voting is the basic form of civic participation, but not all people can vote. For example, non-citizens, citizens under the age of 18, the certified insane, and citizens with felony convictions are denied the privilege of voting. Do you agree or disagree with these restrictions? What other restrictions might be placed upon voting? How would you defend these restrictions?
2. Many observers of American politics have noted with concern that voter turnout in national elections has declined steadily since the 1920s. What could be some reasons for the decline in turnout? Do you think this decline is a bad thing?
3. One response to the decline in voter turnout has been to make voter registration easier. For example, so-called "motor-voter" laws have enabled citizens to register when they renew their licenses or car registrations. In contrast, some European countries even make voter registration automatic. Should the United States do this? What changes in American attitudes and political conditions would be necesary to make automatic registration possible?
4. In some countries (Australia, for example), voting is not only a privilege but an enforcable duty: those who don't vote on election day are fined as if nonvoting were a traffic violation! Should the United States adopt a similar law in order to encourage voter turnout?

For more information on this topic, visit the following websites:

`http://www.cdsresearch.org`
Center for Democracy Studies

`http://www.ned.org`
National Endowment for Democracy

`http://www.igc.apc.org/cvd/`
The Center for Voting and Democracy

The Future of Democracy

EDITORS OF *THE ECONOMIST*

Here is the nightmare. A country, having succumbed to the lure of electronic democracy, and duly wired its voters into the Internet, decides that it will henceforth make its laws by letting anybody who so desires send a proposal into the information highway, after which every adult citizen will be invited to vote on these ideas, each Saturday evening. On Friday night a race riot in, say, Bradford—or Buffalo or Beziers or Bochum—kills half a dozen white people. The Internet hums, the e-mail crackles. Zap comes next day's empurpled answer: out with all Pakistanis/Hispanics/Algerians/Turks.

And here is the rose-tinted dream. The people's elected representatives, having yet again failed to balance the budget, suddenly realise that the sensible thing to do is to put the problem to the people themselves. All the various possibilities are electronically presented to the voters. The voters express their assorted preferences. The contradictions in their answers are laid out for their further examination. They vote again. After a couple of months or so of furrowed-brow button-pressing, bingo, a budget virtuously balanced to the majority's satisfaction.

Neither nightmare nor dream is likely to become reality. Most ordinary men and women are probably not foolish enough to risk the first or technologically arrogant enough to believe they can manage the second. Yet between these extremes of what technology might do to politics lies some fascinating new territory, well worth exploring.

The great electronic leap forward of the 1990s . . . is clearly going to make it even harder for the machinery of democracy to remain in its present steam-engine stage. For the past couple of centuries—except in Switzerland, and to some extent recently in Australia and parts of the United States—democracy has meant a system by which the people vote every few years to elect a handful of representatives, who in between these elections make all the important decisions. For two reasons, this sort of democracy may no longer be sufficient. Something more direct, more fully democratic, may have to be more universally attempted: decisions by vote of the whole people.

Reprinted by permission. *The Economist*, June 17, 1995. Vol. 335, Issue 7919, p. 13.

ANTI-DEFERENCE, ANTI-LOBBYIST

Reason number one is that the gap between ordinary people and parliamentarians is far narrower now than it was in Edmund Burke's days, and indeed for a long time after Burke. During the 20th century, most people in the democracies have become much better educated than they used to be, and much richer, and have more spare time in which to think about what goes on around them. Above all, they are on the whole a great deal better informed. First books and newspapers, then the radio, then television and now the artillery of the Internet bombard them with ideas, facts and figures. They are regularly asked what their opinion is about important matters, and their representatives in parliament know they had better pay attention to what the opinion polls report.

This is probably the chief explanation of why politicians are currently in such bad odour in so much of the democratic world. It is not just that, as is often said, government has failed to provide what the people want. Governments have failed in some countries; in others they are doing their job with reasonable efficiency. The point is that, everywhere, ordinary people are now in a better position to examine what their representatives are up to, observe their errors, smirk or snarl about their sexual and financial peccadillos, and wonder whether it is really a good idea to let such a collection do so much of the business of politics. The people are no longer so ready to proffer the deference their representatives used to expect—and too often still do.

The second reason for taking a serious look at direct democracy is that it may be better than the parliamentary sort at coping with one of the chief weaknesses of late-20th-century democracy. This is democracy's vulnerability to lobbyists. In the relatively humdrum, de-ideologised politics of post-communist days, the lobbyist is getting even more powerful than he used to be; and democrats are right to be worried.

There is in principle nothing wrong with lobbying; the people who make decisions, in any field, should be the target of as much argument and persuasion as possible. Lobbying goes wrong when special interests use their money to cross the line between persuading politicians and buying them. In dealing with a relative handful of elected politicians, the lobbyist has many ways of doing that, ranging from "entertainment" to the straight insertion of cash into the parliamentarian's pocket or the legal pouring of millions into the coffers of American politicians' campaign funds. When the lobbyist faces an entire electorate, on the other hand, bribery and vote-buying are virtually impossible. Nobody has enough money to bribe everybody.

It is true that rich propagandists, even though they cannot bribe the mass of voters, can gull them into taking foolish decisions. Silvio

Berlusconi did it in Italy last Sunday . . . . It has happened, spectacularly, more than once in California. But the nervous can take heart from the record of Switzerland, which has long put most of its big decisions to the vote of the whole people. The Swiss have developed an admirable ability to resist the blandishments of both Big Money and cheap emotion. In particular, the fear that special interests will use direct democracy to get themselves budget-busting goodies should be eased by the fact that Switzerland has not only a tolerable budget deficit but also one of the rich world's smaller public debts. Unless you believe that God designed the Swiss differently from everybody else, it is hard to argue that only they can do these things. The Swiss have just had more practice.

If other countries want to move deeper into direct democracy, they should note how it is best done. Some subjects are more amenable than others to the whole-people vote. Great constitutional issues ("Do you want your country to be part of a federal Europe?") and specific local decisions ("Shall we expand the town's hospital or its high school this year?") fall more naturally into this category than arcane financial measures, some of which even the Swiss treat with care. And a solid list of signatures should be needed to bring any subject to the vote.

Nothing unconstitutional can of course be laid before the people, though the people can change the constitution if they wish. It is necessary to vote fairly frequently—the Swiss trudge to the polls four times a year—if the voters are to do their task properly (which includes learning how to spot what the selfish propagandist is up to, and correcting the voters' own earlier mistakes without too much delay). Above all, trudging to vote is far better than just prodding a button, because it gives you more time to think. The new electronics is an excellent way of putting more information at the voters' disposal, but it is not the best way for those voters to express the conclusion they come to. Much better, having digested the arguments for and against, that they should walk calmly to the polling station.

Done with care, direct democracy works. The more political responsibility ordinary people are given, the more responsibly most of them will vote. This helps to produce something closer to true government by the people. And that, after all, is the way the logic of the 20th century points. If democrats have spent much of the century telling fascists and communists that they ought to trust the people, can democrats now tell the people themselves that this trust operates only once every few years?

The Arguments that Won't Wash

BRIAN BEEDHAM

Most objections to direct democracy are, when you look closely, objections to democracy.

AH YES, the objectors say at once: perhaps the Swiss can do these things, but that does not mean anybody else can; the Swiss, you see, have a unique gift for direct democracy. To which the answer is: come off it. There is nothing special about the Swiss. They are a perfectly ordinary mixture of west-central European peoples (and the fact that they are a mixture makes it harder, not easier, for them to run their country in this way). They too yawn at the blearier aspects of politics; the turnout goes down with a bump when there is nothing of particular interest on the referendum list. They too get sudden bees in the bonnet; it was the Swiss, in 1989, who asked themselves whether they should abolish their army, and found 35.6% of themselves saying yes. Here are no models of zealously dutiful civic rectitude.

If the Swiss can manage this richer form of democracy, it is not because they have always had it. There were some fine early examples of pastoral democracy high up in the Alps in the later Middle Ages. But other parts of the world have had similar things—the town meetings of New England, for instance—and it was not until the 1860s that a countrywide Swiss system of direct democracy got itself organised. Nor is the explanation that the Swiss are an especially sophisticated lot. They are now the second-richest people in Europe, and give themselves a good education; but for the first 60 or 70 years of their democratic experiment—its most vigorous period, many would say—they were largely rural, not very well-to-do, and as politically unpolished as any other people of the time.

Least of all should the Switzerland-is-special school be allowed to get away with the argument that Switzerland can do it because "it is such a small country, where they all know each other." That is half-true of the smallest cantons and communities, but nobody who knows the place would say it was true of Switzerland as a whole.

In a country with nearly 6m citizens and four different languages, the ordinary voter in Zurich knows no more about the political thought-processes of the ordinary voter in Geneva or Lugano than the New Yorker does about the San Franciscan's, the Londoner about the Glaswegian's. The German-speaking and French-speaking parts of the country,

Reprinted by permission. Ecerpted from "Full Democracy," *The Economist*, Dec. 21, 1996. Vol. 341, Issue 7997, p. 3.

in particular, are quite often at angry odds with each other: the 1992 vote about membership of the European Economic Area is only one recent example. The Swiss are not a natural unity, born to chat things over easily on referendum day. Do not believe that the god of direct democracy has selected them as his chosen people.

REMEMBER, POLITICS IS POLITICS

The other attempts to demolish the idea of direct democracy are, with one exception, no more convincing than the notion that only the Swiss can do it. Some people argue, for instance, that letting all the voters share in the decision-making process is bound to be inefficient, because it defies the division-of-labour principle.

In the world of economics, these people explain, it would never be suggested that everybody should grow his own food, make his own shoes and construct his own lap-top computer. The sensible way to organise things is to let people specialise, so that each thing is produced by those who do it best; the consumer then has a far wider range of goods to choose from, much more cheaply. So, in the world of politics, if the specialists of the political class are allowed to get on with the complex business of decision-making, the ordinary chap will end up much better off.

To this the reply is: sorry, but politics is different from economics. The world of politics is not divided between consumers and producers (unless you agree with people like Lenin and Stalin, who thought they knew exactly what needed to be done to create a happy world, and so decreed that their Politburo should be the sole producer of political decisions). In democratic politics, everyone is a consumer, and by the same token everyone can join in the production process. There is no evidence that widening the production process to let ordinary people take part in decision-making in the years between parliamentary elections leads to a narrowing of the range of goods on offer, or increases their price. On the contrary: direct democracy seems to expand the choice, most of the newly recruited producers are happy to do their work for free, and with luck the members of parliament will cost less.

A variation of this attempt to confuse politics with economics is an argument, also used by adversaries of direct democracy, which confuses politics with science. You would not entrust your health to the advice of your next-door neighbour, runs this argument, or ask the other passengers on the train taking you to work how to set about building a nuclear reactor. You go to a doctor or a physicist, somebody trained in the science of medicine or atomic energy. So in politics you should turn to somebody who understands the science of politics—namely, your elected representative.

But politics is not a science, either. Parts of it require some detailed knowledge of various subjects, not least economics, and this is one reason why it makes sense to keep parliaments in existence, places where people are paid to burrow into such details. But the heart of democratic politics is the process of finding out which of the various possible solutions to a problem is the one most people think the best. The quickest and most efficient way of finding that out, surely, is to ask the people directly, rather than leaving the choice to a handful of parliamentarians who may well discover at the next parliamentary election that most people think they got it wrong.

The claim that there is such a thing as a science of politics is deeply revealing. Those who make it are in fact claiming that the policies they think best are the ones that should be followed, even if most of the rest of the country disagrees, because the rest of the country is "scientifically" wrong. That is not unlike the sort of thing you hear from conservative mullahs in the Muslim world, who say that since politics is a branch of religion only the "scholars of Islam" are equipped to puzzle out God's political intentions. Such a claim is not just anti-direct-democracy; it is anti-democracy.

THE DISTORTING EFFECT OF MONEY

There is a bit more substance, but only a bit, in the worry that money can shape the outcome of a referendum. When a question is put to a vote of the whole people, those whose interests are affected naturally want the vote to go their way, and are prepared to spend a lot of money on the signature-collecting and the propagandising which are designed to bring that about.

Studies in both Switzerland and those American states which use direct democracy suggest a pretty frequent link between the amount of money spent and the result of the referendum. The link is by no means always there. The Swiss took their decision about Europe even though most of the big money had been trying to persuade them to vote the other way. The voters of several American states have passed anti-gun legislation despite the gun-lobby's opposition. Italy's voters helped to torpedo the country's old political system in 1991 and 1993 while the system's two main parties watched ashen-faced. But the connection between money and votes seems persistent enough to justify concern.

There are two reasons, however, for thinking it does not decisively tilt the argument between direct and representative democracy. One is the fact that the voters can if they wish set limits on the amount of propaganda money spent at referendum time.

The Swiss have not done so, because the sums spent in Switzerland are (by American standards) still fairly small, and the Swiss do not think they have ever produced a result outrageous enough to require a remedy. The voters of California, on the other hand, in 1974 overruled the resistance of special-interest groups to pass Proposition 9, which set some firm spending limits. Proposition 9 was then squashed by the federal Supreme Court in the name of the constitutional right to freedom of speech. This November the voters of Montana had a shot at doing the same thing in a way that might escape the Supreme Court's veto. In a direct democracy, the voters can set the rules under which referendums take place, so long as these rules respect the country's constitution—which, in a direct democracy, the voters can themselves change.

The other reason for not letting the money issue decide the argument is that money-power almost certainly distorts the old sort of democracy more than it does the new sort. In a direct democracy, the lobbyists have to aim their money at the whole body of voters. Since most of the money is spent on public propaganda campaigns, it is hard for them to conceal what they are up to. In a representative democracy, however, the lobbyists' chief target is much smaller—just the few hundred members of the government and the legislature—and so it is much easier for them to keep what they are doing secret. They have at their disposal a whole armoury of devices ranging from the quietly arranged free holiday in a sunny corner of the world "for information-gathering purposes" through cash-with-a-wink for saying the right things in parliament to straight bribery for getting your government to order the bribe-giver's make of aeroplane.

There have been too many recent examples of all those things all over the democratic world. This is why, when somebody says he is worried about the influence of money over referendums, the correct retort is: "At least you can't bribe the whole people."

Most of the other criticisms of direct democracy are, like this one, equally applicable to the rival version. Does a new referendum designed to solve one problem sometimes carelessly create a new problem? To be sure it does; and the same applies to many an act of parliament. Are some referendums obscurely worded? Yes, and so is some of the work of professional draftsmen; think of the Maastricht treaty. Can the man in the street be counted on to understand tricky economic issues? No, but neither, quite often, can the supposed experts; recall Britain's doomed plunge into Europe's exchange-rate mechanism. None of these objections is fatal. . . .

PART II
Rights and Liberties

Issue 3
Abortion

INTRODUCTION

Of the issues that divide Americans, none is more vexing than the legality and morality of abortion. The modern debate about the issue dates from the Supreme Court's decision in *Roe v. Wade* (1973), which in the name of a woman's privacy, overturned state laws against abortions. Far from settling the issue, the Court's ruling has ensured that the abortion question is still very much alive in American politics. As the harsh rhetoric of the following selections from the *Progressive* and the *National Review* illustrate, simply talking about the issue calmly is a difficult feat. This introduction seeks to outline why this situation is so.

Much of the heat generated by this debate arises from the peculiar combination of constitutional and moral disagreement. Did the Court go too far in construing a "right" to privacy that isn't in the Constitution? People who disagree with *Roe v. Wade* usually do so because they oppose abortion on the grounds that a fetus is a human being. However, the underlying constitutional principle is not about whether abortion is legal or moral. Instead, it has to do with whether or not it is legitimate for the Court to infer a right to privacy that is not explicitly stated in the Constitution. As such, the debate over abortion is as much about the nature and limits of national power as it is about the definition of life. Can the Court create such rights as that of privacy and then require the government to protect this right by nullifying state laws forbidding abortions?

At the time of *Roe*, abortion was not uniformly illegal. Some states allowed it, whereas other states did not. What *Roe* did was take away the states' discretion to legislate on the matter. This judicial activism bothered many people. It bothered those who think that abortion is murder and those who do not care about the privacy issue. It bothered those who do not think abortion is murder yet who are uncomfortable with the idea of the Court's inventing new rights. Ultimately, there seem to be five possible solutions to the abortion debate.

The first solution is that the Court would continue to prohibit abortion as part of a constitutionally protected right to privacy—the current (and not widely accepted) solution. The second solution is that the Court would prohibit abortion on equal protection or due process grounds. This alternative implies that the Court declares a fetus to be a human being. The third is that the Court might reverse *Roe* so as to allow states to pass their own laws about abortion, with no Court-imposed permissions or prohibitions. The fourth is that again assuming no involvement by the Court, the federal government might pass its own laws, pro- or anti-, about abortion. The fifth is that the nation as a whole might enact a constitutional amendment either allowing or prohibiting abortion.

Note that the first two alternatives are legal, the second two are political, and the last alternative is constitutional in nature. Solutions enforced by the Court leave unresolved the question as to whether an unelected judiciary is the most legitimate branch for dealing with divisive social issues. Legislative solutions leave open the question of enforcement. State-level bans on abortion merely oblige women to seek the procedure in other states, whereas a nationwide ban would dramatically expand the intrusive powers of the federal government—itself an unwanted prospect by most conservative opponents of abortion. A constitutional amendment would achieve both the best and the worst of the legal and the legislative worlds. Unlike a court ruling, an amendment represents the will of the people. Yet, as the experience of Prohibition shows in the United States, the difficulty of enforcing an amendment against determined opposition itself erodes respect for constitutionalism.

Until parties to this debate even agree on how to disagree, anger over abortion will continue to fester in American politics.

As you read the articles, consider the following questions.

Discussion Questions

1. The Supreme Court in *Roe v. Wade* legalized abortion by declaring that the Constitution supported a "right to privacy." Had there been no "right to privacy," could access to abortion facilities be defended on other constitutional grounds?
2. To call abortion "murder" merely declares it to be a criminal act with no particular constitutional significance. Could an abortion ban be defended with reference to the current text of the Constitution (i.e. without an anti-abortion amendment)?
3. An anti-abortion amendment would resemble constitutional prohibition in the sense that both use the Constitution as an instrument of social policy, rather than

as a framework for lawmaking. What other parts of the Constitution share this character as social policy?

4. Abortion-rights supporters have recently sponsored the production of an American version of the French drug RU-486. This drug induces abortion at the earliest stages of pregnancy without invasive procedures. How would the availability of this drug affect the abortion debate?

For more information on this topic, visit the following websites:

http://www.prochoice.org
National Abortion Federation

http://www.prolifeinfo.org
Ultimate Pro-Life Resource List

http://www.plannedparenthood.org
Planned Parenthood

http://www.operationrescue.org
Operation Rescue

Preachers of Hate

EDITORS OF *THE PROGRESSIVE*

There is a battle raging right now for the soul of this country. Will we be a democracy that's dedicated to liberty, equality, individual rights, and the separation of church and state, or are we headed down the icy slope toward theocracy?

This question demands asking in the wake of the October murders of Matthew Shepard and Dr. Barnett Slepian and the ongoing violence against homosexuals and abortion providers.

More than 500 people attended a rally here in Madison, Wisconsin, to protest the murder of Shepard, the young man in Wyoming who was pistol-whipped, hung up on a fence for hours, and left to die because he was gay. One after another, people took the megaphone to decry this horrible act of violence, to recount their own experiences of being harassed, or to tell of a friend or loved one who had been beaten by bigots. Speaker after speaker understood that there are powerful religious and political forces in this country that are dead-set on depriving gays, lesbians, bisexuals, and transgendered people of their inalienable rights to life, liberty, and the pursuit of happiness.

Conservative evangelicals and politicians have fomented this violence. Pat Robertson, James Dobson, Lou Sheldon, Gary Bauer, Pat Buchanan, Trent Lott, John Ashford, and Jesse Helms—they are the ones who incubated the murderers of Matthew Shepard.

And even after this terrible crime, there were still those who preached from the prayerbook of hate. "It should be remembered that the new saint of the gay movement was a twenty-two-year-old man engaged in sexual perversion who was apparently cruising a bar for the purpose of finding a partner or two to commit vile acts which also violate the laws of nature's god," said the Reverend Ralph Ovadal of Wisconsin Christians United.

This is the epitome of theological callousness. And that same kind of callousness greeted the assassination of Dr. Slepian.

It was Friday night, and Dr. Barnett Slepian had just returned from synagogue, where he attended a yahrzeit service commemorating the death of his father, *The New York Times* reported. While standing in the kitchen of his home, while enjoying domestic tranquility with his wife and one of his sons, Dr. Barnett Slepian was shot dead.

Reprinted by permission. *The Progressive*, Dec. 1998, p. 8(1).

Dr. Slepian's murder bore all the markings of a political crime, carried out by a fanatical adherent to the "pro-life" cause who refuses to obey the law of the land, refuses to respect women's constitutional right to privacy, refuses to respect the sanctity of the patient-doctor relationship, refuses to respect doctors' rights even to live, and insists on imposing his religious beliefs on the rest of us.

The rhetoric of the anti-abortion forces justifies this kind of violence. When they go around saying that abortion is murder, and that doctors are baby killers, and when they shove pictures of the bloodied fetuses in people's faces to show how cruel and inhumane the doctors are, it is not surprising that some of their more belligerent members will take it upon themselves to kill the "baby killers."

Some members of the "pro-life" movement actually applauded the murder of Dr. Slepian. The Reverend Donald Spitz, founder of Pro-Life Virginia, called the killer of Dr. Slepian "a hero." Spitz said, "We as Christians have a responsibility to protect the innocent from being murdered. Whoever shot the shot protected the children."

Spitz was not the only one articulating this ugliness. Slepian "got what was coming to him," one person put it in an e-mail message to *The Progressive*.

Religious fundamentalism is morphing into religious vigilantism before our very eyes.

These fanatics want to kill off enough doctors and scare away many more so that the reproductive health care needs of women can no longer be met. These fanatics want to make life unbearable for gays and lesbians.

"Militant anti-abortion activists," warns Clarkson, "are increasingly making common cause with neo-Nazi groups on matters ranging from abortion and homosexuality to the 'New World Order.'"

The scale of the violence is staggering. "Over the past two decades, there have been seven murders, at least sixteen attempted murders, more than 200 bombings and arsons, 750 death threats and bomb threats, and hundreds of acts of vandalism, intimidation, stalking, and burglary of abortion providers across the country," writes Frederick Clarkson in a recent commentary. Clarkson is the author of a book called *Eternal Hostility: The Struggle Between Theocracy and Democracy* (Common Courage Press, 1997).

The most recent threat occurred on October 30, when "five abortion clinics in three states received letters claiming to contain deadly anthrax, forcing the evacuation of an Indianapolis clinic and sending at least twenty-nine people to hospitals" for precautionary purposes, the A.P. reported.

In 1997, there was a "67 percent increase in bomb threats and bombings to the gay, lesbian, bisexual, and transgendered community," reports the National Gay and Lesbian Task Force. "There were 2,445 reported episodes of anti-gay harassment and violence in fourteen U.S. cities."

This is terrorism. It is akin to the lynchings and cross-burnings during and after Reconstruction. And it has no place in our democracy.

On our side, though, we must be careful not to label all of our opponents as bigots or fanatics or neo-Nazis. It is just not that simple.

Most people who are anti-abortion did not condone the murder of Dr. Slepian. And most people who oppose homosexuality did not condone the murder of Matthew Shepard.

If we fail to distinguish the followers from the fanatics, we're not going to convince anybody. We need to make our case on the merits. And the merits are unassailable.

Gays and lesbians have as much right as any other Americans to walk around freely, without fear of discrimination, persecution, or death. The Fourth Amendment does not guarantee "the right of heterosexuals to be secure in their persons, houses, papers, and effects"; it guarantees that right to all the people. The equal protection clause of the Fourteenth Amendment does not apply only to heterosexuals; it applies to "any person" in "any state."

Many good, moral people are troubled by abortion. But what anti-abortion activists don't understand is that women will still be getting abortions even if they are illegal. They did before *Roe v. Wade,* and they will do so again if *Roe* is ever overturned. The only differences will be whether they get safe, clean abortions, or whether they get dangerous, dirty ones. It should not be up to the state to tell women, who may be risking their lives, whether they can have an abortion or not. The demand that women be forced to carry to term, no matter what, is a gross infringement on their liberty and privacy rights.

But we can argue the merits until the shingles fall off the roof, and we won't change everybody's mind. That's fine. That's democracy. But the opposite of democracy is to wage terrorist attacks after losing an argument. And that, today, is what some on the far right are doing.

As the century closes, gays and lesbians, along with doctors who perform abortions, are on the front lines of the freedom struggle. Matthew Shepard and Dr. Barnett Slepian are martyrs in this struggle, just as Chaney, Goodman, and Schwerner were when they were gunned down in Mississippi, just as the four black girls—Cynthia Wesley, Carole Robertson, Addie Mae Collins, and Denise McNair—were when they were killed in the bombing of the Sixteenth Street Baptist Church in Birmingham.

But for this freedom struggle to triumph, all of us must organize peacefully against the forces on the right who want to turn this democracy of ours into a theocracy of theirs.

Dead Reckoning

EDITORS OF THE *NATIONAL REVIEW*

A quarter-century has passed since the Supreme Court struck down the laws of every state in the nation, in the name of a constitutional right to abortion it had just discovered. In *Roe v. Wade,* the Court prohibited any regulation of abortion in the first trimester, allowed only regulations pertaining to the health of the mother in the second, and mandated that any regulation in the third make an exception for maternal health. In the companion case of *Doe v. Bolton,* the Court insisted on the broadest definition of health—economic, familial, emotional. Legal scholar Mary Ann Glendon describes the result as the most radical pro-abortion policy in the democratic world. It permits abortion at any stage of pregnancy, for any reason or for no reason. It has licensed the killing of some 35 million members of the human family so far.

The abortion regime was born in lies. In Britain (and in California, pre-*Roe*), the abortion lobby deceptively promoted legal revisions to allow "therapeutic" abortions—and then defined every abortion as "therapeutic." The abortion lobby lied about Jane Roe, claiming her pregnancy resulted from a gang rape. It lied about the number of back-alley abortions. Justice Blackmun relied on fictitious history to argue, in Roe, that abortion had never been a common-law crime.

The abortion regime is also sustained by lies. Its supporters constantly lie about the radicalism of *Roe:* even now, most Americans who "agree with *Roe v. Wade*" in polls think that it left third-term abortions illegal and restricted second-term abortions. They have lied about the frequency and "medical necessity" of partial-birth abortion. Then there are the euphemisms: "terminating a pregnancy," abortion "providers," "products of conception." "The fetus is only a potential human being"—as if it might as easily become an elk. "It should be between a woman and her doctor"—the latter an abortionist who has never met the woman before and who has a financial interest in her decision. This movement cannot speak the truth.

Roe's supporters said at the time that the widespread availability of abortion would lead to fewer unwanted pregnancies, hence less child abuse; it has not. They said that fewer women would die from back-alley abortions; the post-1940s decline in the number of women who died from abortions, the result of antibiotics, actually slowed after *Roe*—probably because the total number of abortions rose. They said it would reduce illegitimacy and child poverty, predictions that now seem like grim jokes.

Reprinted by permission. *National Review,* Jan. 26, 1998. Vol. 50, No. 1, p. 11(3).

Pro-lifers were, alas, more prescient. They claimed the West had started down the slippery slope of a progressive devaluation of human life. After the unborn would come the elderly and the infirm—more burdens to others; more obstacles to others' goals; probably better off dead, like "unwanted children." And so now we are debating whether to allow euthanasia, whether to create embryos for experimental purposes, whether to permit the killing of infants about to leave the womb.

And what greater claim on our protection, after all, does that infant have a moment after birth? He still lacks the attributes of "personhood"—rationality, autonomy, rich interactions—that pro-abortion philosophers consider the preconditions of a right to life. The argument boils down to this assertion: If we want to eliminate you and you cannot stop us, we are justified in doing it. Might makes right. Among intellectuals, infanticide is in the first phase of a movement from the unthinkable to the arguable to the debatable to the acceptable.

Everything abortion touches, it corrupts. It has corrupted family life. In the war between the sexes, abortion tilts the playing field toward predatory males, giving them another excuse for abandoning their offspring: She chose to carry the child; let her pay for her choice. Our law now says, in effect, that fatherhood has no meaning, and we are shocked that some men have learned that lesson too well. It has corrupted the Supreme Court, which has protected the abortion license even while tacitly admitting its lack of constitutional grounding. If the courts can invent such a right, unmoored in the text, tradition, or logic of the Constitution, then they can do almost anything; and so they have done. The law on everything from free speech to biotechnology has been distorted to accommodate abortionism. And abortion has deeply corrupted the practice of medicine, transforming healers into killers.

Most of all, perhaps, it has corrupted liberalism. For all its flaws, liberalism could until the early Seventies claim a proud history of standing up for the powerless and downtrodden, of expanding the definition of the community for whom we pledge protection, of resisting the idea that might makes right. The Democratic Party has casually abandoned that legacy. Liberals' commitment to civil rights, it turns out, ends when the constituency in question can offer neither votes nor revenues.

Abortion-on-demand has, however, also called into being in America a pro-life movement comprising millions of ordinary citizens. Their largely unsung efforts to help pregnant women in distress have prevented countless abortions. And their political witness has helped maintain a pro-life ethic that has stopped millions more. The conversions of conscience have almost all been to the pro-life side—Bernard Nathanson, Nat Hentoff, Elizabeth Fox-Genovese. The conversions of convenience have mostly gone the other way, mainly politicians who wanted to get ahead in the Democratic Party—Jesse Jackson, Dick Gephardt. The fight against abortion has resulted in unprecedented dialogue and cooperation between Catholics and Protestants, first on moral values and now increasingly on theological ones. It has helped transform the Republican Party from a preserve of elite WASPs into a populist and conservative party.

True, few politicians of either party—with honorable exceptions like Henry Hyde, Chris Smith, Jesse Helms, Bob Casey, Charles Canady, and Rick Santorum—have provided leadership in the struggle. Not because opposition to abortion is unpopular—throughout the *Roe* era, 70 per cent of the public has supported laws that would prohibit 90 per cent of abortions—but because politicians, and even more the consultants and journalists and big-money donors to whom they listen, tend to move in elite circles where accepting abortion is de rigueur and pro-life advocacy at best an offense against good taste. Since everyone they know favors legal abortion, they understandably conclude that everyone does. But there is progress even here. The pro-abortion intellectual front is crumbling. Supporters of the license increasingly concede that what they support is, indeed, the taking of human life. Pro-lifers, their convictions rooted in firmer soil, have not had to make reciprocal concessions.

There can be little doubt that, left to the normal workings of democracy, abortion laws would generally be protective of infants in the womb. The main obstacle on our path to a society where every child is welcomed in life and protected in law, then, remains what it has always been: the Supreme Court. There abortionism is well entrenched; and last year the Court appeared to slam the door on the legal possibility of a congressional override of its decisions on abortion or anything else. By defining a practice at odds with our deep and settled moral convictions as part of the fundamental law of the land, the Supreme Court has created a slow-motion constitutional crisis. This is what comes of courting death.

Issue 4
Gun Control

INTRODUCTION

For good or for ill, guns loom large in the American imagination. From Davy Crockett to Dirty Harry, guns have been regarded not merely as an accessory useful for fighting coyotes or crooks, but as a veritable extension of American (masculine) identity. Whether for the exuberant frontiersman or the alienated urban loner, gun ownership expresses a self-reliant individualism that resonates with core American values of autonomy and freedom.

Guns are also deadly instruments. At once a deterrent and an incentive to crime, the widespread availability of guns creates a tension between the ideals of individualism and the demands of community order. The individual who owns a gun for self-protection or self-esteem in effect signals to the community that he or she does not trust the competence of the community to police itself. An increase in the personal security of the gun-owning individual may well come at the cost of a decline in security for the entire community. Indeed, the highest—and perhaps the most paranoid—justification for gun ownership remains the standing guarantee that it provides for limited government. A government that has deprived its citizens of the right to bear arms, so the argument goes, is a government that has deprived its citizenry of the ultimate defense against tyranny.

As a matter of public policy, then, the debates over gun ownership partake of an equal mix of myth, reality, and legalism. The self-reliant individual may be an American myth, but it is a powerful myth that gains reality through its persistence in the public mind. As a practical matter, the availability of guns raises a number of questions that ought to have answers. Does gun ownership deter criminal predators, or do guns themselves contribute to crime? Is there some optimal mix of ownership restrictions (on the type of guns, the type of owners) that would maximize the beneficial effects of guns yet avoid their drawbacks? Finally, myth and fact are overshadowed by what seems to be a constitutional protection for gun ownership. The Second Amendment's guarantee of the "right to bear arms" suggests at least some legal forbearance for citizen militias, if not for the armed individual.

Together, these three aspects of the gun debate contribute to its distinctly acrimonious quality. Given the symbolic potency of guns in American culture, attempts to regulate their purchase and use provoke absolutist collisions over whether or not there exists a right to gun ownership. In particular, the gun debate is particularly prone to "slippery-slope" arguments, whereby small regulatory measures are viewed with alarm by pro-gun forces such as the National Rifle Association (NRA), which see them as opening wedges for more extensive restrictions on gun ownership. One model for such measures is the so-called Brady Bill, named after James Brady, once President Reagan's press secretary until he was crippled by an assassin's bullet. Brady bills in their various versions mandate some form of gun licensing, as well as waiting periods before guns may be purchased, so that buyers may be subjected to police background checks. Much as it seems sensible to attempt to restrict gun ownership to responsible individuals, even Brady bills are opposed by the NRA as harbingers of government oppression.

In this climate, pro-gun and anti-gun advocates tend to disagree past each other more than they do with each other. The following selections highlight how difficult it is to find common ground even to debate the gun question. "How we die in America says a lot about how we live together in America," asserts Kevin Clarke. For Clarke, guns themselves bear responsibility for the "epidemic" of violence that rages in America's inner cities. In contrast, Thomas Cole reports that gun supporters regard their weapons as a deterrent and not as a cause of crime. Moreover, widespread gun ownership is the ultimate bulwark against a government that would oppress its citizens. Even to suggest a ban on handguns is tantamount, in the words of one gun owner, to proposing "cultural genocide."

As you read the articles, consider the following questions.

Discussion Questions

1. Events like the massacre at Columbine High School in Littleton, Colorado have focussed public attention upon the issues of gun availability and ownership. In your opinion, how has the Columbine massacre changed the debate about guns?
2. Guns can be dangerous instruments, but so can a great many things if used the wrong way—cars, for example. Why should guns be singled out and treated any differently?
3. Opponents of tobacco have made headway by filing lawsuits accusing the industry of selling a dangerous product. Opponents of guns have begun to pursue the same strategy. What similarities or differences do you see between the two situations?

4. Defenders of gun ownership frequently look to the Constitution to uphold the legality of gun ownership. Read the second amendment. How must that amendment be interpreted to defend the right to own guns? What other parts of the Constitution either reinforce or contradict the defense of guns?

For more information on this topic, visit the following websites:

http://www.nra.org
The National Rifle Association

http://www.paxusa.org
PAX

http://www.ccrkba.org
Citizen's Committee for the Right to Keep and Bear Arms

http://www.gunfree.org
Coalition to Stop Gun Violence

Don't Withhold Treatment on This Epidemic

KEVIN CLARKE

I was making my way through the Monday evening remnants of the Sunday paper the other night when I heard a sound that has become almost a normal part of the background noise in the Chicago community where I live. It was the irregular popping of a handgun sounding somewhere in the night. Close enough to be heard, far enough away not to pose much of a danger—I didn't bother to call police to report it as I might have done when I first moved here. I don't know if that represents a surrender of civic responsibility or just a surrender to reality, I just know it represents some kind of a surrender.

The dry pop, pop, popping I heard the other night may have been a handgun; it may have been firecrackers. Let's hope it didn't represent the wounding or killing of another young person in my community. We're all familiar with the numbers of us that fall to cancer and heart disease or die in car accidents each year. These are after all the primary ways we die in our culture.

But track down our national cultural tree to those less familiar parts of the diagram among America's subcultures and see what you discover. Among 15- to-24-year-olds in the United States, the second leading cause of death is homicide. Among 15- to 24-year-old African American and Hispanic males, it is the leading cause of death. In 1994 nearly 90 percent of homicide victims 15 to 19 years of age were killed with a firearm. Annual rates of firearm homicide for youth 15 to 19 years of age increased 155 percent between 1987 and 1994.

We may not have done so well in this year's World Cup, but American men are second to none in the world when it comes to killing each other with firearms. The homicide rate among U.S. males is 10 times higher than in Canada, 15 times higher than in Australia, and 28 times higher than in France or Germany. What these Center for Disease Control statistics represent is an epidemic of a treatable disease—gun violence. This is how the CDC is attempting to train the American public to react to gun violence. It's one strategy to awaken us from the kind of cultural stupor that allows us to continue to read a newspaper even as a handgun reports somewhere in the night.

Kevin Clarke is managing editor of online products at Claretian Publications, Chicago, Illinois.
Reprinted by permission. *U.S. Catholic*, Sept. 1998. Vol. 63, Issue 9, p. 25.

As a public-relations gimmick, the notion of gun violence as a treatable epidemic has the utility of being true. I don't know how far the CDC and other medical professional groups will get in corralling gun violence, however, now that Charlton Heston has assumed command of the National Rifle Association and seems determined to repeat a career-making performance by leading the whole country into the wilderness. But this approach to the problem of firearm violence seems a useful alarm to wake the country up to the problem.

It also got me wondering about what other treatable but unnamed epidemics are out there in American life and death. Could we declare an epidemic of child abuse or domestic violence for instance? Or an epidemic of infant mortality, an epidemic of hunger? And couldn't all of these problems reflect aspects of a larger epidemic of poverty? I wonder what our nation's mortality profile would look like if we filtered our death rates through the dilemma of poverty. Clearly those of our fellow citizens who die of exposure on our streets each winter or because of heat exhaustion each summer would have to be included among the most obvious victims of this epidemic, but I think a large portion of these youthful firearm-homicide victims could be counted in as well.

A few summers ago here in Chicago, 800 people died during a week-long heat wave. The coroner's report attributed these deaths to the extreme weather, but many of these deaths could have just as easily been attributed to a national epidemic of poverty. How many older people succumbed to this heat wave because they couldn't afford air conditioning or because they were too poor to pay for adequate health care? How many died in stifling apartments because they couldn't afford to live in communities where they didn't have to nail shut their windows to prevent home invasions?

If we came to see poverty in epidemic proportions, could we finally be moved as a society to do something about it? Epidemics require large-scale mobilizations of public resources to respond to an overriding public emergency. Each year, in communities across the United States, an unnatural disaster of poverty unfolds so quietly that we never seem to notice it. But it is no less real for its subtlety.

Our church leaders remind us that our society will be judged by how well the poor and most vulnerable among us were treated. Would it help us better appreciate the reality of life and death among the most vulnerable of us if we began to see that vulnerability reflected more clearly in our national death rates? Would that suffice as a suitable call to action? The "common good" is one of those theological banners Catholics like to wave when they want to drive home a point about American life. Let me raise it again here.

How we die in America says a lot about how we live together in America. Achieving a real common good requires real sacrifice. What would we have to sacrifice to respond to this public emergency, this epidemic of poverty, so that those of us who live in the impoverished pockets of American society can escape it? What would we have to sacrifice if we took the idea of a common good seriously? I fear that it is more than we are willing to offer when we can't even sacrifice a Second Amendment absolutism that allows that pop, pop, popping to continue to sound somewhere in the background of our lives each night.

Extending Brady Background Checks Opposed

THOMAS COLE

Law-abiding gun owners would like to keep guns out of the hands of violent criminals, said professors of law, economics, criminology, and criminal justice who attended a conference hosted by Academics for the Second Amendment in mid November in Washington, DC. However, they were quick to add, handgun control laws may have the opposite effect.

Policies designed to prevent violent criminals from buying guns legally often do more harm than good, said Joseph Olson, JD, professor of law at Hamline University School of Law in St Paul, Minn., and president of Academics for the Second Amendment. Law-abiding citizens may be unwilling to take the time and trouble to apply in person for permits and fill out paperwork to obtain weapons for self-defense. Criminals, on the other hand, can obtain stolen guns on the street at discounted prices with no waiting period, he said.

To deter criminals from acquiring and carrying guns, he said, existing gun laws should be enforced. Olson, who helped write a Minnesota law with severe penalties for illegal gun trafficking, says that the law has been inadequately enforced. Consequently, criminals ignore it.

Gary A. Mauser, professor of business administration at Simon Fraser University in Burnaby, British Columbia, referred to his review of

Thomas Cole, M.D., is *JAMA* contributing editor.

Reprinted by permission. *JAMA, The Journal of the American Medical Association,* Dec. 23, 1998. Vol. 280, Issue 24, p. 2065.

four evaluations of a Canadian criminal background check law. "Three of four studies showed no effect on homicide rates in Canada."

It would be a mistake, said Olson, to extend US federal firearms laws that currently prohibit gun sales to convicted felons to apply to persons convicted of misdemeanor crimes as well. "Many people plead guilty to misdemeanors to avoid having to hire a lawyer and go to court," he said. People charged with misdemeanors may even have been advised to plead guilty by their attorneys, said Olson, because the attorneys believed that there were no adverse consequences to having a misdemeanor conviction on one's record. Now, perhaps never having been convicted of another offense, their clients could have problems getting a handgun legally.

To maximize the likelihood that only violent career criminals are affected, recommended Olson, only persons convicted of felony crimes should be prohibited from buying handguns. If there is strong public interest in extending this prohibition, he added, then perhaps only persons convicted of three or more violent misdemeanors in a 3-year period should be prohibited from buying guns.

Academics for the Second Amendment was established as a tax-exempt educational organization in 1982. According to a request for financial support authored by Olson, the organization "seeks to foster intellectually honest discourse on the Constitution, the Bill of Rights, and, of course, the environment in which academics, judges, politicians, and the public place the rights preserved by the Second Amendment." The organization holds conferences yearly to critique research and expert and popular opinion on gun ownership and use.

SELF-PROTECTION ENDORSED

At the recent conference, speakers argued that self-defense is a practical necessity. "The police cannot protect you," said Don B. Kates, Jr, an attorney and writer from Novato, Calif., who moderated the conference. There aren't enough police to protect each individual citizen, he said, "and yet they are actively working to keep you from protecting yourselves." The major threat to an individual's ability to protect himself or herself from criminal predation or government oppression, agreed participants who spoke at the conference, would be a universal ban on handgun ownership.

Chester L. Britt, PhD, an assistant professor in Pennsylvania State University's Crime, Law, and Justice Program, presented his research challenging the findings of a 1991 evaluation of the Washington, DC, law banning ownership of guns. "When we extended the period of observation of the original evaluation by 2 years and used the city of Baltimore as a comparison population rather than the suburbs of the District of Columbia," said Britt, "we found that the gun ban did not reduce homicide rates as the original evaluation concluded." Commenting on this and other refutations of firearm injury research published in bio-medical journals, Kates concluded that "the gun battle has been won in the criminology literature." However, he added, "it will never be won in the medical literature, because they only publish one side of the story."

David B. Mustard, assistant professor of economics at the Terry College of Business, University of Georgia at Athens, a coinvestigator on a widely publicized study of the effects of concealed weapons laws on crime rates (Lott JR. *More Guns, Less Crime: Understanding Crime and Gun-Control Laws.* University of Chicago Press, Chicago. 1998), pre-sented some of his findings at the conference. In short, concluded Mus-tard, states with laws permitting persons who meet certain criteria (which varies by state) to carry concealed weapons had less crime than states without concealed weapons permit laws.

SELF-RESPECT HONORED

The right to purchase and carry firearms not only protects the gun owner from violent individuals, said Kates, but also from a potentially violent government. The state holds power over its citizens, he said, and the state is made up of individuals—"some evil, all faulty. Those who op-pose gun ownership are engaged in a mythology that denies this." In an-swer to those who may say that governmental oppression is unlikely in a modern, civilized state, Kates responded: "No historian in the year 1900 would have predicted that Germany would kill Jews. It is impossi-ble to predict that cultural genocide won't happen."

Citing recent historical examples of the slaughter of unarmed Cam-bodians and Rwandans, Kates speculated that the outcome might have been different had the victims been armed. "No modern army has been able to overcome a determined citizenry. That's why there is an Ireland, an Israel, a victorious Vietnam," said Kates. Altogether, he said, "116 million people have been murdered by their governments in this century alone. So who's more untrustworthy, the government or the people?"

It may seem futile to fight a modern army with handheld weapons, but even against superior firepower, it is still important for individuals to be armed, insisted Olson. "It's about self-respect," he said, even if you can't win, it is better to resist than to allow yourself to be killed. A gun ban would render the individual citizen defenseless, he said. Conse-quently, many gun owners consider gun bans to be a form of "cultural genocide," he said, "and if we react strongly to that, you shouldn't be surprised."

Issue 5
Affirmative Action

INTRODUCTION

Affirmative action policies encapsulate both the hopes and contradictions of America's struggle with the legacy of slavery. In various ways, affirmative action attempts to remedy the effects of past injustice and of present discrimination by providing racial and other ethnic minorities with preferences in school admissions or hiring. In its overt form, affirmative action entails setting numerical quotas for the number or percent of minority representation in the academy or workplace. Yet in undertaking such policies, Americans' impulse towards social justice collides with their equally keen sense of what is fair play in a competitive society. At some level, most Americans accept that it is right to provide disadvantaged groups with the chances and resources that will enable them to improve their situation. However, when such remedies appear as explicit preferences that directly subtract from the chances of others with equal or greater qualifications, popular support for affirmative action declines, even among the beneficiaries of affirmative action. Preferences can often be a subtle matter of degree. However difficult it may be to sustain in practice, Americans cherish the distinction between equality of opportunity and equality of outcome, even if the first is a hollow ideal without at least some amount of the second.

Curiously, as a policy style, affirmative action for racial and ethnic minorities finds ample precedent in the similar privileges granted to veterans in civil service exams, or to athletes and the children of alumni in college admissions. Although each of these privileges may have their particular justifications, only affirmative action seems to challenge directly America's faith in itself as a functioning meritocracy. Backlash against the affirmative action programs of the 1970s, which has recently taken the form of state referenda such as California's or Washington's, reflects more than just the injured interests of white males. The prospect of institutionalized racial preferences strikes at the country's collective self-image of decency. Even for people of goodwill, permanent affirmative action presents a Hobson's choice. If affirmative action programs are in reality unnecessary, then their persistence represents an abuse of good intentions by selfish interest groups operating under the cloak of political correctness. If, in fact, affirmative action remains perpetually necessary to ensure fair chances for the disadvantaged, then this very fact reveals something uncomfortably harsh about the limits of America's capacity for toleration.

In between the poles of equal opportunity and equal outcome ought to lie the pragmatic possibility for softer forms of affirmative action (based, perhaps, on class rather than race). Otherwise, as Andrew Stephen writes in his gloomy prognosis, the dilemma of affirmative action assures that America will remain "haunted by the ghosts of slavery." Most struggles over racial preferences focus on policies in the public sector. A different and more hopeful view is offered by Boeing President Harry Stonecipher. Of all professions, that of engineering is most closely associated with merit. The real progress that the Boeing Company has made towards integrating racial minorities into scientific work, Stonecipher argues, points to the role that private sector corporations can play in exorcising old ghosts. Indeed, it is not only corporate America's civic duty to encourage diversity in the workplace but also a part of its good business sense. A corporation that accommodates diversity is also one that succeeds in a fast-changing, global market. Ideals of diversity and standards need not be viewed as trade-offs in the struggle to succeed. Indeed, in the truest meritocracy, diversity may be the only means to success.

As you read the articles, consider the following questions.

Discussion Questions

1. The affirmative action debate presumes that we have a reliable way of telling when one person is better at doing something than another person. What are some of the different ways of measuring human performance? How can we tell when these measures are accurate or fair?
2. The affirmative action debate also presumes that we have a reliable way of telling who is black, white, Latino, or Asian, and that these racial and ethnic categories meaningfully reflect past and present experiences of discrimination. What happens to the debate when these categories are not clear cut, or conceal further differences within groups?
3. Is diversity at school or in the workplace really necessary, so long as the most talented succeed?
4. Affirmative action policies typically involve imposing costs upon the present generation of the privileged in order to remedy the past (and present) effects of

discrimination against the underprivileged of previous (and present) generations. Is this fair? Why, or why not?

For more information on this topic, visit the following websites:

`http://www.bamn.com`
Coalition to Defend Affirmative Action

`http://www.law.harvard.edu/groups/civilrights/resources.html`
The Civil Rights Project at Harvard University

`http://www.southeasternlegal.org`
Southeastern Legal Foundation

`http://www.wdn.com/cir`
Center for Individual Rights

A Place to Stand:

Reaffirming Affirmative Action
from a Market-Based Perspective

HARRY C. STONECIPHER

"Give me a lever . . . and a place to stand . . . and I will move the world."
So said Archimedes. There are many kinds of leverage—not just physical
or mechanical, but moral and social, personal and political, financial and
economic. Every one represents a means by which the few become capable of lifting the many.

That is something that Dr. George Campbell and others who serve
this organization understand very well. You have demonstrated your
mastery of the concepts of leadership and leverage again and again over
the past 25 years.

The National Action Council for Minorities in Engineering was
founded in 1974 following an event like this one at the National Academy of Engineering. It began as a coalition of leaders from government,
academia and business who saw a need for positive action in creating
greater opportunities for minorities inside the profession.

Tonight is an occasion for celebrating a quarter of a century of
progress under NACME's leadership. It is also a time for rethinking old
strategies, for brainstorming . . . and for considering new challenges.

Let us begin by recognizing how far we have come . . . and how far
we have yet to go.

In 1974, African Americans, Latinos and American Indians made up
a grand total of one percent of the engineering workforce. One percent!

Today minorities account for about 10 percent of all Bachelor of
Science and Engineering graduates at U.S. colleges and universities.

No fewer than 6,700 out of roughly 70,000 non-Asian minority engineers today obtained their degrees with the help of NACME scholarships.

By any yardstick, there is still a great shortage of people from minority groups within the engineering profession. NACME is reaching out to
groups that make up 28.5 percent of the population and a third of the birth
rate. Notwithstanding the progress that has been made, less than six percent of the engineering workforce of today comes from these groups.

Some people would say: What is wrong with that? Should every profession, every career path, precisely reflect the population distribution?

Harry C. Stonecipher is president of the Boeing Company.
Reprinted by permission of Boeing Company and *Executive Speeches*, Oct./Nov.
1998, Vol. 13, Issue 2, p. 9.

In his address to the NACME Forum last year, Dr. Campbell addressed that very question. He pointed out a crucial difference between the relatively small number of minority engineers and—as a counterpoint—the small number of white male basketball players in the NBA. There is a clear "legacy of exclusion" on the one side. Whites have had every opportunity to compete in basketball from grade school on up.

Let me add a couple of thoughts from my own perspective.

As the president of an engineering-based company that is one of this country's largest exporters, I know that I cannot afford to compete with one hand tied behind my back—and that is the situation when we as a nation conspicuously fail to tap much of the intellectual and creative potential of large segments of the population.

We need great engineers, and we need to draw them from every group. Engineering is problem-solving . . . and creativity . . . at a high level. To get the best results, we must have the clash . . . the interplay . . . and the resolution . . . of many different viewpoints and perspectives.

Second, as someone who first went to college on a "Grandma scholarship," which is to say, on the savings that my grandmother had accumulated as a school teacher in Tennessee hill country, I know something about the value of an engineering or science degree (mine was in physics) to someone who comes from a less-than-affluent background.

I skipped two grades and graduated from high school at age 16, but I was two years behind some of my original school mates in graduating from college—as a result of a four-year interval in which I worked as lab technician and went to summer school and night school.

A degree in engineering or science is a bootstrap that eliminates poverty by pulling up multiple generations of people. Among my friends who are engineers, I can think of a number who worked their way through school, but none who were unable, unwilling, or less than totally dedicated, to putting capable children on their own through college or even graduate school.

Like many of my friends, I was lucky. I grew up in a family that prized books and learning. From first grade on, I went to schools that were rigorous, disciplined and, in their own way, caring. Every child in this country should have those advantages. But we all know that is, emphatically, not the case.

The $64,000 question is: What are we going to do about it?

The original coalition that NACME began with in 1974 is still intact—and, indeed, bigger and better than ever. We must take advantage of that. Right here in this room, we have a plenitude of resources . . . comprising minority engineers who have been there and done that, and leaders from academia, business and government who retain the ability to act as powerful access providers.

Today, we see a continuing backlash against affirmative action programs in courts and legislatures around the country. Already we have seen a sharp decline in minority engineering enrollments in California due to the impact of Proposition 209. At Boeing, we are strongly opposed to any measures that reduce the national commitment to hiring and promoting people from minority groups. Boeing is among the companies that have stood up and asked to be counted in opposing a negative initiative of this type in the state of Washington.

At the same time that we do battle against a variety of measures aimed at rolling back affirmative action, we should recognize that today's world is awash with new possibilities for progress. If there is going to be less push on the legislative and judicial side in support of greater participation by minorities, then there can be . . . and there must be . . . more push coming from business and industry.

Companies everywhere are looking to become more creative and entrepreneurial. Surely we can apply more of the same kind of thinking in accelerating the recruitment and development of minorities in engineering and other fields.

That is certainly what we are trying to do at The Boeing Company.

We are taking more and more of a results-oriented approach versus the old way of making uncommitted funds available for scholarships and grants. We should all look for the highest possible Return-On-Investment on money spent in this area.

We are tying Boeing scholarships more closely to summer internships with the clearly understood goal of having the inside track on hiring outstanding graduates. We see these scholars and interns as an important part of our future in 10 or 20 years time.

In addition to supporting NACME with $640,000 in giving over the years, we are active with NACME in a wide variety of projects aimed at school reform and insistence on high academic standards for all students at the K-12 level. Each year we bring NACME scholars into our company to work side by side with Boeing engineers.

We have close working relations with 16 Historically Black Colleges and Universities and other Minority Institutions. In addition to providing more than $250,000 in annual scholarship support to the HBCUs, we are moving into new and promising growth areas in our relations with them.

For instance, at our Phantom Work advanced research and development center, we are outsourcing more than $600,000 a year, or nearly 5% of our annual government research dollars, with HBCUs. This includes a total of $200,000 in contract awards over the past two years to Tennessee State University and Central State University for doing advanced modeling work to assist Boeing in the development of lean design and manufacturing processes.

This is a win-win-win situation. It helps us. It helps the schools. And it helps the students. And it brings all three of us into a working partnership that takes on a life of its own, leading to new opportunities and projects.

One of the areas where you see the worst under-representation of minorities is in doctoral engineering programs, where they account for just two percent of all doctoral candidates.

Can we do something about that? You bet we can.

Now we are preparing to award contracts of as much as $50,000 to individual students at HBCUs that they will be able to take with them in applying for admission in masters and doctoral programs at Stanford, MIT and other prestigious universities. In going forward in their studies, these students will continue to do work for us in such areas as development of advanced sensors or solid state electronics. We intend to grow this program to eight or nine students a year.

Those are some of the things that we are doing at the Boeing Company. I expect that many of you have exciting programs of your own, and I look forward to discovering more about them. There should be no patents on good ideas in this organization.

There are many things we can do to put new drive and impetus into all the things that NACME stands for.

In a sense, it is payback time for American business. If, back in 1974, NACME and its supporters in the business world had a lever . . . and a place to stand . . . it was due to the Civil Rights movement.

American business has never properly recognized the debt we owe to the Civil Rights movement. This is something that goes beyond diversity and inclusion . . . important as they are. It goes to the heart of our ability to think and act in new and better ways.

Concepts such as empowerment and self-directed work teams have roots in the Civil Rights campaigns of the 50s and 60s. So, too, does the basic, activist idea that big organizations are capable of large-scale change; and that people, even within the bowels of a big organization, can determine their own destinies.

In closing, then, I would like to quote the eloquent words of Martin Luther King.

As he put it so well, "The greatest progress we have made . . . and the greatest progress we have yet to make . . . is in the human heart."

Still Haunted by the Ghosts of Slavery

ANDREW STEPHEN

Not so long ago I found myself in a curiously heated exchange with an American academic. We had just listened to his wife, who was head of one of the country's most prestigious women-only colleges, deliver a pep talk about why we should all be giving donations to her college: it was pursuing policies of "affirmative action" and "diversity," she said, amid a plethora of similar buzzwords and PC-speak. White males have no place in today's society, seemed to be the gist of what she was saying.

Doubtless because I'm one of those dreaded white males, I reacted viscerally. I asked Mr Academic if he agreed with what Mrs (or do I mean Ms?) Academic had just said: "Of course," he replied. It so happened that he was just about to take up a visiting professorship at Oxford, the culmination of a distinguished scholastic career of which he was justly proud. "So you," I went on, "would be quite willing to give up your Oxford professorship to a woman or black man even if they were less academically qualified than you?"

I've never seen anybody so angry: it had simply never occurred to him that policies he decreed to be good for society should apply to him as much as to anybody else.

I recall this encounter not because it was funny, nor because I found it gratifying to see this man's progressive credentials explode in such a flurry of self-interest. Rather I recount it because it illustrates the confusion America is experiencing over its affirmative-action policies—started by LBJ more than 30 years ago and further solidified by Richard Nixon's Labor Department after it found that blacks were being denied lucrative construction jobs in northern cities because of their colour.

But now—like bussing before it—a policy that has been seen as unquestionably progressive and enlightened is being challenged both legally and politically, by the left as well as the right. In last month's elections, a little-noticed referendum—overlooked in what is being seen as the great rout of the Republicans—was overwhelmingly carried by the voters of Washington state. Initiative 200, as it is called, effectively outlaws affirmative action there; it became the second US state to vote to reverse the generally accepted wisdom of three decades, Californian voters having passed Proposition 209 two years ago. The day after last month's vote, the University of Washington announced that it was

Andrew Stephen is a regular contributor to the *New Statesman*.
Reprinted by permission. *New Statesman*, Dec. 4, 1998, Vol. 127, Issue 4414, p. 30.

immediately taking measures to halt admission quotas based on racial or gender differences.

Bill Clinton says merely that "we must mend, not end" affirmative action—without saying quite what he has in mind. Strictly speaking, affirmative action is meant to benefit the minority—specifically blacks, Hispanics, Asian/Pacific islanders, American Indians and females—only where qualifications are equal to those of competing whites. But hardly anyone, especially among the angry new middle-class whites, believes that this is how the laws have been applied; the voters of Washington state are 90 per cent white, and polls show that by a ratio of six to one, whites believe they are being discriminated against in the job market, and their children in education.

The intensity of the white backlash is, indeed, frightening. Last weekend the *Washington Post* ran a story which said that more and more high-school pupils are refusing to specify their race when providing personal information for the standardised academic tests that decide college places. The clear implication (though, characteristically, not spelled out): white kids fear that they will be given lower marks if they reveal they are white.

The huge irony of this mess, with its ugly racist overtones, is that affirmative action no longer appears to be helping those it was designed to help: the descendants of the American blacks who (let us never forget) the Supreme Court ruled in 1857 could not count as US citizens because they were "subordinate and inferior beings."

The 1986 Immigration Reform and Control Act effectively made it mandatory that immigrants benefit as much as Americans from affirmative action. Now that there are no fewer than 25 million immigrants in the US today, Latino and Asian newcomers are rushing to fill minority quotas at the expense of the blacks who have been here for 300 years.

This means that in racial melting pots such as Los Angeles, struggles already rage between the black minority (who currently hold 30 per cent of municipal jobs) and what in many areas is already the Hispanic majority. The 1991 riots in LA, when America's second largest city was out of control for three days, were triggered by police treatment of a black driver, but it was the simmering animosity between upwardly mobile Korean immigrants and blacks that really fuelled them. Astonishingly, Asian-Americans—with an average annual income of $43,000—are now the most prosperous racial grouping in America, including whites.

So when middle-class whites congratulate themselves that progressive policies to reverse discrimination are working, they have to ask: for whom? America's racial landscape is changing at a dizzying rate. And the sad truth is that the racism exemplified by that grotesque Supreme Court ruling is so deeply embedded in American culture that the white majority still prefers to see Asian and Latino newcomers accelerate ahead of native blacks. Lynchings may be no more, Jim Crow laws may be history: but affirmative-action laws have not succeeded in the way that was intended either.

The ghosts of slavery and oppression continue to haunt America—and one day they will have to be exorcised, once and for all.

Issue 6
Sexual Harassment

INTRODUCTION

Civil rights victories of the 1950s and 1960s relied upon the courts for expansive interpretations of the Constitution. For example, the pathbreaking case of *Brown v. Board of Education* (1954) attacked racial segregation by overturning the precedent set by *Plessy v. Ferguson* (1896), which had held that "separate but equal facilities" were legal under the equal protection clause of the Fourteenth Amendment. In contrast, more recent extensions of constitutional protections into the realm of private behavior have occurred through new interpretations of congressional statutes. Title VII of the Civil Rights Act of 1964, for example, forbids employment discrimination on the basis of sex (gender). Although Title VII was intended to remedy many traditional forms of discrimination against women in the workplace, does this remedy apply to more than just the contractual terms and conditions of female employment? Gender relations in the workplace are often tinged by sexual attractions that may be so uninvited and offensive as to amount to employment discrimination on the basis of sex. Can Title VII be construed to regulate such behavior, even if the employee is acting in a private capacity, without the authorization or even the knowledge of superiors? To what extent can an employer be held liable for the bad manners of his or her employees?

On the one hand, the tradition of common law holds that an employer is liable for the tortious acts of an employee if those acts fall within the scope of employment. On the other hand, holding an employer responsible for torts that are not only unrelated to an employee's duties but that provide no benefit to the employer himself or herself presumes that the employer must assume the costs of remedying sexual harassment as a normal risk of doing business. These alternatives are complicated by the role played by supervisory authority in facilitating sexual harassment. Supervisors who harass subordinates make use of their authority not merely to extract crude quid pro quos, but to avail themselves of the discretion to engage in harassing behavior short of outright sexual coercion. Is an employer liable, in this sense, for an employee's misuse of supervisory authority even if that misbehavior resulted in no tangible damage to a plaintiff's employment status?

In recent rulings, the Supreme Court has sought to balance women's and men's rights to a workplace free of sexual harassment against the danger that the judicial system will become an intrusive chaperone of human nature. The following excerpts from Justice Kennedy's opinion and Justice Thomas's dissent in *Burlington Industries v. Ellerth* (1998) outline the divergence of thinking that currently exists on the highest bench. In *Burlington,* the majority held that the company Burlington Industries could be held liable for the harassment inflicted on Kimberly Ellerth, a salesperson, by her supervisor, Ted Slowik. Ellerth, who quit her job after a year and a half, filed a civil suit against the company, alleging that during her employment, Slowik had created a "hostile work environment" by repeatedly directing lewd and sexually derogatory remarks toward her. Although Ellerth neither made use of the company's harassment complaint procedures nor suffered retaliation (indeed, she was even promoted), the Court nonetheless found that Burlington Industries could be held "vicariously liable" for the behavior of its supervisory employees, subject to the possibility of an "affirmative defense" on the basis of its own efforts to correct harassing behavior.

In his vigorous dissent, Justice Thomas (joined by Justice Scalia) insists on a more limited definition of workplace discrimination as understood under Title VII. In the absence of any adverse employment consequence such as loss of rank or job, employers cannot be held liable for the behavior of supervisory employees if the employer was reasonably proactive in anticipating possible harassing situations. "Sexual harassment," Thomas writes, "is simply not something that employers can wholly prevent without taking extraordinary measures . . . that would revolutionize the workplace in a manner incompatible with a free society."

As you read the articles, consider the following questions.

Discussion Questions

1. Thomas's dissent expresses a distinctly restricted understanding of sexual harassment. Nonetheless, are the underlying assumptions of the dissent and the majority opinion very far apart? In what sense might a "sexually hostile atmosphere" be understood as an "adverse employment consequence"?
2. The dissent insists that sexual harassment in the workplace be treated in the same way as harassment based on race. Why does the majority opinion treat these two kinds of harassment differently?
3. While asserting a broad understanding of sexual harassment, Kennedy's opinion recognizes the danger of a standard so general that it transforms Title VII into a

"general civility code." Does Souter's opinion provide useful grounds for distinguishing between true sexual harassment and merely teasing or rude behavior? Or is sexual harassment merely in the eyes of the beholder?

4. The ruling in *Burlington* hinged on the fact that the harasser was facilitated by his supervisory authority. What are the implications of this ruling for situations in which a "hostile work environment" is alleged between coworkers of otherwise equal rank? Could the findings of this case extend to other sections of the Civil Rights Act of 1964 to cover similar behavior in other nonsupervisory situations— for example, among students?

For more on this topic, visit the following websites:

http://www.eeoc.gov
The U.S. Government's Equal Employment and Opportunity Commission

http://www.hermesweb.com
Hermes' Web—Supreme court cases on the internet.

http://www.ij.org
Insitute for Justice

Justice Kennedy's Opinion in *Burlington Industries, Inc., Petitioner v. Kimberly B. Ellerth*

Opinion of the Court
No. 97—569
Burlington Industries, Inc., Petitioner v. Kimberly B. Ellerth
On Writ Of Certiorari To The United States Court Of Appeals For The
Seventh Circuit
[June 26, 1998]
Justice Kennedy delivered the opinion of the Court.

We decide whether, under Title VII of the Civil Rights Act of 1964, 78
Stat. 253, as amended, 42 U.S.C. § 2000e et seq., an employee who refuses the unwelcome and threatening sexual advances of a supervisor,
yet suffers no adverse, tangible job consequences, can recover against the
employer without showing the employer is negligent or otherwise at
fault for the supervisor's actions.

    I. Summary judgment was granted for the employer, so we must
take the facts alleged by the employee to be true. United States v.
Diebold, Inc. 369 U.S. 654, 655 (1962) (per curiam). The employer is
Burlington Industries, the petitioner. The employee is Kimberly Ellerth,
the respondent. From March 1993 until May 1994, Ellerth worked as a
salesperson in one of Burlington's divisions in Chicago, Illinois. During
her employment, she alleges, she was subjected to constant sexual harassment by her supervisor, one Ted Slowik.

    In the hierarchy of Burlington's management structure, Slowik was
a mid-level manager. Burlington has eight divisions, employing more
than 22,000 people in some 50 plants around the United States. Slowik
was a vice president in one of five business units within one of the divisions. He had authority to make hiring and promotion decisions subject
to the approval of his supervisor, who signed the paperwork. See 912
F. Supp. 1101, 1119, n. 14 (ND Ill. 1996). According to Slowik's supervisor, his position was "not considered an upper-level management position," and he was "not amongst the decision-making or policy-making
hierarchy." Ibid. Slowik was not Ellerth's immediate supervisor. Ellerth
worked in a two-person office in Chicago, and she answered to her office
colleague, who in turn answered to Slowik in New York.

    Against a background of repeated boorish and offensive remarks
and gestures which Slowik allegedly made, Ellerth places particular em-

phasis on three alleged incidents where Slowik's comments could be construed as threats to deny her tangible job benefits. In the summer of 1993, while on a business trip, Slowik invited Ellerth to the hotel lounge, an invitation Ellerth felt compelled to accept because Slowik was her boss. App. 155. When Ellerth gave no encouragement to remarks Slowik made about her breasts, he told her to "loosen up" and warned, "[y]ou know, Kim, I could make your life very hard or very easy at Burlington." Id., at 156.

In March 1994, when Ellerth was being considered for a promotion, Slowik expressed reservations during the promotion interview because she was not "loose enough." Id., at 159. The comment was followed by his reaching over and rubbing her knee. Ibid. Ellerth did receive the promotion; but when Slowik called to announce it, he told Ellerth, "you're gonna be out there with men who work in factories, and they certainly like women with pretty butts/legs." Id., at 159—160.

In May 1994, Ellerth called Slowik, asking permission to insert a customer's logo into a fabric sample. Slowik responded, "I don't have time for you right now, Kim—unless you want to tell me what you're wearing." Id., at 78. Ellerth told Slowik she had to go and ended the call. Ibid. A day or two later, Ellerth called Slowik to ask permission again. This time he denied her request, but added something along the lines of, "are you wearing shorter skirts yet, Kim, because it would make your job a whole heck of a lot easier." Id., at 79.

A short time later, Ellerth's immediate supervisor cautioned her about returning telephone calls to customers in a prompt fashion. 912 F. Supp., at 1109. In response, Ellerth quit. She faxed a letter giving reasons unrelated to the alleged sexual harassment we have described. Ibid. About three weeks later, however, she sent a letter explaining she quit because of Slowik's behavior. Ibid.

During her tenure at Burlington, Ellerth did not inform anyone in authority about Slowik's conduct, despite knowing Burlington had a policy against sexual harassment. Ibid. In fact, she chose not to inform her immediate supervisor (not Slowik) because "'it would be his duty as my supervisor to report any incidents of sexual harassment.'" Ibid. On one occasion, she told Slowik a comment he made was inappropriate. Ibid.

In October 1994, after receiving a right-to-sue letter from the Equal Employment Opportunity Commission (EEOC), Ellerth filed suit in the United States District Court for the Northern District of Illinois, alleging Burlington engaged in sexual harassment and forced her constructive discharge, in violation of Title VII. The District Court granted summary judgment to Burlington. The Court found Slowik's behavior, as described by Ellerth, severe and pervasive enough to create a hostile work environment, but found Burlington neither knew nor should have known about the conduct. There was no triable issue of fact on the latter point, and the Court noted Ellerth had not used Burlington's internal complaint procedures. Id., at 1118. Although Ellerth's claim was framed as a hostile work environment complaint, the District Court observed there was a quid pro quo "component" to the hostile environment. Id., at 1121. Proceeding from the premise that an employer faces vicarious liability for quid pro quo harassment, the District Court thought it necessary to apply a negligence standard because the quid pro quo merely contributed to the hostile work environment. See id., at 1123. The District Court also dismissed Ellerth's constructive discharge claim.

The Court of Appeals en banc reversed in a decision which produced eight separate opinions and no consensus for a controlling rationale . . .

II. At the outset, we assume an important proposition yet to be established before a trier of fact. It is a premise assumed as well, in explicit or implicit terms, in the various opinions by the judges of the Court of Appeals. The premise is: a trier of fact could find in Slowik's remarks numerous threats to retaliate against Ellerth if she denied some sexual liberties. The threats, however, were not carried out or fulfilled. Cases based on threats which are carried out are referred to often as quid pro quo cases, as distinct from bothersome attentions or sexual remarks that are sufficiently severe or pervasive to create a hostile work environment. The terms quid pro quo and hostile work environment are helpful, perhaps, in making a rough demarcation between cases in which threats are carried out and those where they are not or are absent altogether, but beyond this are of limited utility.

Section 703(a) of Title VII forbids "an employer—(1) to fail or refuse to hire or to discharge any individual, or otherwise to discriminate against any individual with respect to his compensation, terms, conditions or privileges of employment, because of such individual's . . . sex." "Quid pro quo" and "hostile work environment" do not appear in the statutory text . . .

The question presented for certiorari asks: "Whether a claim of quid pro quo sexual harassment may be stated under Title VII . . . where the plaintiff employee has neither submitted to the sexual advances of the alleged harasser nor suffered any tangible effects on the compensation, terms, conditions or privileges of employment as a consequence of a refusal to submit to those advances?" Pet. for Cert. i.

We do not suggest the terms quid pro quo and hostile work environment are irrelevant to Title VII litigation. To the extent they illustrate the distinction between cases involving a threat which is carried out and offensive conduct in general, the terms are relevant when there is a threshold question whether a plaintiff can prove discrimination in violation of Title VII. When a plaintiff proves that a tangible employment action resulted from a refusal to submit to a supervisor's sexual demands, he or she establishes that the employment decision itself constitutes a change in the terms and conditions of employment that is actionable under Title VII. For any sexual harassment preceding the employment decision to be actionable, however, the conduct must be severe or pervasive. Because Ellerth's claim involves only unfulfilled threats, it should be categorized as a hostile work environment claim which requires a showing of severe or pervasive conduct. See Oncale v. Sundowner Offshore Services, Inc., 523 U.S. __, __ (1998) (slip op., at 6); Harris v. Forklift Systems, Inc., 510 U.S. 17, 21 (1993). For purposes of this case, we accept the District Court's finding that the alleged conduct was severe or pervasive. See supra, at 3. The case before us involves numerous alleged threats, and we express no opinion as to whether a single unfulfilled threat is sufficient to constitute discrimination in the terms or conditions of employment.

When we assume discrimination can be proved, however, the factors we discuss below, and not the categories quid pro quo and hostile work environment, will be controlling on the issue of vicarious liability. That is the question we must resolve.

III. We must decide, then, whether an employer has vicarious liability when a supervisor creates a hostile work environment by making explicit threats to alter a subordinate's terms or conditions of employment, based on sex, but does not fulfill the threat. We turn to principles of agency law, for the term "employer" is defined under Title VII to include "agents." 42 U.S.C. § 2000e(b); see Meritor, supra, at 72. In express terms, Congress has directed federal courts to interpret Title VII based on agency principles. Given such an explicit instruction, we conclude a uniform and predictable standard must be established as a matter of federal law. We rely "on the general common law of agency, rather than on the law of any particular State, to give meaning to these terms." Community for Creative Non-Violence v. Reid, 490 U.S. 730, 740 (1989). The resulting federal rule, based on a body of case law developed over time, is statutory interpretation pursuant to congressional direction. This is not federal common law in "the strictest sense, i.e., a rule of decision that amounts, not simply to an interpretation of a federal statute . . . , but, rather, to the judicial 'creation' of a special federal rule of decision." Atherton v. FDIC, 519 U.S. 213, 218 (1997). State court decisions, applying state employment discrimination law, may be instructive in applying general agency principles, but, it is interesting to note, in many cases their determinations of employer liability under state law rely in large part on federal court decisions under Title VII. . . .

Section 219(1) of the Restatement sets out a central principle of agency law: "A master is subject to liability for the torts of his servants committed while acting in the scope of their employment."

An employer may be liable for both negligent and intentional torts committed by an employee within the scope of his or her employment. Sexual harassment under Title VII presupposes intentional conduct.

While early decisions absolved employers of liability for the intentional torts of their employees, the law now imposes liability where the employee's "purpose, however misguided, is wholly or in part to further the master's business." . . .

As Courts of Appeals have recognized, a supervisor acting out of gender-based animus or a desire to fulfill sexual urges may not be actuated by a purpose to serve the employer. See, e.g., Harrison v. Eddy Potash, Inc., 112 F.3d 1437, 1444 (CA10 1997), cert. pending, No. 97—232; Torres v. Pisano, 116 F.3d 625, 634, n. 10 (CA2 1997). But see Kauffman v. Allied Signal, Inc., 970 F.2d, at 184—185 (holding harassing supervisor acted within scope of employment, but employer was not liable because of its quick and effective remediation). The harassing supervisor often acts for personal motives, motives unrelated and even antithetical to the objectives of the employer. Cf. Mechem, supra, §368 ("for the time being [the supervisor] is conspicuously and unmistakably seeking a personal end"); see also Restatement §235, Illustration 2 (tort committed while "[a]cting purely from personal ill will" not within the scope of employment); §235, Illustration 3 (tort committed in retaliation for failing to pay the employee a bribe not within the scope of employment). There are instances, of course, where a supervisor engages in unlawful discrimination with the purpose, mistaken or otherwise, to serve the employer. E.g., Sims v. Montgomery County Comm'n, 766 F. Supp. 1052, 1075 (MD Ala. 1990) (supervisor acting in scope of employment where employer has a policy of discouraging women from seeking advancement and "sexual harassment was simply a way of furthering that policy"). . . .

In order to accommodate the agency principles of vicarious liability for harm caused by misuse of supervisory authority, as well as Title VII's equally basic policies of encouraging forethought by employers and saving action by objecting employees, we adopt the following holding in this case and in Faragher v. Boca Raton, post, also decided today. An employer is subject to vicarious liability to a victimized employee for an actionable hostile environment created by a supervisor with immediate (or successively higher) authority over the employee. When no tangible employment action is taken, a defending employer may raise an affirmative defense to liability or damages, subject to proof by a preponderance of the evidence, see Fed. Rule Civ. Proc. 8(c). The defense comprises two necessary elements: (a) that the employer exercised reasonable care to prevent and correct promptly any sexually harassing behavior, and (b) that the plaintiff employee unreasonably failed to take advantage of any preventive or corrective opportunities provided by the employer or to avoid harm otherwise. While proof that an employer had promulgated an anti-harassment policy with complaint procedure is not necessary in every instance as a matter of law, the need for a stated policy suitable to the employment circumstances may appropriately be addressed in any case when litigating the first element of the defense. And while proof that an employee failed to fulfill the corresponding obligation of reasonable care to avoid harm is not limited to showing any unreasonable failure to use any complaint procedure provided by the employer, a demonstration of such failure will normally suffice to satisfy the employer's burden under the second element of the defense. No affirmative defense is available, however, when the supervisor's harassment culminates in a tangible employment action, such as discharge, demotion, or undesirable reassignment.

IV. Relying on existing case law which held out the promise of vicarious liability for all quid pro quo claims, see supra, at 7, Ellerth focused all her attention in the Court of Appeals on proving her claim fit within that category. Given our explanation that the labels quid pro quo and hostile work environment are not controlling for purposes of establishing employer liability, see supra, at 8, Ellerth should have an adequate opportunity to prove she has a claim for which Burlington is liable.

Although Ellerth has not alleged she suffered a tangible employment action at the hands of Slowik, which would deprive Burlington of the availability of the affirmative defense, this is not dispositive. In light of our decision, Burlington is still subject to vicarious liability for Slowik's activity, but Burlington should have an opportunity to assert and prove the affirmative defense to liability. See supra, at 20—21.

For these reasons, we will affirm the judgment of the Court of Appeals, reversing the grant of summary judgment against Ellerth. On remand, the District Court will have the opportunity to decide whether it would be appropriate to allow Ellerth to amend her pleading or supplement her discovery.

The judgment of the Court of Appeals is affirmed.

Justice Thomas's Dissent in *Burlington Industries, Inc., Petitioner v. Kimberly B. Ellerth*

Thomas, J., dissenting
SUPREME COURT OF THE UNITED STATES
No. 97—569
BURLINGTON INDUSTRIES, INC., PETITIONER v. KIMBERLY B. ELLERTH
ON WRIT OF CERTIORARI TO THE UNITED STATES COURT OF APPEALS FOR THE SEVENTH CIRCUIT
[June 26, 1998]
Justice Thomas, with whom Justice Scalia joins, dissenting.

The Court today manufactures a rule that employers are vicariously liable if supervisors create a sexually hostile work environment, subject to an affirmative defense that the Court barely attempts to define. This rule applies even if the employer has a policy against sexual harassment, the employee knows about that policy, and the employee never informs anyone in a position of authority about the supervisor's conduct. As a result, employer liability under Title VII is judged by different standards depending upon whether a sexually or racially hostile work environment is alleged. The standard of employer liability should be the same in both instances: An employer should be liable if, and only if, the plaintiff proves that the employer was negligent in permitting the supervisor's conduct to occur.

I. Years before sexual harassment was recognized as "discriminat[ion] . . . because of . . . sex," 42 U.S.C. § 2000e—2(a)(1), the Courts of Appeals considered whether, and when, a racially hostile work environment could violate Title VII.[1] In the landmark case Rogers v. EEOC, 454 F.2d 234 (1971), cert. denied, 406 U.S. 957 (1972), the Court of Appeals for the Fifth Circuit held that the practice of racially segregating patients in a doctor's office could amount to discrimination in "'the terms, conditions, or privileges'" of employment, thereby violating Title VII. Id., at 238 (quoting 42 U.S.C. § 2000e—2(a)(1)). The principal opinion in the case concluded that employment discrimination was not limited to the "isolated and distinguishable events" of "hiring, firing, and promoting." Id., at 238 (opinion of Goldberg, J.). Rather, Title VII could also be violated by a work environment "heavily polluted with discrimination," because of the deleterious effects of such an atmosphere on an employee's well-being. Ibid.

Accordingly, after Rogers, a plaintiff claiming employment discrimination based upon race could assert a claim for a racially hostile work environment, in addition to the classic claim of so-called "disparate treatment." A disparate treatment claim required a plaintiff to prove an adverse employment consequence and discriminatory intent by his employer. See 1 B. Lindemann & P. Grossman, Employment Discrimination Law 10—11 (3d ed. 1996). A hostile environment claim required the plaintiff to show that his work environment was so pervaded by racial harassment as to alter the terms and conditions of his employment. See, e.g., Snell v. Suffolk Cty., 782 F.2d 1094, 1103 (CA2 1986) ("To establish a hostile atmosphere, . . . plaintiffs must prove more than a few isolated incidents of racial enmity"); Johnson v. Bunny Bread Co., 646 F.2d 1250, 1257 (CA8 1981) (no violation of Title VII from infrequent use of racial slurs). This is the same standard now used when determining whether sexual harassment renders a work environment hostile. See Harris v. Forklift Systems, Inc., 510 U.S. 17, 21 (1993) (actionable sexual harassment occurs when the workplace is "permeated with discriminatory intimidation, ridicule, and insult") (emphasis added) (internal quotation marks and citation omitted).

In race discrimination cases, employer liability has turned on whether the plaintiff has alleged an adverse employment consequence, such as firing or demotion, or a hostile work environment. If a supervisor takes an adverse employment action because of race, causing the employee a tangible job detriment, the employer is vicariously liable for resulting damages. See ante, at 15. This is because such actions are company acts that can be performed only by the exercise of specific authority granted by the employer, and thus the supervisor acts as the employer. If, on the other hand, the employee alleges a racially hostile work environment, the employer is liable only for negligence: that is, only if the employer knew, or in the exercise of reasonable care should have known, about the harassment and failed to take remedial action. See, e.g., Dennis v. Cty. of Fairfax, 55 F.3d 151, 153 (CA4 1995); Davis v. Monsanto Chemical Co., 858 F.2d 345, 349 (CA6 1988), cert. denied, 490 U.S. 1110 (1989). Liability has thus been imposed only if the employer is blameworthy in some way. See, e.g., Davis v. Monsanto Chemical Co., supra, at 349; Snell v. Suffolk Cty., supra, at 1104; DeGrace v. Rumsfeld, 614 F.2d 796, 805 (CA1 1980). This distinction applies with equal force in cases of sexual harassment.[2] When a supervisor inflicts an adverse employment consequence upon an employee who has rebuffed his advances, the supervisor exercises the specific authority granted to him by his company. His acts, therefore, are the company's acts and are properly chargeable to it. See 123 F.3d 490, 514 (1997) (Posner, C. J., dissenting); ante, at 17 ("Tangible employment actions fall within the special province of the supervisor. The supervisor has been empowered by the company as a distinct class of agent to make economic decisions affecting other employees under his or her control").

If a supervisor creates a hostile work environment, however, he does not act for the employer. As the Court concedes, a supervisor's creation of a hostile work environment is neither within the scope of his employment, nor part of his apparent authority. See ante, at 10—14. Indeed, a hostile work environment is antithetical to the interest of the employer. In such circumstances, an employer should be liable only if it has been negligent. That is, liability should attach only if the employer either knew, or in the exercise of reasonable care should have known, about the hostile work environment and failed to take remedial action.[3]

Sexual harassment is simply not something that employers can wholly prevent without taking extraordinary measures—constant video and audio surveillance, for example—that would revolutionize the workplace in a manner incompatible with a free society. See 123 F.3d 490, 513 (Posner, C.J., dissenting). Indeed, such measures could not even detect incidents of harassment such as the comments Slowick allegedly made to respondent in a hotel bar. The most that employers can be charged with, therefore, is a duty to act reasonably under the circumstances. As one court recognized in addressing an early racial harassment claim:

> "It may not always be within an employer's power to guarantee an environment free from all bigotry. . . . [H]e can let it be known, however, that racial harassment will not be tolerated, and he can take all reasonable measures to enforce this policy. . . . But once an employer has in good faith taken those measures which are both feasible and reasonable under the circumstances to combat the offensive conduct we do not think he can be charged with discriminating on the basis of race." De Grace v. Rumsfeld, 614 F.2d 796, 805 (1980).

Under a negligence standard, Burlington cannot be held liable for Slowick's conduct. Although respondent alleged a hostile work environment, she never contended that Burlington had been negligent in permitting the harassment to occur, and there is no question that Burlington acted reasonably under the circumstances. The company had a policy against sexual harassment, and respondent admitted that she was aware of the policy but nonetheless failed to tell anyone with authority over Slowick about his behavior. See, ante, at 3. Burlington therefore cannot be charged with knowledge of Slowick's alleged harassment or with a failure to exercise reasonable care in not knowing about it.

II. Rejecting a negligence standard, the Court instead imposes a rule of vicarious employer liability, subject to a vague affirmative defense, for the acts of supervisors who wield no delegated authority in creating a hostile work environment. This rule is a whole-cloth creation that draws no support from the legal principles on which the Court claims it is based. Compounding its error, the Court fails to explain how employers can rely upon the affirmative defense, thus ensuring a continuing reign of confusion in this important area of the law. In justifying its holding, the Court refers to our comment in Meritor Savings Bank, FSB v. Vinson, 477 U.S. 57 (1986), that the lower courts should look to "agency principles" for guidance in determining the scope of employer liability, id., at 72. The Court then interprets the term "agency principles" to mean the Restatement (Second) of Agency (1957). The Court finds two portions of the Restatement to be relevant: §219(2)(b), which provides that a master is liable for his servant's torts if the master is reckless or negligent, and §219(2)(d), which states that a master is liable for his servant's torts when the servant is "aided in accomplishing the tort by the existence of the agency relation." The Court appears to reason that a supervisor is "aided . . . by . . . the agency relation" in creating a hostile work environment because the supervisor's "power and authority invests his or her harassing conduct with a particular threatening character." Ante, at 18.

Section 219(2)(d) of the Restatement provides no basis whatsoever for imposing vicarious liability for a supervisor's creation of a hostile work environment. Contrary to the Court's suggestions, the principle embodied in §219(2)(d) has nothing to do with a servant's "power and authority," nor with whether his actions appear "threatening." Rather, as demonstrated by the Restatement's illustrations, liability under §219(2)(d) depends upon the plaintiff's belief that the agent acted in the ordinary course of business or within the scope of his apparent authority.[4] In this day and age, no sexually harassed employee can reasonably believe that a harassing supervisor is conducting the official business of the company or acting on its behalf. Indeed, the Court admits as much in demonstrating why sexual harassment is not committed within the scope of a supervisor's employment and is not part of his apparent authority. See ante, at 10—14.

Thus although the Court implies that it has found guidance in both precedent and statute—see ante, at 9 ("The resulting federal rule, based on a body of case law developed over time, is statutory interpretation pursuant to congressional direction")—its holding is a product of willful policymaking, pure and simple. The only agency principle that justifies imposing employer liability in this context is the principle that a master will be liable for a servant's torts if the master was negligent or reckless in permitting them to occur; and as noted, under a negligence standard, Burlington cannot be held liable. See supra, at 5—6.

The Court's decision is also in considerable tension with our holding in Meritor that employers are not strictly liable for a supervisor's sexual harassment. See Meritor Savings Bank, FSB v. Vinson, supra, at

72. Although the Court recognizes an affirmative defense—based solely on its divination of Title VII's gestalt, see ante, at 19—it provides shockingly little guidance about how employers can actually avoid vicarious liability. Instead, it issues only Delphic pronouncements and leaves the dirty work to the lower courts:

> "While proof that an employer had promulgated an anti-harassment policy with complaint procedure is not necessary in every instance as a matter of law, the need for a stated policy suitable to the employment circumstances may appropriately be addressed in any case when litigating the first element of the defense. And while proof that an employee failed to fulfill the corresponding obligation of reasonable care to avoid harm is not limited to showing any unreasonable failure to use any complaint procedure provided by the employer, a demonstration of such failure will normally suffice to satisfy the employer's burden under the second element of the defense." Ante, at 20.

What these statements mean for district courts ruling on motions for summary judgment—the critical question for employers now subject to the vicarious liability rule—remains a mystery. Moreover, employers will be liable notwithstanding the affirmative defense, even though they acted reasonably, so long as the plaintiff in question fulfilled her duty of reasonable care to avoid harm. See ibid. In practice, therefore, employer liability very well may be the rule. But as the Court acknowledges, this is the one result that it is clear Congress did not intend. See ante, at 18; Meritor Savings Bank, FSB v. Vinson, 477 U.S., at 72.

The Court's holding does guarantee one result: There will be more and more litigation to clarify applicable legal rules in an area in which both practitioners and the courts have long been begging for guidance. It thus truly boggles the mind that the Court can claim that its holding will effect "Congress' intention to promote conciliation rather than litigation in the Title VII context." Ante, at 19. All in all, today's decision is an ironic result for a case that generated eight separate opinions in the Court of Appeals on a fundamental question, and in which we granted certiorari "to assist in defining the relevant standards of employer liability." Ante, at 5.

Popular misconceptions notwithstanding, sexual harassment is not a freestanding federal tort, but a form of employment discrimination. As such, it should be treated no differently (and certainly no better) than the other forms of harassment that are illegal under Title VII. I would restore parallel treatment of employer liability for racial and sexual harassment and hold an employer liable for a hostile work environment only if the employer is truly at fault. I therefore respectfully dissent.

NOTES

1. This sequence of events is not surprising, given that the primary goal of the Civil Rights Act of 1964 was to eradicate race discrimination and that the statute's ban on sex discrimination was added as an eleventh-hour amendment in an effort to kill the bill. See Barnes v. Costle, 561 F.2d 983, 987 (CADC 1977).

2. The Courts of Appeals relied on racial harassment cases when analyzing early claims of discrimination based upon a supervisor's sexual harassment. For example, when the Court of Appeals for the District Columbia Circuit held that a work environment poisoned by a supervisor's "sexually stereotyped insults and demeaning propositions" could itself violate Title VII, its principal authority was Judge Goldberg's opinion in Rogers. See Bundy v. Jackson, 641 F.2d 934, 944 (CADC 1981); see also Henson v. Dundee, 682 F.2d 897, 901 (CA11 1982). So too, this Court relied on Rogers when in Meritor Savings Bank, FSB v. Vinson, 477 U.S. 57 (1986), it recognized a cause of action under Title VII for sexual harassment. See id., at 65—66.

3. I agree with the Court that the doctrine of quid pro quo sexual harassment is irrelevant to the issue of an employer's vicarious liability. I do not, however, agree that the distinction between hostile work environment and quid pro quo sexual harassment is relevant "when there is a threshold question whether a plaintiff can prove discrimination in violation of Title VII." Ante, at 8. A supervisor's threat to take adverse action against an employee who refuses his sexual demands, if never carried out, may create a hostile work environment, but that is all. Cases involving such threats, without more, should therefore be analyzed as hostile work environment cases only. If, on the other hand, the supervisor carries out his threat and causes the plaintiff a job detriment, the plaintiff may have a disparate treatment claim under Title VII. See E. Scalia, The Strange Career of Quid Pro Quo Sexual Harassment, 21 Harv. J. L. & Pub. Policy 307, 309—314 (1998).

4. See Restatement §219, Comment e; §261, Comment a (principal liable for an agent's fraud if "the agent's position facilitates the consummation of the fraud, in that from the point of view of the third person the transaction seems regular on its face and the agent appears to be acting in the ordinary course of business confided to him"); §247, Illustrations (newspaper liable for a defamatory editorial published by editor for his own purposes).

PART III
The Political Process

Issue 7
Ideology

INTRODUCTION

While political labels may be accidents of history, their underlying meanings persist despite changes in name. As Mitchell Cohen points out in the first article, the terms "left" and "right" date from the seating practices of the National Assembly during the French Revolution, when republican and royalist opponents arrayed themselves on opposite sides of the chamber. Even more so than their counterparts in English history, these categories have become the models for what we call political ideologies. An ideology is a system of thought that unfolds the logic of one big idea, such as freedom, equality, security, or piety. Ever since the French Revolution, conflicts over interest and principle in the Western political tradition have been complicated by the question of exactly what the words left (or liberal) and right (or conservative) mean. In public policy-making, such labels are useful since they orient supporters and opponents alike. Political labels, and the ideology behind them, are a kind of useful shorthand. They tell us who we are and even how to think, especially when issues and circumstances change.

At the same time, the logic of big ideas is always threatened by the reality of political power. Power is the ability to get people to behave in the way we want them to. We need power to get things done in public life. Yet, as we usually understand it, power is merely a means to something more, rather than an end in itself. Power itself can be a dangerous thing, since having too much of it encourages the delusion that we can simply force other people to live by our own big ideas. It is even worse when our big ideas become merely an excuse for the pleasure of exercising power. At bottom, big ideas like equality and freedom are true only to the extent that people accept them willingly. Power does not merely corrupt big ideas; it inverts them. Forced equality can be the crudest kind of oppression, whereas forced freedom can be the most exquisite kind of cruelty.

In the United States of the late twentieth century, the Democratic left stands for the idea of equality, whereas the Republican right stands for the idea of freedom. From these beginnings, political ideologies intersect in interesting ways. For Democrats, equality is the basis for true freedom, since it is only through equal access to resources like food, shelter, or education that citizens can be free to realize their human potential. For Republicans, freedom is the basis for true equality, since it is only through the free use of our capacities and our property that we express our common humanity. At its worst, the Democratic ideology of equality leads to envy—to the hatred of freedom because it produces difference. For its part, at its worst, the Republican ideology of freedom leads to contempt—to the hatred of equality because it stands in the way of wealth, achievement, and distinction.

Big ideas like freedom and equality become the lenses with which to focus on smaller issues and to recognize group interests. Thus, a Democrat tends to favor larger government, greater economic regulation, expanded civil rights, and a therapeutic approach to crime because of an overriding impulse to use public power to enforce greater equality of condition. Yet these measures also favor Democratic interests such as labor unions, public sector employees, so-called public interest advocates, and ethnic pressure groups. In contrast, a Republican tends to favor smaller government, less economic regulation, and a punitive approach to crime because of an overriding impulse to guard freedom against the abuses of public power. Not coincidentally, these particular positions also benefit the interests of corporations and the wealthy, as well as address the passions of social conservatives.

Note also how, in practice, the Democratic and Republican positions express ambivalence about the proper scope and exercise of public power. Beneath their rhetoric about justice and freedom, both Mitchell Cohen and Pete Dupont see power as necessary but threatening. While advocating greater government regulation of the economy and the society, Democrats nonetheless believe that government should both respect and protect the civil liberties of individuals, even to the extent of inventing rights such as that to privacy. Yet this concern does not extend to a similar enthusiasm for the protection of property. Social justice, yes—but whose justice? Much as they call for less economic regulation and for a wider return of governing authority to state and local control, Republicans still favor greater government coercion in the realm of personal behavior. Thus, to Republicans the use of drugs, the viewing of pornography, or the practice of homosexuality represents not the exercise of freedom but the indulgence of moral depravity. Limited government, yes—but for what, and for whom?

As you read the articles, consider the following questions.

Discussion Questions

1. In contrast with Republicans and Democrats, a libertarian is someone who believes in a minimal government that should regulate neither social or economic life. A populist is someone who believes in a strong government that regulates both social and economic life. Why are there no important libertarian or populist parties in American politics?
2. The readings in Issue Two addressed the future of democracy. Given a choice between direct and representative democracy, which form of government do you think a liberal and a conservative would prefer?
3. Power can corrupt ideals if it is used to force people to live by those ideals. Nonetheless, in what ways can ideals themselves be powerful?
4. Why care about ideology at all, as long as the stock market keeps going up and everyone feels richer?

   For more information on this topic, visit the following websites:

   http://www.conservative.org
   The American Conservative Union

   http://www.free-market.com
   The Freedom Network

   http://www.democratic.org
   The Democratic National Committee

Why I'm Still Left

MITCHELL COHEN

Should the word "left" matter any more? Identify with it nowadays and the reaction is apt to be a perplexed, crinkled nose. As if to say, "The word's in bad odor, why use it? In any event, you'll be taken for a left-over." Frankly, "left" has never had happy associations, olfactory or otherwise, on American shores. One reason, undoubtedly, is that we, unlike most Western countries, never had a mass socialist party—sharply distinguishing itself from communism—as a normal feature of our politics. Then there was the cold war itself, in which "the left" was habitually, often maliciously, identified with Leninism or Stalinism.

It could be said that the word "left" was victim of a double intellectual mugging. The right, always quick to denounce communist mendacity, decided that on this one point—that "left" meant Soviet-style dictatorship—communist parties always spoke truthfully. The latter happily concurred, because they wanted to be arbiters of what "left" meant, precluding a pluralist left. This was not achieved—Bolshevik conduct, from early on, was censured by many leftists, leading Marxists included—but success was substantial enough.

This gave birth to a de facto and paradoxical propaganda alliance of communists and conservatives. That communists called themselves "democratic" as well as "left" never complicated things. But why take their word in one case and not in the other? Or, since tens of thousands of self-identified "leftists"—social democrats, democratic socialists, left-liberals, independent Marxists, Trotskyists, anarchists—were persecuted, imprisoned, or murdered by Leninist and Stalinist states, why not draw the obvious conclusion that these regimes were anti-left? At issue is not simply a word. "Left," after all, has no intrinsic worth; what matters are the politics and ethos it properly evokes. But then a word's resonance also depends on its associations, its use or misuse. Once "liberal" pointed to honored features of our society; now it is the "L-word," a powerfully disqualifying epithet, comparable (well, not quite) to the S-word, socialist. So the problem is clearly not just "left" but the fact that all political words and ideas to the left of the right have run into trouble.

I want, in what follows, to look at words and values. "Modern English . . . ," as Orwell observed, "is full of bad habits which spread by imitation and which can be avoided if one is willing to take the necessary

Mitchell Cohen is coeditor of *Dissent*. He teaches politics at Baruch College and the Graduate Center at the City University of New York.

Reprinted by permission. *Dissent*, Spring 1997. Vol. 44, No. 2 .

trouble. If one gets rid of these habits one can think more clearly, and to think clearly is a necessary first step towards political regeneration." "Left" is, admittedly, a vague term, and this permits its easy abuse not only by foes but a little too often by friends. Still, my aim is not, in response to corruptions or ambiguities, to provide a canonical definition. It is probably not possible and in any event it wouldn't be very fruitful. What a future left needs is surely not codified language, much less thought, but a combination of discrimination and openness in its intellectual conversation. Its concepts should be receptive to adjectives—as in liberal socialist or democratic left. There is nothing wrong with modifiers. It is in this spirit that I want to rearticulate and to reassert some basic left-wing values; and I'll affirm that we who have identified ourselves as "left" should still do so, not out of fidelity to a maligned term or to a site on political maps, but on behalf of those values. "Left" is no left-over only if those values remain vital to the idea of a decent society, to social justice.

I. I'm still "left" because I'm committed to an ethos that is democratic and humanist, equality-friendly and inclusive—not only in the political domain but in social and economic relations too. This ethos presumes that an egalitarian sensibility, not a conformist mentality (be it expressed as rigid collectivism or abstract individualism), should animate our social, economic, and political life. And it presumes that it is inequality that must be justified by its proponents or apologists.

The origins of "left" as a political term date to the French revolution, most famously when delegates with royalist, clerical, and aristocratic leanings settled to the right side of the National Assembly and those of more republican and democratic persuasion moved left. Eventually these chance spatial positions also assumed social hues, with "right" more associated with the upper classes and emigres and "left" with most everyone else. An egalitarian reconstitution was, in fact, occurring, pressed forth by the idea of equal citizenship: the hierarchy of the old regime's three estates—Church, Nobility, Everyone Else (the Third Estate)—had been toppled, to be succeeded by a more level division of left, center, and right.

Those who, in the future, called themselves "left" usually embraced the legacy of "Liberty, Equality, Fraternity," but almost always with an eye to expanding its meanings and domains. If the precise sense of and the balance among the three ingredients were to be disputed often enough, they still stood together in contrast to the conservative trinity of order, hierarchy, and tradition. Later, especially for socialists, socioeconomic egalitarianism gave wholeness to the emancipatory project begun in the age of democratic revolution, to the summons to human liberty signaled initially by the "Declaration of Independence" and the "Declaration of the Rights of Man and the Citizen." "Left," briefly, was a stance more than a hard concept. First it meant advocacy of political and social equality. Later it meant siding with working people and the dispossessed, especially against private economic power; and that, consequently, democracy ought to pervade socioeconomic in addition to political domains of life so that, to expropriate one pithy premise, the conditions for the freedom of one would be the conditions for the freedom of all. This was—it seems to me, still is—an attractive, regulative idea. To be "left"—my sort of left, anyway—is to be committed still to a triad of liberty, equality, and solidarity; not as a slogan but as entwined imperatives, each distinct yet each in need of the others to flourish. Lest liberty be operative mostly for those who can afford it; lest equality stifle diversity or autonomy; lest solidarity be hierarchical.

Of the three French revolutionary terms, the left has been supremely identified with the second, equality. Often, leftists are caricatured as proponents of a simplistic leveling of society, a forced "equality of all outcomes." Certainly the left has had its simpletons—it hardly surpasses the right or center in this distinction—but some of its most trenchant thinkers actually argued against reducing justice to one denominator. This included Marx himself. Think about his axiom for an egalitarian community: "From each according to his abilities to each according to his needs." This proposes that different individuals contribute to and receive from a classless society different things.

What, then, moves people "left" if not "equality of outcomes"? I think it is the discovery, over and again, that it is not simply "free choice" or "fairness" or "nature" but structures of power and legacies of history, all of them human doings, that have fashioned our society—fashioned it so that the life-possibilities of a few are great and those of most people much more limited. This judgment raises questions about assumptions that, unfortunately, are too common: that "those who have, deserve"; that those who don't are culpable for their want; that such is the "natural order of things." It doesn't take a lot of historical reflection to discern that "natural order" looked quite different in other times and places, although it is almost always invoked to justify hierarchy by those on its top.

So when issues of justice arise, it becomes necessary to talk not just about "personal achievement" in the abstract but of how unchosen inequalities shape the lives of individuals. What is the impact of economic classes and social organization and how do structured, often dramatic, discrepancies of power affect a democratic society? Or to be blunt: why is it that corporate profits rose over 200 percent in the last decade and a half, while the United States "is slipping into a category of countries—among them Brazil, Britain and Guatemala—where economic stratification is most pronounced"? How come "the ratio of the top 20% of American incomes to the poorest 20% is now nine to one"?

Why does the stock market plunge 171 points when employment rates go up—in a world that awards $90 million severance to an executive ousted after fourteen months on the job? Once these things seem to add up to more than a sum of statistical facts, once their causes and impact are not perceived as just happenstance but as somehow integral to our Western societies, then right-wing—no less neoliberal—pronounce-ments about "individual autonomy" and "merit" sound suspect. This has nothing to do with a foolish notion that indolence warrants the same, be it material plenty or life chances, as hard work. Respect for labor, after all, was always a cardinal left-wing virtue; it grounded a basic socialist charge against capitalism, that privileges enjoyed by its domi-nant strata usually rest on the work of others. No, the problem is other-wise—in the pretense that unmerited privilege and social power don't exist; in accepting that a few minutes' gamble on a stock or currency or "futures" market "merits" one person millions, while a full day of fac-tory labor "merits" another individual the minimum wage times eight. We are, as John Rawls among others has argued, subject to a birth lot-tery. Our parents are a matter of chance, not choice. Unless you can be said to have rated your progenitors, why should advantages or disabili-ties that attend accidents of birth be translated into social privileges? Surely, a pneumonia-afflicted six year old with lazy or limited parents doesn't rate lesser medical care than the child of assiduous or gifted souls. Unless, that is, she merits the comportment, not to mention genes, of her parents—whom she did not "freely choose." And if our af-flicted child's health shouldn't depend on her parents' industriousness (or lack thereof), neither should it hinge on their affluence or social class. Similarly, no shiftless son of a rich alumnus deserves admission to an elite university, however much money Father contributes (an affirma-tive action that rarely provokes ire). Nor does he merit the social power that may later be conferred by inherited stocks and bonds.

In short, we don't inhabit a world of rugged individuals. As some on the left are wed to simplistic notions of egalitarianism, so it becomes obvious that many on the right embrace simplistic notions of person-hood. But it is only a complex notion, one of social individuality, that makes sense. People don't simply fashion themselves out of themselves. Their lives as well as their talents as individuals are—or are not—brought to richness or riches through a pre-existing web of social, eco-nomic, political, and cultural relations. We make our own history, but not simply of our own will, not in conditions we select; we do so, as a nineteenth century thinker, now unpopular, once said, "under given and inherited circumstances." Those circumstances permit or impede this or that access, enable this or that education, avail of this or that financial resource, allow time to cultivate natural talents or not. We are, in other words, born into structured, unequal conditions, a world configured by unchosen social—among which I include gender and racial—inequalities. One cannot speak honestly about "equality of opportunity" without addressing—redressing—them. If you've reached this judgment, you may also recognize that you've been deliberating in a left-wing way. It's remarkable, you note, that conservatives, so insistent on their hard-nosed grasp of the "realities of power," become slippery when considering inequalities of socioeconomic power, their reproduction and consequences. Don't interfere with the market's "freedom," they urge. Liberty will be threatened if egalitarian correctives are deployed to remedy social suffering caused by its "natural" workings.

But when has the growth of socioeconomic equality (through, say, initiating a welfare state) led to an overthrow of liberal democracy? Precisely nowhere. Threats to democracy and liberty are more likely to come from burgeoning inequality. In fact, while it is difficult to think of historical cases in which increasing equality led to revolt against liberty, one can recollect numerous instances of democracy subverted by privileged strata or powerful economic institutions fearful of expanding equality. Liberty is fortified when social and economic fairness, rather than the hunger of corporations and banks for profits, takes priority. And significant inequality in socioeconomic power translates into political inequalities—into the disfiguring of democracy. Democracy's vistas, therefore, need to project deeply within, to socioeconomic equity. It's an old "left-wing" point: socioeconomic questions are also political. So the tools of political democracy are properly deployed to enhance social and economic democracy

This doesn't mean abolishing markets. Attempts to do so have not enhanced well-being anywhere. But I don't see how the dictatorship of markets does so either. True, a considerable segment of the historical left believed a command economy was a panacea for capitalism's ills. However, other left traditions—social democratic, market and guild socialist, liberal-left—did not equate socialization with nationalization. They recognized that an economy cannot be planned fully from its center, certainly if democratic decision making from below (in the workplace, for instance) is valued. They understood that trying to administer all economic life from the center is likely to result in an attempt to administer the citizenry from there too.

These other left traditions rejected as simplistic the radical opposition of planning to markets and incorporated markets into their thinking. Unlike classical liberals, however, they did not fetishize them. They recognized that markets are means, not ends or self-sufficient creators of human values, let alone a basis for natural theodicies. In any event, they recognized too that we interfere with nature in diverse ways; sometimes the results are happy, sometimes not.

What if we accept the claim that market mechanisms are "natural"? Does that mean "naturalness" should be an all-determining criterion for human action? There are "natural" events (floods, for instance) that jeopardize countless lives. Would it be "unnatural" to arrest them if we could? And since markets operate in historical and social contexts and not in "natural" vacuums—and as they are never "free" because freedom is an attribute of beings who make choices and markets are not beings—the left has claimed the moral right to intervene in the economic sphere.

Markets, then, should be subject to qualitative human requirements, to standards external to themselves—not vice versa. We need to discriminate between public goods they produce and "public bads" (I borrow from John Roemer), be they social suffering or pollution. Commodification does not define the human good. A sick person, L.T. Hobhouse remarked long ago, should be treated according to the illness, not the individual's "worth" on a labor market. That notion captures the left socioeconomic ethos neatly; also, to a considerable extent, why I'm still "left."

II. It is obvious that a left ethos doesn't much inform our society today; nor are its immediate prospects so promising. When I speak of "the left" it is, admittedly, somewhat of an imaginary entity, more hope than actuality, although a potential nucleus is real enough (in labor, civil rights, and feminist ranks).

But why not just become a "liberal" of some sort? Liberalism has, of course, had varied meanings. In the classical European formulations it was associated, albeit with divergent accents, with ideas like individualism, the market, equality before the law, and laissez-faire. On one hand it embodied an impulse to freedom against absolutist politics and economics; on the other it customarily legitimized capitalist cruelty. The left—my sort of left, anyway—conceives itself as heir to liberalism's better impulses, all while repudiating its manifest flaws. Hence it speaks of social individualism and solidarity as opposed to simple individualism; of qualitative values that should discipline the market; of creating conditions that make equality before the law equally meaningful for rich and poor; and of the myths of laissez-faire. I, for one, don't object to being called liberal when the word is used as an adjective. As I'm for democracy that is not atomized but social, I'm for a leftism that is liberal. It is useful to recall that while classical liberalism helped historically to point the way to modern democracy, it didn't necessarily favor it. You can support civil liberties, equality before the law, and "free" markets without sanctioning universal suffrage. In contrast, most of the left championed the vote for all in most European countries. Once achieved, universal suffrage set down roots deep in the political culture—so penetrating that the political culture was transformed and undoing political equality became, finally, unthinkable (except for fascists, and the like). By the early twentieth century most classical liberals embraced political equality firmly but, generally speaking, they wanted egalitarianism to go no further. As earlier liberals divorced legal from political equality, these liberals favored segregating political from social or economic rights. Since equality's reach was for them properly circumscribed by the ballot box, the form of political life—liberal democracy—and the content of social life were separated one from the other.

On the other hand, a social liberalism that believed in government action to ameliorate social and economic problems also emerged over the last century. This is what Americans commonly call liberalism—a legacy of programmatic ideals associated with the New Deal and Great Society. My kind of left is not so distant from this social liberalism in important ways. The latter championed a welfare state and was content with its outlines. The democratic left also supported a welfare state but wanted to go "beyond" it—beyond government-managed redistributory policies and institutions—to democratizing economic and social structures and the conditions of daily work. "Beyond" was not, perhaps, the best word, because the idea was to thicken democracy in our society, so much so that a return to greater socioeconomic inequalities would be as unthinkable as, say, a return to property qualifications for the franchise.

Of course it never went that far. It seems to me that this is one reason why, now that the welfare state is besieged, its resilience is modest. Social liberals do sanction considerable intrusion by politics (or law) into social and economic life, but they resist some of the implications. Hence Ronald Dworkin, a leading social liberal thinker, proposes that liberal equality requires political decisions to be "independent of any particular concept of the good life or what gives values to life." But what if values promoting a bad life for considerable numbers of people are entrenched in a society, reinforcing or serving structures of unmerited, unjustifiable privilege and power? Must they not be countered by a broad ethos marking out an alternative good life? An idea of the good life—which always means a good life among individuals living together—need not legislate for all dimensions of existence; it does, however, imply an ingrained orientation to living within a community, an orientation that animates public culture and governing institutions. In fact, one can interpret the historical fate of the welfare state as an illustration of how social liberal achievements, because they tried to remain on the political level, were inherently vulnerable.

Post–World War II Western society is often described as a "class compromise." In simplest terms (I am being schematic and telescope features from different countries), this meant that capital and labor were both exhausted and conceded some of each other's priorities. Capital acquiesced to a welfare state, some measure of redistribution, and collective bargaining, while labor accepted capital's hierarchical prerogatives in the workplace and retreated from radical demands for public ownership and extensive redistribution. Class conflict became class sparring, enabling economic growth and social welfare legislation in an atmosphere of social peace. Policies tilted according to election victors, yet there was no dramatic alteration as major parties, whether left or right leaning, didn't contest the basics.

It was, one might say, a pragmatic settlement. After the sacrifices of depression and war, even the dominant strata recognized that things couldn't return entirely to antebellum patterns of hierarchical entitlement. Concurrently, labor discovered that industrial workers would not be the "universal class." Since they never had composed—and never would constitute—the vast majority in Western capitalist societies, workers needed allies in the middle strata to create a decent, or at least better, society. This, in turn, required social coalitions, not just for the near future but in the long run. Compromises in goals, not just tactics, were unavoidable.

The more this settlement seemed to consolidate, the less did social liberals or social democrats feel a need to think beyond it (with some exceptions, notably in Sweden). This gave rise to the 1950s version of a theme that is again popular nowadays: "there is no basic difference between left and right," because ideological history (at least within the West) has ended. But two decades later the compromise crumbled as economic problems multiplied, triggered by the 1973 oil embargo. Importantly, the welfare state was besieged just as globalization and revolutions in technology and communications gained momentum, making it easier for capital to reconsider its past concessions. Changes in the political constellation elucidate the story neatly.

The politicians who were governing as difficulties proliferated were upholders of the pragmatic order, first on the center-right (for example, Heath in the United Kingdom and Nixon and Ford here) and then on the center-left (Callaghan and Carter). They represented the supposed nullification of weighty differences between left and right on socioeconomic questions. But when they proved unable to master the crisis of their compromise, they opened the way for its principled foes, the radical right exemplified by Thatcher and Reagan, to take over their parties, then governments, and to initiate war on the welfare state. This was a historical breakthrough for a conservative agenda based on the sort of harsh classical liberal ideology that had been routed half a century earlier by the Great Depression.

Success required some conservative stealth along with (social) liberal weakness in shaky times. This meant targeting taxes instead of the various social benefits most citizens wanted to conserve. As taxes paid for those benefits, the issues had to be recast—as the "culture of poverty"; or "welfare cheats" who, coincidentally, all had a common skin color; or "the 1960s," "sexual permissiveness," and "countercultural threats" to "middle-class" values. Of course, the counterculture was, by the late 1970s, mostly a thing of the past, and the middle class of what conservatives now proclaimed the "golden age"—the 1950s, not the 1920s—had actually been created by the very social liberalism they opposed (that is, it was the product of state action when markets failed to function "naturally," social welfare legislation, and strong trade unionism). With social liberals unable to conserve, repair, or advance beyond their own past achievements, and conservatives advocating classical liberalism but speaking nostalgically of an America fashioned by social liberalism, the public meanings of all political labels, together with the values associated with them, were easily muddled. They were muddled to the advantage of the political right, which was now intellectually self-confident. (The business class invested heavily in producing an intellectual stratum in the 1970s and 1980s.) Indeed, the moral vocabulary of the welfare state lost its public hold with remarkable rapidity—liberalism became the "L-word"—even while citizens still coveted many of its programs (like Social Security and Medicare in the United States). As right-wingers once acceded to left social standards in the form of the welfare state, now Bill Clinton, Tony Blair, and their admirers accept ideological bottom lines drawn by the Reagan/Thatcher era. Instead of pulling the center to the left, they chase a center that has been pulled far right by conservative dominance.

You would think that today, more than half a century after the welfare state was launched, its experience would have dislodged some earlier ideological predispositions (the myth of "rugged individualism" or simplistic notions of meritocracy, for examples). Yet they remain entrenched. This is one reason why, from a left viewpoint, social liberalism, with its disinclination to address "the good life," was too limited. Indeed, the greatest flourishing of its political philosophy—for instance, the work of Rawls and Dworkin—in this country came in the 1970s—just before liberal welfare states descended into deep crisis. Next thing, taxes were cut to up the upper crust; corporations were given more and more freedom, with unions correspondingly weakened; domestic spending and aid to the poor were curtailed dramatically. In short, traditional (that is, pre-welfare state) economic values flourished. They helped to create a poor life for a lot of people. In the meantime, social liberalism barely inches on to the far left end of today's political spectrum, because the "center" is so far right.

III. Liberal democracy as a whole, and not just social liberalism, may soon find itself in hard times. This may seem a strange assertion just a few years after the conclusion of the cold war. Didn't Francis Fukuyama tell us that after 1989 liberal democracy is our unsurpassable horizon? This is what he meant when he said that history had "ended." And there were obvious implications: communism's fall meant that ideology also had ended (yet again!); consequently, closure had come to fundamental debates about Western societies; obviously, then, left and right are rendered meaningless as political categories.

Great events—like 1989—tend, quite naturally, to focus our attention. They can, however, also make us myopic. Only if one sees communism as the exclusive question of the century and beyond can one make liberal democracy a final horizon. Indeed, in this globalizing era the relation between liberal democracy and economic power is increasingly complex, with new and unsettling problems arising that have nothing to do with the late Soviet Union. It may well be that lacking a radically new perception of horizons, liberal democracy's past, very considerable achievements will be jeopardized.

Let me explain. The political horizons of liberal democracy and the nation-state have overlapped considerably. A glance at modern history shows how dependent the former was on the emergence of—more precisely, the demand for political equality within—the latter. Liberal democracies, whatever their international entanglements (political, economic, and so on) were bounded; their governments had levers to pull in order to shape domestic life. The more democratic, the more, in principle, citizens ought to have been able to see their wills take tangible form in policies. But classical liberal economics, resting on the relentless pursuit of markets and profits everywhere, conflicts with liberal democracy—if the latter means that citizens have a say in determining the basic conditions of their lives.

What happens when economic globalization, augmented and driven on by revolutions in technology and communications, increasingly deprives democratic governments of those levers? What meaning can self-government then have? According to one recent study, multinational corporations now account for 30 percent of gross global output, 70 percent of world trade, and 80 percent of international investment. There is much debate about the ramifications of such figures and about globalization in general, particularly for the United States, with its large internal market. Still, this seems ominously credible: the more capital's "economic liberty" spreads internationally—the more transnational financial institutions and corporations rather than popular mandates define priorities for a country's domestic condition—the more the value of liberal democratic government may be "downsized" in the eyes of citizens. Why? Its inability to respond meaningfully to democratic expectations and social needs. The serious question is not how to live after history's "end" but how, if liberal democratic self-sufficiency is declining, do we discipline the processes of globalization on behalf of democratic precepts and (non-market) human needs and values?

IV. The difficulties raised for liberal democracy and social liberalism by the late twentieth century are shared to a significant extent by the democratic left. I wish I could say that it has come up with persuasive responses where social liberals or just liberal democrats have not. I can't—and this indicates its real crisis today, not communism's demise (we wanted those dictatorships to fall as much as anybody, except perhaps people living under them). The predicament—how to formulate a convincing strategic program grounded in a left ethos—shouldn't be underestimated.

Neither should it be devouring. Intellectual quandaries can require a good deal of time to be sorted out. We are in a historical moment that is inhospitable to left-wing values; those of us who are still "left" must keep them above water, think aloud and hard about them. But in the end, the need for an ethos of intelligent egalitarianism will remain because indefensible inequalities, like those I considered earlier in this essay, are still very much with us. And if there is one thing we should have learned from our era, it is that history harbors surprises, not that it ends. So we should have some patience with our times, though impatience with such intellectual shortcuts as "Left and right are now meaningless terms" or "We're all centrists now." They are prescriptions for a new age of intellectual conformity. We ought, instead, to present regulative ideas for a better society, and do so continuously. We need to project an America with a sense of moral commonality both deeper and differently configured than that which was proposed by liberals. Not a consummated utopia, certainly not an "end-state" enveloped by sameness, but the extension of democracy well beyond the political domain into social and economic life. So that equality in one would not be threatened by inequality in another and all citizens would actually have the means of individual liberty.

We need to speak of an America in which social goods are not simply entitlements that individuals protect for themselves but social rights grounded in mutuality, in a culture of cooperation, in a dialectic of "I" and "we." Consequently, an important linkage would have been secured in the minds of citizens—between social goods (like Social Security, education, and health care) and the idea of social citizenship. Markets, then, would be kept to their proper station and unchosen inequalities would be rendered increasingly immaterial to human relations. Not only through the redistribution of goods but by making the general conditions permitting the free development of one social individual the general conditions permitting free development of all social individuals. The regulative terms of socioeconomic, no less than political, conversation would be equality-friendly so that the ethos of a Reagan or a Milton Friedman, not to mention the priorities of transnational corporations, would produce perplexity—and crinkled noses. Their values would seem as far-fetched to most Americans as, well, as many left (not to mention liberal) values seem today.

Imagine if elections in twenty-first century America were contested not by Democrats ready to slash the poor's safety net and Republicans proposing welfare for the rich via tax cuts, but by Social Democrats advocating a classless society and Social Liberals upholding some version of the welfare state. The latter might still want to avoid disputes about the good life, but at least there would be a new context. Daily politics would concern dimensions of social citizenship, not the extension of social cruelty. Another way of saying this is: the "center"—indeed, the vistas of our society—would have moved decisively left.

I still want that movement to happen; and that is also why I am still "left."

The Conservative Manifesto

PETE DUPONT

> "We hold these truths to be self-evident, that all men are created equal, that they are endowed by their Creator with certain Unalienable Rights, that among these are Life, Liberty, and the pursuit of Happiness. That to secure these rights Governments are instituted among men, deriving their just powers from the consent of the Governed."
>
> —The Declaration of Independence, July 4, 1776

However many times these words are quoted, they still sound fresh. Thomas Jefferson's eloquence provided the spark for one of the most successful revolts against a tyrannical state in history.

The idea of the divine nature of the individual and his or her superiority to the state has not come easily or cheaply. The blood of millions has been shed in defense of this seemingly simple idea. But the idea of man's superiority to the state will not die, because it is grounded in the

Peter DuPont, the former governor of Delaware, is chairman of the Committee for American Leadership.

Reprinted by permission. *National Review*, March 21, 1994. Vol. 46, Issue 5, p. 32.

divine nature of man—not of kings. Man is endowed by his Creator—not by the state—with "certain Unalienable Rights."

From Hitler to Stalin and Honecker, Duvalier and Castro, Saddam Hussein and Milosevic, as the challenges to our creator-endowed freedoms have become clear, individuals have risen up to throw off the shackles of tyranny. It took seventy years in the Soviet Union, but the inevitable revolution occurred.

Sometimes, however, the threat posed by the state to man's freedom is not so clear. Sometimes it comes gradually, offered in tempting packages put forward by well-meaning people who believe with all their hearts that they know better how to improve the lot of all. All that is necessary is that we provide them with certain powers, and that we sacrifice only a few of our freedoms, to provide a better and more equal world for all. A better world, of course, as viewed by them.

The arrogance of the notion that an elite corps of the best and the brightest can make society better and more equal continues to be lost on the Left. So has the inevitable failure of their efforts and the suffering their suffocating ideology has brought to millions of its victims. But that has not deterred them.

Even in America, amidst the greatest success of political and economic freedom in the history of the world, generations of central social and economic planning have finally fostered a new culture—a culture of dependency, rampant crime, single parenthood, broken families, triballike group competition, and a turn away from personal responsibility.

Our political leaders preach a message of class envy and so demand collective solutions to our problems. They tell us we can individualize opportunity and collectivize risk; that we may enjoy the benefits of our society but have no responsibility for its costs; that the less than successful are helpless victims of unfairness. But they are wrong. The balkanization of society into competing ethnic or economic groups treads upon the dignity of the individual and it is only individual effort and ingenuity that will support a prosperous society. The fundamental bargain of a free society is that progress and opportunity require individual discipline and responsibility.

But if conservatives are to be proved right sooner than later, we must rise once again to the challenge of demonstrating that a course of personal freedom, moral responsibility, and individual opportunity will inevitably provide for a more bountiful, a more rewarding, and, yes, a more just and equal society than any alternative known to man.

The election of 1992 revealed a deep dissatisfaction among voters. Government is seen to be corrupt, self-aggrandizing, and disconnected from individual concerns and understanding. Reform is not enough. Conservatives must offer an alternative that is not just the opposite of liberalism—small government where they favor large, individualism where they favor group entitlements, free markets where they favor regulation—but a profound and fundamental "re-visioning" of the philosophy of American government.

President Clinton's Administration has already embarked on a program of higher taxes and greater government involvement in our lives. To oppose that course is important, for reducing the power of government and concurrently increasing the power of the individual are essential tasks in reimplementing this conservative vision. But that is not enough. The conservative vision offers a government subservient to and reinforcing the spiritual and economic imperatives of the individual. We must reject outright the collectivism of liberal government and advocate the Jeffersonian vision of personal freedom, moral responsibility, and individual opportunity upon which the success of democratic capitalism rests.

STRONG FOREIGN POLICY

> *To protect our liberty, America must be the world's predominant economic and military force, able to project overwhelming military power anywhere around the globe. But that power must be used only to advance America's direct national interests.*

The first duty of government is to protect the safety of its citizens. The traditional expression of this responsibility is a strong defense. Despite the end of the Cold War and the diminished threat of the former Soviet Union, military strength has not lost its relevance.

History teaches that rapid disarmament following a perceived elimination or reduction in the threat to freedom inevitably has tragic consequences. From the Congress of Vienna to the Treaty of Versailles, free nations have paid a terrible price for letting down their guard in times of diplomatic euphoria.

America stands poised to repeat this tragic mistake. The peace children of the 1970s are disarming the United States at a frightening pace. The Clinton defense program would have this country spend a smaller percentage of its GNP on national defense than at any time since Pearl Harbor.

In an age when missiles can traverse the globe in minutes, threats to U.S. security are unlikely to develop so gradually that incremental military build-ups are sufficient. The United States must be prepared, hour by hour, to defend its interests.

Threats to U.S. security are diminished, not removed. The Russian reforms have become paralyzed. Response to unrest in the boundary states of the former Soviet Union is increasingly a military response.

The Soviet transition is far from complete; so too is that of the People's Republic of China. Both may end where they began; it is too soon to be sure. But it is not too soon to ensure that America sustains the military capability she will need should the future turn out to be a reflection of the past.

Strengthening U.S. security in this uncertain world requires:

—Restoring our defenses to end of the Cold War capability. A defense budget of at least 5.5 per cent of GDP (compared to 4.7 per cent in FY93) will be needed to maintain the capacity to conduct a Desert Storm operation, deploy an adequate navy to protect the sea lanes, and develop a strategic defense.

—Having the United States unilaterally maintain command and control of U.S. military forces; the lives of American military men and women should not be put at risk for anything less than the direct national interest of the United States. America's security interests must not be subordinated to international consensus or UN supervision. The mirage of multilateralism has no place in national defense policy.

—Building a strategic defense capability to protect American territory and interests against missile attack. Tonight we sleep defenseless against a single missile launched from anywhere by unknown terrorists.

—Continuing to support economic reforms, but preparing to confront an expansionist Russia, for the passions of nationalism, totalitarianism, and economic expansion have not been extinguished. U.S. policy must oppose the use of Russian force in the former Soviet states and support the legitimate defense needs of Poland, the Czech Republic, Hungary, and the Baltics.

SAFE STREETS, RESTFUL SLEEP

The safety of our streets and neighborhoods is the first domestic priority of American society. It is achieved by removing from the streets the recidivists committing a large portion of crimes, and increasing the capability of law-enforcement entities.

The greatest threat to the safety of American citizens today comes not from foreign enemies, but from domestic crime. Some 24 million people each year are the victims of serious crime. Crime has increased fivefold since 1960; violence has exploded. A young black male is more likely to die by violence than any other cause, and, as George Will has written, millions of our children go to bed each night to the sound of gunfire.

Vast sectors of our cities are effectively controlled by criminals, while in too many neighborhoods crime overwhelms all else; school, home, and work environments are often helpless in its grip. This violence is imposing a terrible physical, psychological, moral, and economic cost upon society, in pain, suffering, trauma, and dollars.

Yet the perpetrators of much of America's crime freely walk the streets of our cities and towns. According to former Attorney General William P. Barr, some 30 per cent of all murders, 25 per cent of all rapes, and 40 per cent of all robberies are committed by men out on bail, probation, or parole. William Bennett's Index of Leading Cultural Indicators documents that the median prison sentence served for conviction of a serious crime is just eight days.

For thirty years the liberal response to the rising tide of criminal violence has been therapeutic: understand, help, and rehabilitate the criminal. It is a tattered vision, rent by the reality of intentional, repeated, and malevolent violence.

The conservative response is different: certain punishment for proven crime, compassion for victims, and prevention of crime by removal from society of its perpetrators and increased resources for law enforcement.

Conservatives also believe law enforcement is the constitutional responsibility of state and local government and should remain so.

To make America safe again we must:

—Remove from the streets that small class of recidivist violent criminals—perhaps fewer than half a million of them—who commit the preponderance of the criminal acts.

—Lengthen the time served in prison by convicted criminals, mandating life sentences without parole for multiple violent felony convictions.

—Restrict parole for violent offenders and prisoners testing positive for drug use. Increase the use of pretrial detention for dangerous and second-offense defendants. Try repeat violent juvenile defendants as adults.

—Strengthen law enforcement by constructing 500,000 new prison beds and training 100,000 additional police officers.

—Make sure that illegal drug use and sale remain criminalized. The Federal Government should continue its drug interdiction and seizure programs.

—Reaffirm our allegiance to the Second Amendment's right to bear arms. Unilateral disarmament of law-abiding citizens in the face of armed criminals is as ill-conceived a policy as disarmament of a nation faced with international aggression.

ECONOMIC PROSPERITY

> *Encouraging a market economy—history's only mechanism through which ordinary citizens can benefit from rising living standards—is the nation's first economic priority. Lower tax rates, limited government regulation, and open international markets will encourage economic prosperity.*

At the core of the spectacular success of the American experiment in democratic capitalism lies a market economy. The tragedy of the liberal hour has been its rejection of market economics and its embrace of the arrogant belief that the best and brightest at the helm of the ship of state can steer a more prosperous economic course than the market can steer for us. As we have witnessed, particularly in the decade of the 1980s, the millions of daily decisions made by free people in a marketplace of choices will maximize both opportunity for individuals and the prosperity of the nation as a whole.

To accomplish these goals, conservative economic policy is founded upon six principles.

1. No economic program can be successful without low inflation and sound money. The marketplace is best served by a predictable growth of the money supply, tied to a commodity basket or some other stable indicator, that will rise only as the economy expands. Political manipulation of the money supply must not be one of the tools of government.

2. Tax policy should focus upon creating the greatest possible economic growth and collecting revenue in the fairest, simplest, and least economically distorting fashion. Current tax policy, heavily weighted against the successful, the productive, and the innovative, must be reversed. Repealing the Bush and Clinton tax increases and setting a top marginal tax rate of less than 25 per cent (fully indexed for inflation) are our immediate objectives.

3. Vigorous international trade must be encouraged by expanding the NAFTA concept beyond Canadian and Mexican markets. Protectionism is a statist policy; the government by tariff and quota both regulates and retards economic growth. Further, keeping foreign goods out of America is unfair to all of us. It reduces the choices we have in the market, raises the price we pay for goods, and costs us jobs in export and domestic industries.

4. Limiting federal and state regulation of enterprise to what is necessary to provide information to consumers and ensure transactional fairness will increase private-sector innovation and opportunity. Individ-

uals are better served by a refereed marketplace than by politically motivated, centrally directed economic planning. Every industry, from airlines to trucking, that has been deregulated has become more efficient
and offered lower prices to consumers. Deregulation of financial-services
institutions will promote more customer opportunity and security;
deregulating telecommunications services will provide higher quality
and less expensive service. Market solutions to environmental challenges will provide a cleaner earth at a fraction of the cost.

5. Similarly, ending market-distorting production subsidies and
price supports will reduce consumer prices and increase opportunity. An
economic freedom, constitutional amendment in the Milton Friedman
mold will guarantee these opportunities:

> Neither Congress nor any state shall make laws abridging the free-
> dom of sellers of goods or labor to price their products or services.

Such an amendment would end all sorts of collectivist tinkering,
from New York City's (and other locations) rent-control statutes, to agri-
cultural price supports.

6. Reform a legal system that is placing heavy burdens upon society through both litigation delays and liability costs. Placing the burden
of legal fees on the losing party (as in Britain), assessing full cost for use
of the courts for those who can afford to pay, and sharply restricting
punitive damages would begin reform.

LESS IS MORE

> *Government cannot fulfill people's lives; only the energy and
> freedom of individuals striving to excel can do that. Govern-
> ment policy must help them by reducing its intrusive role
> and reinvigorating federalist principles.*

One hundred years after the founding of the Republic, the Federal Government spent less than 3 per cent of GNP. Fifty years later, in 1937, it
consumed only 9 per cent of GNP. Today the figure has reached 24 per
cent. Hospital cost controls, mandated family leave, environmental
standards, welfare regulations, are all enacted in Washington to limit authority in our hometowns. Federal courts decree the location of community public housing, regulate the disposal of municipal garbage, order the
busing of young children to distant schools, and override state constitutions in taxing citizens to pay the bill. The idea of federalism and limited
government, the philosophical underpinning of our Constitution, is slipping away.

Much of the responsibility for the erosion of the Constitution's dual sovereignty compact lies with the Supreme Court. The surest opportunity to return to America's founding philosophy therefore lies with the Court as well. It should begin with disapproval of federal gerrymandering of local legislative district boundaries to achieve specific racial or ethnic election outcomes, in contravention of Article I, Section 2, of the Constitution. The Court should overturn *Roe v. Wade,* an exercise in denial of state authority as abundant in political support as it is lacking in constitutional nexus.

But legislative opportunities to reduce the intrusive role of the public sector in private life are legion.

—A constitutional restraint to limit Federal Government spending to less than 20 per cent of GNP is the first step. In the meantime, fiscal policy should restrain the annual growth of federal spending to less than the rate of GNP growth, so that the public sector shrinks as a percentage of GNP.

—The marketplace should be used to provide the delivery of basic services to individuals and families. The problem in America is not that we do not spend enough alleviating our problems, it is that the systems we are using to alleviate them are wasteful, unworkable, and unresponsive to individual needs.

Health-care IRAs and tax credits for individual health-care expenditures offer a sensible, market approach to paying for health services; they permit greater individual choice and demand greater individual responsibility. It is a simple truth that until people begin using their own earned dollars to pay for health care, it will be overpriced and overused.

Nor should the Federal Government be providing retirement income for the vast majority of citizens capable of providing for themselves. There is an urgent need for a market-based retirement option that will increase benefits for the retired and avoid impending massive payroll tax increases that will destroy job opportunities for the young.

Finally, parents should be empowered to choose whatever school—public, private, or religious—is best for each of their children. Educational funding should follow the student to whatever school parents select, for it is adoption of market principles that will inject competition-driven improvements in our schools. The current system, with its lame emphasis on self-esteem, as opposed to substance, and its mediocre performance is a standing injustice to our children. It cannot be reformed. It can only by replaced—by a system based upon the market and responsive to the individual.

A series of federal statutes should be enacted to allow states to govern all matters which, in Madison's words, "extend to all the objects which, in the ordinary course of affairs, concern the lives, liberties, and properties of the people, and the internal order, improvement, and prosperity of the State." Thus state employee wages, wetlands, and welfare regulation, for example, are left to state government. Uniform national rules, as proposed in President Clinton's health plan, for example, are not beneficial to society. They limit individual freedom, and retard both innovation and improvement in the quality of goods and services.

—Limiting the terms of elected officials will also serve to limit the power of government and thereby enhance the power of individuals. Upholding the power of voters to enact term limits will provide an early test of the Supreme Court's renewed commitment to federalist principles. No stronger admonition can be delivered to those abusing federalism than to empower their victims to limit their opportunity to do so.

The American experiment, to use de Tocqueville's phrase, has created the most rewarding society in the history of mankind. It has offered the individual freedom and a virtually unbounded opportunity to excel.

The fundamental bargain of a free society is that progress and opportunity require personal discipline and responsibility, and this requirement extends to every individual, not just to the successful and advantaged members of society.

On the one hand, our social compact offers freedom to the individual, education to help people develop their skills, and compassionate assistance to weather the rough times of structural change, economic contraction, and poverty.

But there is a second half to the compact, too—the individual's responsibility to society. In return for America's opportunity, we are expected to accept responsibility for our own lives and to conform to social norms. Drug use is outside the pale; so is violent behavior. The ultimate responsibility of the citizen in the social compact is to be a law-abiding contributor to the whole, not an outlaw demanding entitlement to his or her own vision of ordered civility. If you want society's help, you work, you don't do drugs, have more welfare babies, rob, assault, or kill.

To strengthen this social compact:

—Reaffirm the two-parent family as the norm in American culture and respect the primacy and authority of the family unit. Government must defer to the authority of parents regarding the teaching and raising of children. Stop championing unwed motherhood as an alternative lifestyle, make divorce more difficult to obtain, and raise the child-care tax deduction to $7,000 in order to restore its value to postwar levels. Use the power of the law to enforce fathers' economic responsibility for their children.

—Replace the failed policies of the welfare state with the work ethic. The perverse incentives of liberal social policies, which reward illegitimate births, idleness, and family breakdown have destroyed families and devastated the social underclass.

The replacement of the work ethic by the welfare state has destroyed the opportunity, the dignity, and the cohesion of poor families in America. No marginal improvement in tax rates, no health- or day-care benefits or transportation vouchers can repair a system based upon the destructive premise of permanent welfare assistance. The work ethic is at the core of a healthy society, and the individual responsibility of doing a job, earning a living, and striving for improvement is crucial to restoring opportunity and self-respect to underclass Americans. We must replace welfare with work. For all able to work, America's social compact demands work; public compassion is balanced by private responsibility.

—Reaffirm the Fourteenth Amendment's guarantee of equal protection of the laws by erasing preferences based upon race, religion, origin, and gender.

Thirty years ago America turned a corner in race relations, acknowledging and repudiating the racism in its past and taking the first steps on the path toward equality of opportunity for all. But the civil-rights revolution soon abandoned its emphasis on individual rights, and embraced racial and ethnic identification as the talisman for rights and remedies in everything from jobs to jury selection to the drawing of voting district boundaries.

The quota system has become so pandemic in universities, businesses, and government today in America that an entire philosophy—multiculturalism—has had to be invented to justify it. The truth is that affirmative-action quotas are both unjust and untenable. They are unjust because they punish those who have done nothing wrong. They are untenable because they undermine the concept of merit and the individual pursuit of excellence.

The conservative vision must challenge the very basis upon which we help the poor and the underclass, rejecting the affirmative-action quota model outright, and returning to the concept of race-blind impartiality and fairness for each individual, to Martin Luther King's dictum that a man should be judged not by the color of his skin but the content of his character.

—Extend the social compact only to legal immigrants, and control our borders so that only legal immigrants enter. America owes no duty to citizens of other nations; excepting the occasional political refugee, our policy should limit immigration to the skilled and energetic, those individuals most likely to contribute to our society.

Finally, government must abandon the statist, utopian concept of equality of results, and emphasize instead the critical importance of individual opportunity and economic growth to assuage society's inevitable inequality of outcomes. For as Michael Novak has noted:

> Real differences in talent, aspiration, and application inexorably individuate humans. Given the diversity and liberty of human life, no fair and free system can possibly guarantee equal outcomes. A democratic system depends for its legitimacy, therefore, not upon equal results but upon a sense of equal opportunity.

CONFIRMING AMERICA'S CULTURE

A cohesive society requires a set of shared beliefs that define the behavioral norms of all its members. Our governmental policies must positively reinforce the American culture; they must abandon moral neutrality in public policy and affirm such values as our common language, the role of religion in our lives, and the individual pursuit of excellence.

Our common language is the most obvious element of America's culture. More profound are our religious heritage, the subservience of the state to the individual, the two-parent family as the foundation of society, and the concept of merit.

That is not to say there are not Americans who, for example, believe in no God at all, speak languages other than English, or choose not to have families. But to be a part of America's culture one accepts that the state will not be neutral regarding every set of ideas, from incest to abortion. Our culture's values, customs, and beliefs must be reinforced by the institutions of our society.

Thus, disparaging the role of religion in our lives or undermining the authority of parents has no place in public policy. What does have a place is requiring that public schools teach in English, allowing an invocation before graduation, and encouraging grades on merits. Marriage is reserved for heterosexual couples, and affirmative action used in its original meaning—that everyone is invited to participate in our society. Freedom of expression is guaranteed for the anti-religious or pornographic artist, but government funding is not.

Moral neutrality in public affairs has propelled us down the slippery slope of cultural decline. The climb back up requires a cultural renaissance in our families, neighborhoods, churches, and schools. But it cannot succeed unless the public sector abandons its indifference to moral choices and affirms the cultural values shared by our citizenry.

Confirming America's culture requires a fundamental shift in public-policy thought:

—Reject the neutrality of governmental institutions and policies regarding moral values. They must reinforce the fundamental values of American culture: diligence and self-discipline, honesty and virtue, compassion and respect for others. Our policies must lead people to choose marriage over single parenthood, encourage adoption and discourage abortion, and promote personal discipline as a higher value to society than libertine lifestyles.

—Reject multiculturalism, the belief that every cultural concept is of equal moral value and must be accepted as a valid lifestyle choice. It is undermining our values and endangering our society.

—Reward the pursuit of excellence. Both brain surgeons and bricklayers must be committed to excellence if our society is to prosper. Academic excellence must be the first priority of the public school classroom, and merit the basis of employer hiring and promotion standards. Race norming of test scores and adjustment of standards to equalize results among racial, ethnic, or age groups undermines effort, merit, and equality of opportunity.

TAKE THE OFFENSE

Only in liberty can nations and individuals prosper. The tyranny of the state over the masses struggling to be free is a sadly recurring twentieth-century theme. But if common men, ennobled by the divine spark of their Creator, are, in Winston Churchill's phrase, to "move forward into broad, sunlit uplands," they must do so one-by-one, striving to advance their individual progress toward that uplifting goal. There are no collective means to individual prosperity.

The collectivist, tribal, morally neutral policies of the Left will no more be successful in solving the nation's problems in the future than they have been in the past. They will fail to achieve the liberal promise; they will make problems worse, not better.

But conservatives cannot succeed in capturing the imagination and support of the American people by simply opposing the policies of the Left. We must offer a vision which speaks to the best in people, not the worst; to the hopes and aspirations of our citizens, not to their greed and their fears. Americans have historically understood that governments are a threat to personal freedom. They instinctively distrust policies which denigrate personal responsibility. They realize that too much of

American life has been corrupted by political manipulation. Our challenge is to offer a conservative alternative to the liberal order, and nothing less than these fundamental reforms will do.

Several years ago, I served on the Blue Ribbon Commission advising post-Communist Hungary on its route to prosperity. The Commission's conclusion reflects the essence of the conservative vision:

> Government cannot fulfill people's lives. What a wise governmental system can do is to create the trustworthy, confidence-inspiring institutions that permit individuals to fulfill their own lives.

Issue 8
Political Parties

INTRODUCTION

The two-party system is a central feature of American politics. National politics since the early nineteenth century has been characterized by two large parties contending for elected office. Party names and issues may change: Abortion wasn't an issue in the nineteenth century, just as the tariff does not have the same importance now. Nonetheless, the two-party arrangement remains an enduring feature of the American political scene. Of course, third parties emerge all the time: Ross Perot's Reform Party is only the latest. But these smaller third parties tend to experience one of two distinctive fates. Either they grow large enough to take the place of one of the larger parties (as did the Republicans in the 1850s), or they disappear into one of the larger parties (as did the Progressives by 1916). In either case, America's political equilibrium takes the form of alternating two-party governance.

The reasons for this equilibrium, which are well known, have to do with how we choose our politicians. American politics operates with a winner-take-all rule. The candidate or the party that gets 51 percent of the vote, or even a mere plurality, wins completely. Combined with single-member districts that organize representation on a geographical basis, the winner-take-all rule puts in place a set of incentives that discourages third parties. The winner-take-all rule leads the major parties to broaden their appeals in order to capture the allegiance of the "median voter," or that voter whose views places him or her in the middle of the electorate. Since the major parties need only a bare majority (or even a mere plurality) in order to triumph, they attempt to cover as much ideological ground as possible, even while they seek to retain the allegiance of their ideological cores. As a result, in some cases the difference between a moderate Democrat and a moderate Republican can be far less than that between two members of the same party.

Above all, our system tends to squeeze out third parties, since the two larger ones continually "steal" voters from smaller, emergent parties by adjusting their appeals. Citizens, for their part, face a parallel incentive to ignore small parties, expect perhaps for protest votes. Otherwise, a small party that wins less than a plurality wins nothing. Thus, citizens who wish to maximize the impact of their ballots will rationally choose instead that larger party whose positions are nearest to those of their preferred third party. A winner-take-all rule is only one possibility for electoral representation. Indeed, most other democracies make use of some form of proportional representation (PR). Under PR, parties win office in proportion to the percentage of the population that supports them. Under current American rules, a party winning 10 percent of the vote wins nothing. Under PR, that party winning 10 percent would gain an equal percentage of elected offices.

Each system has its advantages and drawbacks. Winner-take-all encourages a broad-based stability within the major parties, whereas PR stimulates parties to define their positions more clearly (and citizens to vote more precisely). Winner-take-all may lead to tyranny of the majority, if one party dominates national offices; PR, on the other hand, may lead to tyranny of the minority, as influential small parties bargain for disproportionate influence within coalition governments. In his satiric depiction of our electoral system, Michael Lind sees a "Wonderland" quality to the kind of unrepresentative outcomes that winner-take-all can produce. Combined with the political manipulation of geographical voting boundaries, or gerrymandering, our present system too frequently shuts out substantial minorities from political power. In the long run, according to Lind, this sort of unfairness reduces the legitimacy of the political system and discourages voting turnout.

Tiffany Danitz counters that, despite our tendencies towards two-party dominance, third parties are alive and well in contemporary American politics. They may rarely triumph, but their activities do have the important effect of forcing parties to address minority views and concerns that would otherwise remain ignored.

As you read the articles, consider the following questions.

Discussion Questions

1. "In politics," Lind writes, "who wins depends on the rules." For various reasons, Lind disapproves of "pluralist" voting rules. Can you think of any system of voting rules that would be objectively fair?

2. In Issue Two, we encountered the distinction between direct and representative democracy. Which set of rules—the American pluralist rules, or the European proportional rules—seem to correspond most closely to either sort of democracy?

3. In the United States, political representation is organized geographically. Apart from the possibility of "gerrymandering," what are other consequences of geographically based representation?

4. Among the current third-party possibilities in the United States, the most significant seems to be the Reform Party associated with Ross Perot. How have the Republicans and Democrats responded to the emergence of the Reform Party since 1992?

For more information on this topic, visit the following websites:

`http://www.reformparty.org`
The Reform Party of the U.S.A.

`http://www.greenparty.org`
The Green Party of North America

`http://www.lp.org`
The Libertarian Party

Alice Doesn't Vote Here Anymore

MICHAEL LIND

When it comes to the way we elect Congress, we're on the wrong side of the looking glass.

"Oh, my," said Alice, "is it really true that there are elections in Wonderland?"

"Of course, you foolish girl," the Queen of Hearts replied. "This is a constitutional monarchy. The Single Member of the Congress of Wonderland is elected by democratic means. Come, I shall introduce you to the electorate."

Alice followed the Queen to a field, in the middle of which was a table where the Mad Hatter and three of his friends were feasting. "The Mad Hatter's Party, with its four members, is one of the three political parties here in Wonderland," the Queen told Alice. "The other two parties, Tweedledum's Party and Tweedledee's Party, have three members apiece." Sure enough, Tweedledum and Tweedledee stood nearby, each with two followers.

"The electoral system of Wonderland," the Queen continued, "is based on the method of Plurality Voting by Single-Member Districts, sometimes known as Winner Takes All. You understand how that works, of course."

"No," said Alice sorrowfully, "I am afraid I do not."

The Queen shouted, "Off with her head!"

"Please," Alice begged, "I'll do my best to learn about the electoral system of Wonderland, if only you will explain it."

"Very well," the Queen said. "But I must warn you, the more I explain about Plurality Voting, the less you will understand it. For example, the most important part of our system of Plurality Voting by Single-Member Districts is the shape of the district."

"I cannot imagine why," Alice said.

The Queen was shocked. "Have you never heard of the Gerrymander?" At the mention of its name, the Gerrymander, a large and rather fearsome creature somewhat like a cross between a salamander and a Jabberwock, shambled forth. "Go on," the Queen ordered the beast, "draw the Single-Member District for the forthcoming congressional election."

Alice watched as the Gerrymander, dipping its brush in the pot of red paint hanging from its neck, began to outline a square in the grass.

Michael Lind is the author of *Up from Conservatism*, and the editor of *Hamilton's Republic*.

Reprinted by permission. *Mother Jones*, March–April 1998. Vol. 22, No. 2, p. 52.

Soon the square's borders included the three members of the Tweedledum Party and the three members of the Tweedledee Party. But when it came to the four supporters of the Mad Hatter's Party, the Gerrymander painted a red stripe right down the middle of their banquet table.

"There," the Queen said with satisfaction. "Thanks to the Gerrymander, we now have a Single-Member District with two large parties, those of Tweedledum and Tweedledee, with three voters apiece, and one small party, the Mad Hatter's Party, with only two voters."

"But that isn't right!" cried Alice. She rushed to the Mad Hatter. "Aren't you going to do something?"

"Why on earth should I?" he asked.

"You have the biggest party," Alice replied. "Your party has four members, and the other two parties have only three voters apiece."

"Oh, you silly girl," said the Mad Hatter, pointing to the red stripe bisecting the table. "Can't you see that my party has only two voters eligible to vote in the Single-Member District?"

Alice noticed Tweedledum and Tweedledee handing purses full of coins to the Gerrymander. "Don't you see what they've done to you? They've drawn the Single-Member District to minimize the power of your voters!"

"Of course they have," the Mad Hatter chuckled. "We'd have done the same to them, if we could afford to pay the Gerrymander."

"But it isn't fair to your party! Why don't you protest?"

"Protest!" All four members of his party, the two inside the Single-Member District and the two outside, burst into laughter. "Protest? Why, our elections have always been held this way. To protest would be unpatriotic and vulgar." At this, the Mad Hatter and his friends resumed their banquet.

Alice was thinking very deeply. At length she said, "I have devised a strategy by which your party can maximize its influence, even though the Gerrymander has turned you into a minority party."

The Mad Hatter looked up from the table in annoyance. "Are you still here?"

Alice explained her plan. "The Queen of Hearts said that Wonderland has a Plurality Voting System. Therefore, it is all very puzzling, I admit, the winner needs either a simple majority in a two-party race or less than a majority, a mere plurality, in a three-party race. In a plurality election, the greater the number of parties, the smaller the plurality that is necessary to win."

"Yes, yes, yes," the Mad Hatter said, drumming his fingers on the table. "Is there a point to this tedious lesson in political science?"

"Who can get that plurality is very, very important," Alice insisted. "Your two-person party is too small to win. Therefore you must decide which of the other two parties you prefer."

"Oh, that is easy," replied the Mad Hatter. "The positions of the Tweedledee Party are nearest our own positions, whereas we find the Tweedledum platform positively hateful."

"Well, then," Alice responded, "you must vote for the Tweedledee Party, not for your own."

"Not vote for our own party!" the Mad Hatter exclaimed.

Alice explained: "If you vote for the Tweedledee Party, then it will defeat the Tweedledum Party, by five votes to three. But if you vote for your own party, then you increase the chances that the Tweedledum Party will win. It's only rational."

"It may be rational, but this is Wonderland, and I'll have none of it!" the Mad Hatter declared.

There was no time for further argument, for at that very moment the Queen ordered, "Let the ballasting begin!"

A large balloon appeared above the treetops and drifted over the field. The balloonist shouted down to the Mad Hatter's Party: "How do you want your ballast cast?"

"Two for the Mad Hatter's Party!"

The balloonist tossed down two bags of ballast, which crashed in the midst of the table. Following the instructions of the other parties' voters, he cast three bags of ballast at the feet of Tweedledum and three at the feet of Tweedledee.

"The ballasting is complete," the Queen announced, as the balloon, deprived of ballast, drifted up into the sky and disappeared, taking the panicked balloonist with it.

"The election is a tie," Alice observed. "Tweedledum and Tweedledee each have three votes."

"No matter," said the Queen. "Under our Single-Member District Plurality Voting System, the outcome in a close race is often decided by the way the Swing Vote breaks."

"Who casts the Swing Vote?" Alice asked.

"Why, you do, little girl. Guards!"

Two guards appeared and forced poor Alice to climb up a tree containing an old, rotten, and very unsafe swing. With a great deal of anxiety, Alice sat in the swing and hung on for dear life as the guards gave it a push.

Back and forth Alice swung. As she passed overhead, first the Tweedledum Party and then the Tweedledee Party reached up, promising concessions in return for her support. Finally, on the third pass, the Swing Vote broke. Screaming, Alice was hurtled into the arms of Tweedledum.

"I got the Swing Vote!" Tweedledum exclaimed. "I won the election! I won the election!"

"But that isn't fair!" Alice cried. "It isn't fair three ways! It isn't fair the first way because the district was Gerrymandered, so the biggest party, the Mad Hatter's, was turned into a minority. And it isn't fair the second way because the plurality method of voting ensured that either the Tweedledum Party or the Tweedledee Party would win, even though a majority of the voters in the district voted against each party. And it isn't fair the third way because the election was so close that its outcome was settled by a Swing Voter, me, whose views may have nothing in common with what all of the other voters in the district want. It isn't fair at all! It's a travesty of democracy, which means nothing if it does not mean majority rule!"

The Queen gasped. "Little girl, what does democracy have to do with majority rule? In Wonderland, democracy means the Rule of the Largest Minority, helped out by a minuscule Swing Vote, in a Gerrymandered Single-Member District. Majority rule, indeed! Off with her head!"

The electoral system of Wonderland, as described above (with apologies to Lewis Carroll), is, as Alice rightly insists, unjust and perverse. Unfortunately, that electoral system is our own. (Coincidentally, it is one that Carroll himself would not have approved of. A mathematician by training, he was fascinated by voting systems and produced important work on voting theory, including developing elaborate alternative voting procedures that would eliminate bizarre distortions like those in Wonderland, that went completely unnoticed until the 1950s. He used to pass out pamphlets explaining his obscure theories to his Oxford colleagues, none of whom had an inkling as to what he was talking about.)

Plurality voting by single-member districts is how we elect the House, state legislatures, city councils, and other legislative bodies. Our method produces the same undemocratic effects identified by Alice, but they are somewhat less humorous when we tally their political consequences:

GERRYMANDERING. Under the Constitution, state legislatures are permitted to redraw the lines of U.S. House districts every 10 years, following the census. If the Republicans gain control of the statehouses in the midterm elections next November (32 states currently have Republican governors; 18 have GOP-controlled legislatures), this could spell disaster for the Democrats. As Republican National Chairman Jim Nicholson predicts: "The winners are going to determine the political landscape in at least the first decade of the next millennium, because they are the people who are going to preside over the process of reapportionment and redistricting of their respective states as a result of the 2000 census." Because the party of the president usually loses seats in midterm elections, this is an ominous prospect. And Democrats have good reasons to fear a Republican gerrymander: The current 15-seat Republican majority in the House is largely due to cynical GOP efforts during the last round of redistricting in 1991 to forge what some Democrats have called an "unholy alliance" with black and Hispanic Democrats to carve up racially mixed liberal districts into "safe" black and Hispanic seats and equally "safe" Republican seats. The GOP even went so far as to make expensive redistricting software available to minority activist groups as part of its plan to split up the white liberal vote and ghettoize the nonwhite liberal vote.

As a result, there are only four white Democrats in the House from South Carolina, Georgia, Alabama, Mississippi, and Louisiana combined. In Newt Gingrich's Georgia, before racial gerrymandering, there were nine Democrats (eight white and one black) and only one Republican. Today the Georgia delegation numbers eight Republicans, all white, and three Democrats, all black.

SWING VOTE. A relatively modest swing vote breaking rightward has helped make the South a solidly Republican stronghold. A shift of only a few percentage points can move divided districts from the Democratic to the Republican camp. Where the districts themselves are swing districts, holding the balance of power between the two parties in Congress, the votes of a tiny minority of swing voters in a few districts can create a revolution in national politics. Morton Kondracke, a columnist for Roll Call, estimates that less than 12,000 voters nationwide, or six-hundredths of 1 percent of the eligible voting population, swung the vote to the House Republicans in 1996.

PLURALITY WINNERS. The recent rise of third-party politics threatens to strengthen the hold of the two dominant parties in Congress, rather than weaken it. For instance, in a special House election in New Mexico last year, Carol Miller won 17 percent of the vote as the Green Party candidate, splitting the Democratic vote and sending a Republican to Washington to represent a district in which only 42 percent of the voters supported him. She intends to run again in 1998 and is unlikely to fare any better. With more and more Reform, Green, New, and Libertarian party candidates running for congressional seats, perverse results are inevitable: Minuscule returns for a Green Party candidate can throw an overwhelmingly progressive district to the Republicans, just as a spoiler Libertarian Party candidate can ensure the election of a Democrat in predominantly conservative districts. The third-party candidate loses, and the wrong major party candidate wins.

Plurality voting by single-member districts may be crooked, but it's the only game in town, isn't it?

No, as a matter of fact it isn't. Most liberal democracies have rejected plurality voting because of its unfair and paradoxical results. Instead, they elect their legislatures by some version of proportional representation by district.

Here's how proportional representation works: Imagine a region with five adjacent single-member congressional districts. In each district, the electorate is divided between Republicans (60 percent), Democrats (20 percent), and Greens (20 percent). Under plurality voting, even though Republicans are only a slight majority of the electorate, they will get 100 percent of the vote. The region will send five Republicans to Congress, no Democrats, and no Greens. Under proportional representation, the five adjacent districts would be consolidated into one five-member delegation, which would send three Republicans, one Democrat, and one Green. This distribution of seats would more accurately reflect the distribution of sentiments in the electorate. In politics, who wins depends upon the rules.

Note that under proportional representation, the Alice-in-Wonderland results of our system, gerrymandering, plurality winners, and swing votes, simply disappear. State legislatures would abandon partisan gerrymandering, because it could no longer effectively prevent the minority from picking up at least a few seats. Racial gerrymandering would no longer be necessary, either. If people wanted to vote along racial or ethnic lines (which is far from a good idea in principle), then members of significant racial or ethnic minorities would be sure to elect one or two members of a multimember district, even if the white majority itself voted along racial lines.

The plurality winner problem would also vanish. A party with 60 percent of the votes couldn't win 100 percent of the seats in a district, only 60 percent of the delegation.

What about the swing vote? It is most troubling in two-party systems, in which the swing voters hold the balance between the parties. The democracies that use proportional representation tend to have multiparty systems, and it is likely that the United States would as well if proportional representation were adopted here. English-speaking populations are not innately more likely to be divided into two parties than are German-speaking populations. A two-party system is an unintended but almost inevitable byproduct of the plurality electoral system.

Such a multiparty system might also help reduce the polarization of American politics. Because a coalition of two or more parties, not just a single majority party, would probably hold power in the House and Senate, a party would gain little political capital by attempting to demonize the president, or to vilify potential coalition partners in the other parties. The rigid connection between lobbies and parties would dissolve as lobbies found it more useful to try to influence two or more parties instead of identifying themselves wholly with one.

Another benefit of proportional representation is that it could abort the otherwise inevitable emergence of a solid Republican South, or any other region that is "solidly" one party or the other. Right-wing Republicans in Cambridge, Berkeley, or New York's Upper West Side might be able to elect at least one or two members of Congress from their own area. Right now, in many districts, the minority party does not even bother to run a candidate. With five-member districts, any party with a chance at winning one-fifth of the vote could run candidates. It would no longer make sense for parties to write off whole districts, or even whole states. All of America would become politically competitive for the first time in history.

At this point, the defender of the status quo is certain to introduce a parade of horribles: for example, the fractionalization of the electorate into too many ineffectual parties, or the tyranny of small, fanatical parties in the multiparty legislature. The first can easily be dismissed: Under proportional representation, interests tend to coagulate into a handful of substantial parties. And we can eliminate the problem of tiny fanatical parties, which has bedeviled Israel, by insisting that no party can get seats in the legislature unless it wins a certain threshold, say, 5 percent, of the national vote. Thus, even if neo-Nazis win a district in Louisiana, they won't be seated in Congress unless they pass the national threshold.

Proportional representation tends to have a stabilizing effect on democracies, usually because a centrist party, such as the Free Democrats in Germany, moderates the extremist tendencies of its coalition partners. By contrast, elections in plurality democracies such as Britain and the United States tend to produce wild shifts in public policy, even though only a small number of swing voters may have changed their votes.

In the United States, the political history of the last quarter-century probably would have been far less turbulent had we adopted proportional representation to elect the House in, say, the 1950s. What would have happened is, of course, anybody's guess. Mine is that three major parties would have emerged from the wreckage of the Democrats and Republicans: An upscale progressive party based in New England and the Pacific Northwest, a conservative party based in the South, and a working-class populist party, with members who were socially conservative but fiscally liberal. On social issues, the House might have had a populist-conservative majority; on economic issues, a populist-progressive majority. The destruction of federal welfare programs and the balancing of the budget through regressive policies, the work of a centrist Democratic president and a right-wing Republican congressional majority, might never have taken place. The far left would have been just as thwarted, but New Deal liberalism, based on an alliance of Northern progressives, Southern populists, and working-class Catholics, might have endured.

What about the executive branch and the Senate? Proportional representation works only with multicandidate districts. For single-candidate offices, a system known as preference voting (also called the "instant runoff") could thwart Wonderland democracy. Where three or more candidates ran for an office such as the presidency, the voter would be instructed to rank the candidates in order of preference. Thus a voter in our imaginary three-party America who prefers the progressive to the populist candidate on social issues, while preferring the populist to the conservative one on economic issues, would assign the following ranking on the ballot: Progressive (1), Populist (2), Conservative (3). If no candidate wins a majority, the second-choice votes are redistributed among the top two candidates. In extreme cases, it might be possible for a candidate who got the most first-preference votes to lose to a candidate who won an overwhelming majority of second-preference votes.

Preference voting makes it almost impossible for a candidate strongly opposed by most voters to get elected in a three- or four-way race. Even more important, the adoption of preference voting for senatorial and presidential races would give candidates an incentive to seek support beyond their own parties. While elections under the plurality system tend to produce rival moderates exaggerating their differences, elections under the preference voting system would encourage candidates from genuinely different parties to reach out to members of other parties. The candidates would campaign not only for the first-preference votes of their party but for the second-preference votes of the parties that were nearest to their positions on particular issues. There might be coalition cabinets and even fusion tickets, with a president from one party and a vice president from another.

Preference voting can also eliminate two potential problems that multiple parties might pose to the American constitutional system. In a separation-of-powers political system like ours, conflict is endemic, particularly when different parties control the branches. If Congress were divided among multiple parties, it could severely weaken its power relative to the presidency. The president could claim to represent "the people," using that as a pretext to get around a Congress split among a number of squabbling parties. Preference voting in presidential elections might reduce that danger by encouraging the candidates, in campaigning for second-choice votes, to promise a multiparty coalition Cabinet.

Second, preference voting might also decrease the likelihood of another catastrophe that can occur from the collision of multiple parties with a plurality electoral system, the minoritarian president. In some countries with presidential systems, political chaos and even civil wars have erupted when a president supported by only a small minority has won election in a multiple-party race. Preference voting would guarantee that the winning candidate would always receive a majority of second-choice (and perhaps third-choice) votes, meaning that voters would never be stuck with their least favorite candidate.

Can proportional representation ever be more than a fantasy in the United States? It's already used to elect the city council of Cambridge and it was used for many years by the Cincinnati City Council (it was scrapped in the 1950s because it allowed blacks a chance to be elected).

There are no constitutional obstacles to changing our method of voting. The Constitution is silent about electoral systems. Our plurality system was established by statute; it can be replaced by statute. Alternatively, Congress, which has the ultimate say over how its members are elected, might give the states the right to determine how their congressional delegations are chosen. In 1995, Rep. Cynthia McKinney (D-Ga.) introduced the Voters' Choice Act, which would allow states to use proportional representation to elect their congressional delegations.

A supporter of the status quo might argue that our system is somehow uniquely suited to the American character or to our political culture, or that two centuries of tradition have sanctified it. But the Founding Fathers did not actually choose the plurality system in any meaningful sense; they simply adopted the British electoral system they grew up with. No real alternative existed until the 1850s, when an Englishman named John Hare devised one of the first influential versions of proportional representation.

Far from being alien to American society, proportional representation is arguably the only appropriate electoral system for a society as diverse as ours. It encourages social peace by giving every major segment of the population a piece of the action. Proportional representation has proved most successful in ethnically divided societies, such as the Baltic states and South Africa, since it permits every significant minority to elect at least some representatives. The traditional American theory of democracy, majority rule with minority rights, has always been questionable. We cannot count on the federal judiciary to protect the rights of minorities, because its composition, over time, will reflect the partisan majority in the other two branches. Properly understood, democracy means majority rule with minority representation. Under proportional representation, the black or Hispanic or libertarian or socialist or populist minority would have the opportunity to elect the occasional member of Congress, state legislator, or city council member, instead of having to cast a doomed vote.

If the traditionalist argument in support of plurality voting were valid, it ought to be most powerful in Britain, from which the U.S. inherited its archaic electoral method. There, however, Prime Minister Tony Blair made a national referendum on the replacement of plurality voting by proportional representation an important part of his campaign. Australia, New Zealand, and Ireland already have forms of proportional representation in some elections, and Canada recently considered the idea when it attempted to redesign its senate (the plan failed for reasons that had nothing to do with the issue of proportional representation). If Britain and Canada scrap plurality voting, the United States, in a generation or two, might find itself alone among advanced democratic countries in clinging to an electoral procedure rejected as unfair and primitive everywhere else. The "world's greatest democracy" may end up having the least democratic electoral law.

Needless to say, politicians elected under a given voting system are unlikely to change it. In the United States, the best way to force the political class to undertake electoral reform may be to sponsor initiatives in states, such as California, whose constitutions permit this method of direct action. Most electoral reforms, such as the extension of suffrage to women and blacks, were adopted by progressive states before they were enacted by congressional statute or constitutional amendment.

In the 1996 election, less than half of the electorate voted. Under the current electoral system, choosing not to vote is a rational decision by people who do not identify with either of the two parties, or who live in congressional districts or states in which one party has an overwhelming majority. When the system is rigged against you, a boycott makes perfect sense (international comparisons demonstrate, to nobody's surprise, that voter turnout is far lower in democracies with plurality voting than in multiparty democracies using proportional representation).

Though it may be justified, popular alienation threatens democracy itself in the long run. If people believe, correctly, that they are not represented by the American political elite, they will be drawn to the kind of antipolitics represented on left, right, and center by Jerry Brown, Pat Buchanan, and Ross Perot, respectively. At its worst, antipolitics is the opposite of political reform; its goal is to smash constitutional, representative democracy, not to improve it. As Americans grow more alienated from the two-party system that our antiquated voting scheme encourages, they may be tempted to support a charismatic president who, claiming a popular mandate, promises to get things done, with little regard for constitutional niceties or those crooks in Congress. Only a few years ago, a majority of Americans polled said that they would support Colin Powell for president, knowing almost nothing about his political views. That he wore a uniform was apparently sufficient recommendation. A North American version of Latin American-style Peronism or French-style Bonapartism, disguised as presidential prerogative or direct democracy, is all too conceivable in the 21st century.

Time is running out. Soon, we will have to prove to ourselves that the American political system has not discredited democracy itself, only the democracy of Wonderland.

A Warming Trend for Third Parties?

TIFFANY DANITZ

Third parties well may be entering a new age in politics, as current indicators point to an electorate that is disgruntled despite a peaceful and economically prosperous decade.

Are they spoilers or champions of democracy? Third-party candidates have a long, and often unmentioned, place in U.S. history. Firebrand Belva Ann Lockwood, for instance, had gained some notoriety when in 1879 she won the right for women to argue cases in front of the Supreme Court. This more than likely aided her 1884 presidential bid, at age 54, against James G. Blaine and Grover Cleveland. Running on an equal-rights ticket, Lockwood garnered thousands of popular votes from an all-male electorate. She may not have been a spoiler, but she forced a public debate on women's suffrage.

"We get more influence by challenging [the Republicans and Democrats]," says Howie Hawkins, a coordinating-committee member for the environmentalist Green Party, "but maybe that is how to get all voices to have representation in the legislature." David Gillespie, author of *Politics at the Periphery: Third Parties in Two-Party America*, explains that the primary role of the third party has been to popularize ideas before the major parties are ready to address them. But he says the time for a larger role for third parties has come and cites a Maricopa Research Inc. poll which found that more than 60 percent of Americans would like to see a new political party.

"I think the year 2000 may well be a year some third-party movement organizes and comes closer to the mainstream than ever before. This is the movement of the militant center," he says. Historically, he adds, third-party success has depended upon a downturn in the economy or a national crisis. But he tells *Insight* current indicators point to an American electorate that is disgruntled despite a peaceful and economically prosperous decade.

How are third parties gearing up for their big bang into the third millennium? The National Reform Party, a splinter group of the United We Stand America party of Ross Perot, is busy recruiting and training possible candidates for local, state and national offices. It has declared war on the Republican Party for the 1998 congressional elections and is trying to punish the GOP for its alleged failure to fulfill its 1992 promises.

Tiffany Danitz is a general assignment reporter for *Insight* magazine.
Reprinted by permission. *Insight on the News*, Jan. 12, 1998. Vol. 13, No. 2, p. 22.

"Nationwide we are looking at the 50 weakest Republicans in Congress and looking at running Reform candidates against them," says Pat Benjamin, the national vice chairwoman of the Reform Party. "We helped the Republicans gain control of Congress in '94 and there are a lot of unhappy people," she adds, ticking off as problems the 105th's votes on fast-track trade authority, campaign finance and support for the North American Free Trade Agreement.

This war cry may be the reason the Reform Party is heavily courting Morry Taylor to run for governor of Illinois. Taylor is a businessman who sought the GOP presidential nomination in 1996, spending millions out of his pocket in the process. Reform Party members filed petitions in December on his behalf, but he is adamant that they did so without his blessing.

Harry Browne, on the other hand, the Libertarian candidate for president in 1996, is not shy about revealing his interest in running again in 2000. "For us the election cycle never stops," the Libertarian Party's acting national director, Ron Crickenberger, tells *Insight.*

The Libertarians are the first third party to achieve 50-state ballot status in consecutive presidential elections. They ran 800 candidates in 1996 at all levels of government, and took 5.4 million votes with them. Libertarians elected seven of their candidates to office. Then, in the November 1997 election bids, 35 Libertarian candidates were elected. In 1998 their goal is to contest 1,000 races nationwide, and to support this effort they are engaging in a series of training seminars for candidates and party activists, says Crickenberger.

Candidates have to jump a number of state and federal election-law hurdles to get access to the ballot box. The states with the loosest restrictions require only that a presidential contender be formally organized, but in Florida, for instance, third parties must collect 450,000 signatures to qualify for a run, according to Kris Williams, a legal expert for the Libertarian Party.

Gillespie says that while third parties must spend large sums and struggle to remain on the ballot, the two major parties are occupied with qualifying for matching funds from the federal government to finance their elaborate campaigns. In 1996 the Libertarians spent $500,000 to get Browne on the ballot, in all 50 states, compared with Perot's rump 1992 presidential bid, which cost him $17 million.

"If you're a major candidate and people assume you will win and add all this money and automatic ballot access, you are bound to win," says Gillespie. "It is like saying, 'No third-party candidate need apply.'"

But the third-party people may receive a boost from former Libertarian presidential candidate Ron Paul, now a GOP congressman from Texas. Paul and a cosponsor, Ohio Republican Rep. Steven LaTourette, have introduced two bills in Congress which would ease the restrictions that often bump third parties off the federal playing field. The Debate Freedom Act would require presidential debates among all opponents who qualify for the ballot in at least 40 states. The Voter Freedom Act reduces the number of signatures needed to get on the federal ballot in the 50 states from 700,000 to 100,000. Both bills are in the House Government Reform and Oversight Committee waiting for Congress to reconvene.

Paul's spokesman, Michael Sullivan, calls the current standards "immoral," saying citizens deserve to hear the voices of all the people who would represent them when tax dollars are financing campaigns. "Both parties have put up barriers and we are disenfranchising a lot of people. No one should be against opening the doors to political discourse," he adds.

This legislation may be the boost the Green Party needs to run another candidate for president in 2000. Ralph Nader lent his name to the Green ticket in 1996 and might be willing to do so again in 2000. However, the Greens probably will run a different candidate—one without a self-imposed $5,000 spending limit, a factor which Hawkins believes led people to think Nader wasn't serious about the Green bid.

"My understanding is [Nader] is setting the same terms for 2000," says Hawkins, "and across the Green movement people appreciate his name and the legitimacy he lends. But, we want to run a more vigorous campaign."

The Green Party is bigger than a pile of political planks—it is a movement, according to Hawkins. Greens are concerned with organizing the grass roots on a lot of local issues such as deregulation of utilities, or concerns about incinerators or creating a union to arbitrate workfare assignments.

Howard Phillips, the presidential candidate for the conservative U.S. Taxpayers Party in 1992 and 1996, tells *Insight* that his party has not chosen a candidate for 2000. But Phillips is visiting states on behalf of the party and trying to expand its reach and recruit leaders. "We have had workshops on campaign management on a daily basis. We work with people giving consideration to running for office in their states," says this former director of the Office of Economic Opportunity.

Blooming in the winter of their discontent, third parties are having more success on the verge of the millennium. In the last decade, Alaska and Connecticut broke a record held since the Great Depression when each state elected a third-party governor. Gillespie calls 1992 the "Year of Ross Perot." In 1996 Perot was flanked by contenders: Nader, Phillips and Browne. Perot set another record when his sequential third-party presidential bids garnered more than 10 percent of the vote for the first time since the Civil War.

Gillespie doesn't think the newfound interest in third parties breaks from the past since much of it is driven by packages of issues rather than ideological concerns. Benjamin is adamant that she is not a party person, for instance, but instead is driven by the chance to debate on issues—a chance to appeal to a growing voter base.

But for others, ideology and the hoped-for results combine. "There is not a single significant issue from socialized medicine to foreign policy where, in practice rather than rhetoric, the Republican Party is separate from Clinton," fumes Phillips. The Taxpayer Party's spokesman says he wants to see principled politicians make a stand and walk away from the center.

Gillespie says it is healthy for the nation to look for alternatives. "The two parties are saying the same things. We are moving in terms of political technology, toward the possibility of instant response, yet here we have a horse-and-buggy two-party system that doesn't fit participatory democracy in the 21st century. We are becoming far more incisive in our ability to discern things, and technology gives us instant feedback."

The Internet is making a profound impact on third-party membership as well as on their organizing capabilities. As technology buttresses party infrastructure, Gillespie muses, the country will see some third-party "greening" at the local level paralleled with presidential bids, since that is the focus of national media attention. The significance of the rise in third parties, despite a healthy economy, may be that the United States on the cusp of the next millennium is becoming ever more a pluralistic democracy with politically organized interest groups. It could be that third parties, and fourth and fifth parties, are here to stay.

Issue 9
Campaign Finance Reform

INTRODUCTION

Our economic system celebrates the idea that people make as much money as they can, but our political system has great trouble with the idea that people spend money as they please. This, in a nutshell, is the dilemma of campaign finance. A democracy takes seriously the idea of one person, one vote. Yet it is undeniable that some votes speak with a louder voice than others. Those with money are able to buy access to, and influence over, politicians, while those without are left with the meager consolation of the franchise. The problem is not so much that the rich buy politicians in the straightforward sense of personal corruption and venality. Rather, the financial requirements of the modern political campaign—above all, the costs of modern advertising media—create a structural imperative on the part of all candidates to grub for money, driven on by the paramount fear that their opponents may have successfully grubbed for more.

Modern election law dates from the Federal Elections Campaign Act (FECA) of 1974. Yet as Thomas Fleming's entertaining historical overview makes clear, the problem of campaign finance and politics dates from the beginning of the Republic. Indeed, if there are any constants in this colorful and oftentimes sordid story of money and politics, they are, first, that each major party avidly solicits funds, even as they hypocritically rail against the fundraising shenanigans of the other party; and second, that politicians of all stripes are infinitely creative at circumventing the prevailing legal restrictions on raising money. To be sure, the form of fundraising may change. The "tithing" typical of nineteenth century machine politics gave way, under the pressure of civil service reform, to the systematic shakedown of corporate donors perfected by Marcus Alonzo Hanna on behalf of William McKinley's 1896 Presidential campaign. When, in turn, corporate contributions were declared illegal, the power of money in campaign politics merely assumed a different form.

Currently, modern campaign finance prospers despite the intent of the law thanks to two subterfuges. The Political Action Committee, or PAC, serves as a conduit for money that amplifies the donations of individuals and enables corporations and labor unions to get around contribution limits. In addition, a legal distinction between spending for specific candidates' campaigns (limited to $5000) and spending for general activities of party mobilization or 'educational' advocacy (unlimited) has restored to large donors access and influence. This distinction, which gives rise to the notorious terms "hard" and "soft" money, has become increasingly unworkable as unlimited soft-money donations are applied to hard-money purposes. Indeed, the prerogatives of soft money seem to find protection in the Constitution itself. In Justice Potter Stewart's judgment, "money is speech and speech is money." Sanctified by the First Amendment, large amounts of money—over a billion dollars of direct spending in the last Presidential campaign—remain an inescapable reality of modern elections.

While Fleming places this reality in historical perspective, Joseph Lieberman, a practicing politician, nonetheless condemns the influence of campaign money. To Lieberman, the ubiquity and sheer magnitude of such finance bespeaks a larger social corruption. In a society where winning comes at any cost whether in sports, politics, or the economy, the pressure of money crushes other values. Money not only tarnishes the integrity of politicians, Lieberman believes, but also reduces the legitimacy of the political system in the eyes of the general public. For in a world where everything can be bought, no one thing can be very valuable.

As you read the articles, consider the following questions.

Discussion Questions

1. The constitutional argument against campaign finance restrictions rests upon Judge Stewart's claim that "money is speech and speech is money." Does this seem reasonable to you? After all, Stewart's claim is an analogy, not an identity. 'Money talks' is a figure of speech; money is not speech itself. Or is it? Do you express yourself by, say, spending money at the mall?
2. Let's assume that money is indeed speech, and vice versa. If we take seriously constitutional protections of free speech, then shouldn't the government be providing everyone with the money necessary to express themselves? After all, without the money to support all speech, how can any speech be free?
3. If money and politics are inseparable, can you imagine any reform to the campaign finance laws that would place campaign finance on an objective, if not fair, basis?

4. Campaign financing became controversial early on in the presidential campaign for the year 2000. In what ways have our most recent presidential candidates met the letter, and violated the spirit, of the campaign finance laws? Have their tactics differed from those chronicled by Fleming?

For more information on this topic, visit the following websites:

`http://www.brookings.org`
The Brookings Institution

`http://www.fec.gov`
Federal Election Commission

`http://commoncause.org`
Common Cause

`http://www.followthemoney.org`
The National Institute on Money in State Politics

The Long, Stormy Marriage of Money and Politics

... or Why in America Campaign-Finance Reform Never Succeeds

THOMAS FLEMING

In the summer of 1787 a sweaty group of politicians was debating the clauses of a proposed constitution in humid Philadelphia. Endless problems reared their ugly heads: the distribution of power between large states and small states; slavery; the size of a standing army; the powers of the Presidency. The framers solved—or postponed—most of these dilemmas with their famous genius for compromise. But one quandary was solved differently.

A rich young South Carolinian named Charles Pinckney proposed that the Presidency should be limited to people worth $100,000—well over a million dollars in today's money—and the federal judiciary and Congress to those worth half that sum. Pinckney did not get this idea out of thin air. In South Carolina a man had to have $10,000 to be elected to the state senate.

Other Southerners were eager to support the proposal. Even James Madison, the father of the Constitution, was ready to admit that the chief danger in a republic was the likelihood that a majority of poor men would pass laws that penalized the rich and undermined the nation's stability. It was vital to give men of wealth a large, if not controlling, voice in the new nation.

Benjamin Franklin took the floor. He said he was opposed to anything "that tended to debase the spirit of the common people," and he reminded the delegates that the Bible said rulers should be men "hating covetousness." Pinckney watched his proposal drown in a cascade of nays.

Thus did Americans deal with the first argument over the place of money in a republic. Liberal idealism—and Franklin was probably the most liberal member of the constitutional convention—met conservative realism and routed it. It was a totally misleading moment.

Today it may well seem that Pinckney has posthumously vanquished Franklin in this long-running debate. Money lies at the heart of election politics. In the presidential and congressional campaigns of

Thomas Fleming is a novelist and historian. His most recent novel, *The Wages of Fame* (Forge Books, 1998), deals with political corruption in pre–Civil War Washington, D.C.

Reprinted by permission. *American Heritage*, Nov. 1998. Vol. 49, Issue 7, p. 45.

1996, the two major parties spent $990.6 million, more than twice what they spent in 1992. For much of the past year, we have been treated to accounts of how the biggest winner, President Clinton, raised a lot of this cash.

A night in the Lincoln bedroom went for $250,000, while a clubby fifty-guest dinner with the President cost $100,000, and a cocktail party, just $50,000. Unknowns like John Huang and Charlie Trie reportedly funneled hundreds of thousands of dollars from overseas donors. The Democratic National Committee (DNC) squirmed in public while returning at least $3.5 million in tainted dollars.

We have heard less about Republican fundraising practices partly because they do not seem to have been quite so blatant but also, of course, because the GOP controls Congress and is chairing the investigations. In the course of the campaign, the Republican National Committee put heavy pressure on its biggest donors to up their usual $100,000 contributions to a quarter million. In return they were guaranteed invitations to all the GOP's balls and dinners, plus a chance to take home photographs of themselves smiling beside Speaker of the House Newt Gingrich or Majority Leader Trent Lott. At least two dozen executives from major corporations bought this package.

Gifts to candidates are theoretically limited to $5,000 under the 1974 law that set up the Federal Election Commission. But this toothless watchdog, a creature created by Congress with three members from each party to guarantee gridlock, is only the latest mutation in a process that has engaged the best minds in the Republic for generations. If they haven't solved the problem, it is nonetheless worth seeing why they haven't.

In the beginning there were no campaign-finance laws. Franklin notwithstanding, money wasn't regarded as a menace to American politics. That realistic—and rich—man President George Washington firmly backed Secretary of the Treasury Alexander Hamilton's plan to create financial stability in the new nation by reassuring the wealthy. The federal Bank of the United States gave merchants and manufacturers badly needed capital. The assumption of the Revolution's debts at face value established the nation's credit, even though it enormously favored prosperous speculators in government paper. There were a lot of rich men around in 1790; the distribution of wealth was roughly what it is today. The top 10 percent of the population controlled well over half the land and cash.

Thomas Jefferson took up Franklin's cause and organized a political party to oppose Hamilton's Federalists. His ally in New York Aaron Burr soon realized that Hamilton and his friends controlled both the state's only bank and the local branch of the Bank of the United States, and they refused to lend money to anyone who did not back their party. The very canny Burr wangled through the state legislature a banking charter concealed in the Trojan horse of a municipal water company and, thus establishing himself, swung New York's crucial electoral votes behind the triumphant Jefferson-Burr ticket in the year 1800. The contest created a rivalry between two different political orientations that persists to this day (as does the bank Burr created, now known as the Chase Manhattan).

While pulling off his banking coup, Burr also managed to politicize a lower-middle-class chowder and marching group called the Society of St. Tammany. As Tammany Hall it soon dominated New York City's government. Along with polling the dead, stuffing ballot boxes, and hiring Irish immigrant toughs to cast ballots half a dozen times per election and beat up would-be opposition voters, it became a major source of campaign cash.

As the relatively genteel electioneering of the Revolutionary War generation encountered the politics of mass democracy under Andrew Jackson, money became more rather than less important. President Jackson waged war against the Bank of the United States, which, to hear him tell it, had half of Congress on its payroll. It unquestionably had Daniel Webster and other conservatives. The bank and its well-heeled backers spent thousands trying to paint Jackson as a dictator in the election of 1832.

Fighting the rich cost money; the slogan of a New York Jacksonian Democrat, William Learned Marcy, "To the victor belong the spoils of the enemy," suggests one way in which they raised it. Public offices were up for grabs in every election; it seemed logical to expect the officeholders to kick in a percentage of their salaries to protect their jobs.

Jackson and his methods annihilated the opposition in 1832, and by the time James Buchanan ran for President, in 1856, money had become important enough in a campaign to prompt the Republican boss of New York, Thurlow Weed, to define the difference between the winner (Buchanan) and the loser (John C. Fremont) as $50,000. When Abraham Lincoln ran for President four years later, the Republicans were determined not to fall short again. In pivotal states, such as Indiana, local Republicans welcomed money from Weed's ample New York coffers. Lincoln himself once said, "In a political contest, some use of money is both right and indispensable." Early in 1860 he paid out of his own pocket to help one friend visit Chicago to push his candidacy.

Lincoln's uphill 1864 election campaign depended heavily on contributions from thousands of companies that the government had enriched with war-production contracts. The return of peace dried up this flow of cash, but government employees continued to be the major source of campaign funds. In Pennsylvania, where the Republicans developed a formidable political machine under Simon Cameron, every state employee received an annual letter ordering him to contribute 2 percent of his pay; its menacing final sentence read: "After the campaign we shall place a list of those who have not paid in the hands of the head of the department you are in." Cameron's political philosophy can be summed up in the aphorism for which he has achieved a certain fame: "An honest politician is one who when he's bought, stays bought."

Ironically—a word that might well be applied to almost every paragraph of this tale—the Democrats, the party of the common man, introduced the habit of running very rich men for office. This began when they nominated Samuel Tilden for President in 1876. They had already learned the advantages of enlisting the support of the rich. August Belmont, James Buchanan's principal backer in 1856, a suave New Yorker who was the American spokesman for the immensely wealthy Rothschild banking clan, had helped pay for the creation of the Democratic National Committee in 1852.

Tilden, a highly successful corporate lawyer reportedly bankrolled two-thirds of his $150,000 Democratic campaign against Rutherford B. Hayes. Scarred by the scandals of the Grant administration, the Republicans looked vulnerable. But *The New York Times*, the Republican flagship newspaper, led a ferocious counterattack on Tilden's ethics, and the Presidency came down to the electoral votes of three Southern states. Tilden's nephew and several leading Democrats schemed to buy these undoubtedly acquirable assets, foolishly urging one another on in telegrams that the Republicans later obtained and published. Meanwhile, the GOP put men on trains to head south with carpetbags full of money. "Rutherfraud," as hostile newspapers called Hayes, became President by a single electoral vote.

The stench wafting from the 1876 election, combined with the 1881 assassination of President James Garfield, inspired a cadre of Eastern Republicans to take action. Eager to break the grip of the corrupt old guard on the GOP, they portrayed the deranged assassin as an office seeker driven insane by the status quo and used him to belabor the spoils system and the custom of forcing civil servants to finance elections with a percentage of their salaries.

In 1883 they prodded the Pendleton Act through Congress, making some government jobs winnable (and keepable) on merit alone and banning the solicitation of funds from federal officeholders. But Pendleton had no bearing on state and city government employees, and pay-or-else letters continued to flow from Republican bosses in Pennsylvania, while Tammany Hall and other Democratic machines went on collecting their tithes from civil servants and anyone who did business with the city or state.

Now the law of unintended consequences, the only constant mechanism in the story of campaign-finance reform, eased into gear. National politicians, with their access to government workers stymied by the Pendleton Act, turned to corporations and found there the immense wealth generated in the Industrial Revolution by Vanderbilts, Astors, and the like. Boies Penrose, the Pennsylvania Republican boss who succeeded Cameron, summed up the prevailing philosophy when he remarked, "You can't run a party on nothing and when you need money the place to get it is from them that have it." Henry Adams saw the result in starker terms: "The moral law has expired."

A climax of sorts came in the 1896 presidential campaign. Behind the blandly orthodox Republican image of William McKinley stood Marcus Alonzo Hanna, the first authentic genius of campaign finance. His genius was assisted not a little by the radical pyrotechnics of the Democratic candidate, William Jennings Bryan, who attacked the two pillars of Republican prosperity, the gold standard and the protective tariff.

Hanna raised an estimated $7 million from alarmed businessmen to put McKinley in the White House. He levied assessments on companies of all sizes based on his judgment of their "stake in the general prosperity." With a shrewdness that anticipated the fundraisers of our own nineties, Hanna refused to promise any specific favor or service; rather, he sold the glittering concept of "access" and a government that smiled on corporations.

McKinley beat Bryan and then repeated the performance in 1900 at only about a third of the cost. He even returned $50,000 of a reputed $250,000 contribution to Standard Oil because it exceeded what he considered the company's fair share of the national effort. His fundraising tactics soon generated a backlash. The outspent Democrats denounced them as proof that America was going from democracy to plutocracy, and they were joined by muckraking reporters who began writing of corporations buying up entire state legislatures to guarantee their immunity from investigation and control. To Hanna's dismay, the critics were joined by none other than the Republican politician who became President when McKinley was assassinated in 1901.

Like Benjamin Franklin, Theodore Roosevelt had a deep respect for the spirit of the average American, and he sensed that revelations about unchecked corporate power were in danger of making many people cynical toward their country. When he ran for re-election in 1904, he piously returned a $10,000 check from Standard Oil and said he wished he could raise money from average citizens but found the idea unworkable. So he turned to wealthy individuals to fund his campaign. Although their identities remained unknown at the time, four big givers—J. P. Morgan, John Archbold of Standard Oil, George Gould, and Chauncey Depew (spokesman for the Vanderbilts, which means the New York Central Railroad)—covered a fourth of his 1904 expenses.

A year later Republican progressives joined the battle against corporate money in politics. A New York legislative committee under Charles Evans Hughes discovered that the state's giant insurance companies had paid hundreds of thousands of dollars to state and national politicians, often disguised as legal expenses. Hughes summoned to the witness chair Thomas Platt, boss of the New York Republicans, and asked him if candidates felt a moral obligation to big givers. "That is naturally what would be involved," Platt replied.

Among the many large contributions made to the Republican party, Hughes's investigators found one check for nearly $50,000 paid by New York Life to Theodore Roosevelt's 1904 campaign. That revelation made headlines across the country. In his next message to Congress an embarrassed Roosevelt recommended a law banning all corporate contributions. The bill that finally emerged, in 1907, was the result of agitation by the populist senator Benjamin Tillman, of South Carolina. "Pitchfork Ben," a race-baiting demagogue, wanted nothing less than to cripple the Republican party. Nevertheless, public indignation at corporate influence had grown so feverish that even such a law from such a source had a wide appeal. "It is impossible to make a case against the Tillman bill on any other grounds than that boodle has become an indispensable factor in our elections," wrote the Washington Post.

Roosevelt had proposed to ban all contributions to political parties and have elections funded by the government. The Tillman Act was much narrower: It proscribed contributions to federal elections by corporations and national banks. The Republican Senate excised the part that barred business money from state and local elections.

Tillman's success led progressives to browbeat a reluctant Congress into other reforms. In 1910 a Democratic-funded entity known as the National Publicity Bill Organization (NPBO) lathered a law that required federal candidates to disclose the sources of their campaign funds. The next year an amended version barred House candidates from spending more than $5,000 in each election. Senators were limited to $10,000, or a lesser amount established by state laws. None of these reforms was adopted without months of angry debate. Spending limits, in particular, aroused furious objections from many politicians.

It soon became apparent that the Tillman Act did not keep business money out of federal elections. Instead of corporations, wealthy individuals—the end run chosen by Roosevelt—were paying now. The Democrats, who had rallied around Tillman and the NPBO, gratefully took whacking contributions from the likes of Thomas Fortune Ryan and August Belmont, ignoring William Jennings Bryan's declaration that he would not accept more than $10,000 from any individual for his third White House run in 1908.

When Woodrow Wilson ran for President in 1912, he publicly refused to accept a cent from Belmont or Ryan and declared he would raise his funds from contributions of $100 or less. Theodore Roosevelt was quickly proved right; the idea was unworkable, and the small givers ran dry at a total of $318,910. Soon Wilson was taking six-figure donations. In 1916, up against a revived Republican party, he looked the other way while Ryan and Belmont joined the big givers who raised more than $800,000 to finance his narrow victory over Charles Evans Hughes.

Enter the Supreme Court. In 1918 Truman H. Newberry beat Henry Ford in the Republican primary for the U.S. Senate in Michigan and went on to win the general election. Ford's backers demanded Newberry be prosecuted for exceeding the state's meager campaign-funding limitation of $1,875. Newberry was convicted and sentenced to two years in Leavenworth. The senator hired Charles Evans Hughes to represent him on appeal; Hughes argued before the Supreme Court that Newberry had not personally exceeded the spending limit. Rather, his campaign committee had spent $180,000. Hughes also argued that Congress had no jurisdiction over primaries.

The Court accepted the latter argument and overturned Newberry's conviction. But politicians paid more attention . . . to Hughes's ingenious distinction between candidate and committee. Here was a man identified with campaign-finance reform saying it was perfectly all right to pile on the boodle as long as the candidate was not directly involved with its collection and disbursement.

Before the politicians could apply this nice new principle, they were chastened by the Teapot Dome scandal. Certain contributors who had given heavily to the Republican party in an off year when there was no requirement to report anything had been rewarded with access to oil deposits owned by the U.S. government. The resulting public outrage prompted Congress to overhaul the existing finance law in the Federal Corrupt Practices Act of 1925, which required committees and candidates to file quarterly reports every year. Still, they left a law through which campaign managers could, in the words of one newsman, "drive a four horse team."

In the 1930s the leaps-and-bounds growth of the federal bureaucracy under Franklin D. Roosevelt alarmed Republicans and anti-Roosevelt Democrats enough to make them allies in passing the 1939 Hatch Act, also called the Clean Politics Act, which forbade political activities, including fundraising, by all government employees. The Pendleton Act in 1883 had covered only bureaucrats classified by Congress as deserving protection—excluding most federal employees, about 70 percent, who thus could continue to give to their favorite politicians.

In spite of fierce Democratic resistance, Hatch's law was extended the following year to include the many state government employees whose salaries came from federal funds. This was a body blow aimed at Democratic big-city political machines. In an attempt to derail this proposal, angry Democrats tacked on a rider limiting individual contributions to $5,000 and party committee expenditures to $3 million in each presidential election.

Debate on the bill offered a dispiriting glimpse into the hypocrisies of campaign finance as purveyed by both parties. Ignoring their history of running rich men, the Democrats portrayed themselves as the party of the poor, who financed their campaigns from contributions by high-minded public employees. The Republicans expatiated on the danger of cash from publicly financed bureaucrats—as if they had never milked government servants in states like Pennsylvania that they controlled.

In the end Congress amazed itself and everyone else by approving limits on both individual donations and total campaign expenditures. The general counsel to the Republican National Committee reacted promptly: He expanded the Charles Evans Hughes option. There would be nothing wrong, he said, with someone paying $5,000 apiece to several state and local Republican committees; indeed it would also be legal to form several national committees, each of which could spend $3 million. In the 1940 election the Republicans spent $15 million, the Democrats $6 million, breaking all previous records.

In the same Depression decade a new force emerged on the campaign-finance scene: labor unions. Through their dues they could put millions behind chosen candidates. The specter of concentrated worker power alarmed conservatives at least as much as did the potential tyranny of politically active union chiefs, and in 1943 a congressional coalition of Southern Democrats and Republicans prohibited unions from contributing to national political organizations, a ban that was reaffirmed by the Taft-Hartley Act of 1947. The Congress of Industrial Organizations (CIO) responded by forming the first political-action committee, CIO-PAC, a group nominally independent of the sponsoring union. It was an invention labor would learn to regret.

Nothing much was done about campaign finance between 1943 and 1971. Sporadic congressional moral spasms died in committee or were blocked by unenthusiastic Presidents, notably Lyndon Johnson, who appointed a bipartisan panel to overhaul the law and never even acknowledged its report. The big change in these years was soaring campaign costs, driven by the growing power of television. From $21 million in 1940, when radio time went for as little as $25,000 a half-hour, the tab for the TV-saturated Johnson-Goldwater campaign in 1964 rose to $60 million.

In 1968, when Hubert Humphrey fought it out with Richard Nixon, the cost hit $100 million. Single-handedly proving the impotence of the Hatch Act's $5,000 limitation on individual gifts, the insurance magnate

W. Clement Stone gave $2.2 million to a plethora of Republican committees and Nixon front organizations. The Democrats matched this flouting of the law's intent by setting up almost fifty committees to bring in their cash.

It looked as if the politicians and their managers would continue to raise money and spend it in ever-swelling volume unto the millennium. But Democrats were deeply disturbed by Nixon's 1968 triumph, which they attributed to his larger war chest. Echoing Thurlow Weed's 1856 lament, Humphrey's campaign manager, Joseph Napolitan, said that another $300,000 could have won his candidate California and the election.

Sen. Russell Long and several other leading Democrats began calling for an overhaul of campaign-finance laws and the introduction of some form of public funding—the goal, of course, was to upend the Republicans' financial supremacy—and after years of debate and hearings, they produced the Federal Election Campaign Act of 1971. FECA did not contain a public-funding clause, because President Nixon violently opposed the idea, but it continued the ban on corporate and union money, and it set limits on how much a wealthy candidate could spend on his own campaign ($50,000 for a presidential race). It also paradoxically abolished the limit on how much an individual could give to someone else's campaign or how much a committee could contribute. In an attempt to control TV costs, the lawmakers limited how much a candidate could spend on media. FECA also called for far stricter and more detailed disclosures of who was giving and how much.

There was a good deal of hopeful talk about FECA's reducing the costs of campaigns. Instead President Nixon spent twice as much in 1972 as he had in 1968, and his challenger, George McGovern, quadrupled his party's previous outlays. The total bill for both parties in all the races exceeded $400 million, a 33 percent jump over 1968.

Before Congress could begin to reassess FECA, the Watergate scandal generated a new opportunity for reform. The hearings not only revealed a President guilty of obstructing justice but unveiled his election team laundering money in Mexico and performing similar arabesques elsewhere to evade the new election law. Soon one out of every four constituent letters that reached Congress was a demand for campaign-finance revision.

At this point a new player entered the fray, the citizens' advocacy group Common Cause. Using litigation, lobbying, publicity, and other forms of political pressure, these upper-middle-class liberals became a kind of Greek chorus crying for reform. In 1974 Congress responded by producing the first really comprehensive campaign-finance legislation. Described as an amendment to 1972's FECA, it was in fact an almost total overhaul, aimed at creating an era of equality and ethical purity in American politics.

First, and seemingly most important, the lawmakers at last voted for what Theodore Roosevelt had wanted: public money for presidential-election campaigns. It would be paid by people checking off a one-dollar contribution on their tax returns (raised to three dollars in 1993), which would not increase their total bill. Meanwhile, Congress tried to rein in private political spending down the line: Senators were limited to $100,000 per primary and $150,000 per general election; representatives to $70,000. Presidential contests were confined to $10 million for a nomination and $20 million in the general election. National-party committee spending was given a ceiling of $10,000 in House elections, $20,000 in Senate ones, and $2.9 million in a presidential race. The law retained the 1971 limits on personal spending by wealthy candidates and their immediate families and tried otherwise to diminish the influence of large donors by forbidding them to give more than $25,000 per federal election. PACs were allowed $5,000 per candidate. Disclosure rules were again toughened, and to monitor this complicated process, Congress created the bipartisan Federal Election Commission.

President Ford had no sooner signed the new law than an unlikely trio—the very conservative senator James Buckley of New York, the very liberal former senator Eugene McCarthy of Minnesota, and Ira Glasser, executive director of the New York Civil Liberties Union—called a press conference in Washington to assail it from every point of the ideological and political compass. They said the monetary limitations violated their First Amendment rights and the disclosure requirements had the makings of a police state. McCarthy compared public funding of the major parties to declaring that the United States had "two established religions."

The three men sued to overturn FECA, and a year later the case went before the Supreme Court. What came out of this imbroglio was a now-familiar blend of paradox and good intention and pragmatism. The Court threw out all limitations on money used to voice political opinions not directly connected to a candidacy, because prohibiting this kind of spending was a violation of the First Amendment. The same reasoning led the justices to demolish any limitation on what a candidate could spend in his own behalf. In a dictum still reverberating through our political system, Justice Potter Stewart said: "We are talking about speech, money is speech and speech is money, whether it is buying television or radio time or newspaper advertising, or even buying pencils and paper and microphones."

But the justices also ruled that there could be limits on direct contributions to candidates, because that money passed out of the giver's hands and hence no longer belonged to him as speech. They argued that the intent of FECA, to remove the taint of corruption from the political process, made this limitation justifiable.

The frustrating distinction between "hard" money (contributions) and "soft" money (expenditures) was born here. Hard money went directly to a campaign; soft money went anywhere else. Subsequent decisions have widened the soft-money playing field to continental proportions. In 1978 the Court ruled that corporations have First Amendment rights not much different from individuals'; more than a few lawyers concluded that the justices had implicitly declared the 1907 Tillman Act barring corporate contributions unconstitutional. In 1996 the Court ruled that a series of savage advertisements run by the Colorado Republican Federal Campaign Committee against the senatorial candidate Tim Wirth were "independent expenditures" protected by the First Amendment, not "coordinated contributions" to his opponent.

In this relaxed atmosphere PACs, representing business, labor, and assorted special interests such as education and the environment, began to proliferate. In 1974 there were 608 PACs giving $12.5 million. By 1996 there were 4,079 giving $200.9 million. The Federal Election Commission was partly responsible, having issued several opinions that permitted corporations to tap employees as well as stockholders for these artificial entities and even to contribute directly from their treasuries, showing little concern when a PAC and a company were nearly indistinguishable in their interests. PACs have developed habits that do little to increase competition in Congress. They give about 90 percent of their election-year millions to incumbents—that is, to the people who can deliver favors.

In the 1980s, as the Democrats scrambled to catch up with the revivified Republicans under Ronald Reagan, Rep. Tony Coelho, head of the Democratic Congressional Campaign Committee, decided that the party of the people could attract business money by the tens of millions. Inevitably this policy involved the party in deals that looked a lot like bribes. By the time the decade ended, Jim Wright, the Democratic Speaker of the House, had been driven from office by conflicts of interest, and Coelho himself had resigned one jump ahead of the House Ethics Committee. Toward the end of Coelho's tenure, one fundraiser said, "The Democratic party doesn't stand for anything anymore."

In the nineties, labor unions, seeking to regain their old clout, have poured millions into the Democrats' coffers via PACs. Among the biggest givers have been the American Association of State, County and Municipal Employees and the National Education Association. In 1996 they gave $7.3 million. For those with a sense of history, the irony is disquieting. We are back to extracting a percentage of government employees' income to finance political campaigns, but now we call it union dues.

So we come to the money-drenched election of 1996. The $990.6 million total reflects only the visible part of the iceberg, the national committees. There was no requirement to report how much soft money was funneled to state party organizations. Then there was the "issue advocacy" sector, in which theoretically independent groups such as labor unions bought TV and radio time to purvey their views, to the tune of at least $75 million—again with no requirement to report a cent. A study by the nonpartisan Center for Responsive Politics (CRP) estimates that the real total expenditure figure for 1996 is $2.2 billion.

During the campaign, monitors such as CRP virtually threw up their hands. "There are no limits, there are no rules," a CRP spokesman said. Each candidate received $62 million in public funding, but this did not stop each party from raising almost $100 million in soft money. Fred Wertheimer, former president of Common Cause, summed up the spectacle in scathing terms. He said President Clinton had broken his "legally binding commitment to the American people." In accepting public funding, Clinton had agreed to limit the money he raised and spent from other sources. "He exceeded the legal cap by $45 million," Wertheimer says.

In the congressional hearings that probed the election, commentators repeatedly observed that there was no public outrage over this and that Bill Clinton's popularity ratings remained high. Others, though, said that the people do care and that they had already proved it in 1996. On October 6, 1996, after *The Wall Street Journal* broke the first of several stories about questionable White House fundraising (thirty-one donors listed the DNC headquarters as their home address), the Democratic campaign stalled. Instead of continuing to widen his lead over Sen. Robert Dole, the President suddenly had all he could do to maintain a precarious status quo. His hopes of winning a hefty majority of the vote and a mandate to govern vanished. Millions of voters, still unwilling to embrace the Republican candidate, had switched to Ross Perot. Millions more had stayed home, and leading Democratic operators now glumly concede that this voter outrage—such as it was—cost them control of the House of Representatives.

On the other hand, the number of Americans checking off three dollars on their income tax returns to finance public funding of presidential campaigns has dwindled to 12 percent. Some see this as evidence that most people oppose public funding; some as a reflection of disgust at its failure to change anything. Whichever is the case, most Republicans remain opposed to full public funding, with a total ban on private money, partly because they believe this would give the Democrats an unfair advantage. Most of the media, they argue, are Democratic sympathizers, and without paid TV campaigns the GOP would be unable to get its messages to the people. The GOP also opposes reformers' attempts to limit the use of soft money, for the same reason. As we go to press, the Senate has just killed for this year a reform bill, sponsored by Senators John McCain and Russell D. Feingold, a version of which passed the

House in midsummer. If it ever does pass the Senate, most of its provisions, especially those barring soft money, seem certain to be found unconstitutional by the Supreme Court.

Reformers and editorialists who fulminate over congressional hesitation and half-measures ignore a fundamental fact. Until money and free speech can truly be disentangled—which may be simply impossible—the campaign-finance debate is likely to remain academic. It looks as if Americans will go on struggling to reconcile two of our fundamental ideals, freedom and equality, in our elections process—just as we will go on grappling with these often conflicting visions in other areas of our national life. Almost nobody wants to deny the bedrock right to get one's message across, whatever the cost, yet almost everyone dreams of competing messages' getting through on their merits alone. Like much else in our experimental Republic, this tension between realism and idealism will continue both to vex and to reassure.

A Republic—If We Can Keep It

JOSEPH I. LIEBERMAN

The present corrupt system of financing elections, a U.S. senator argues, poses a serious threat to our democracy. The sad lesson of the recent campaign-finance scandals is not only that the laws are vaporous but also that politicians won't change their ways without public pressure.

Of the many remarks uttered during the U.S. Senate investigation of the 1996 national elections that saw the laws on campaign spending and contributions stretched to the point of absurdity, one of the most telling came in a brief comment by the former White House deputy chief of staff Harold Ickes. Challenged about his handling of a questionable transaction during the final week of the 1996 campaign, Ickes defended his conduct in part by pointing to the chaotic atmosphere all around him: "We were like Mad Hatters," he said.

This allusion to the fundraising madness of the 1996 election cycle seems apt to many good people who were running around like Mad Hatters doing all kinds of bad things. There was a surreal quality to the

Joseph Lieberman, a two-term Democratic senator from Connecticut, serves on the Senate Governmental Affairs Committee.
Reprinted by permission. *The Atlantic Monthly*, Aug. 1, 1998. P. 14(1).

whole scandal, with its bizarre cast of characters, the tortuous logic that many participants employed to rationalize their actions, and the sense as the investigation went on that the polity has fallen down a long, dark hole into a place that is far from the vision and values of those who founded our democracy.

In that strange place the law appears to be written in invisible ink. It is somehow possible for wealthy donors to give hundreds of thousands of dollars to political campaigns, even though the law is clearly intended to limit contributions to a tiny fraction of such sums. It is possible for labor unions and corporations to donate millions to political parties at the candidates' request, despite a decades-old prohibition on the involvement of unions and corporations in national elections. It is possible for tax-exempt groups to run millions of dollars' worth of television ads that clearly endorse or attack particular candidates, even though these groups are barred by law from engaging in such partisan activity. And it is possible for presidential nominees to continue putting the touch on contributors, even though they have pledged under the law not to raise any more money for their campaigns after receiving enormous lump sums ($62 million apiece for Bob Dole and Bill Clinton in 1996) in public funds.

The fundraising scandal of 1996 was a very real tragedy, with very real consequences for our democracy. People at the highest levels in both political parties did more than just strain credulity: they betrayed the public trust. In their breathless, unbounded rush to raise even more money for even more television advertising, they effectively hung a giant FOR SALE sign on our government and the whole of our political process.

They also gave Americans, already beset by cynicism, good reason to doubt whether citizens have a true and equal voice in their own government. The dangers here must not be dismissed: corruption is a great killer of experiments in self-government. In 1787, as he left Independence Hall at the close of the Constitutional Convention, Benjamin Franklin was asked what kind of government the country now had. He replied, "A republic, if you can keep it." Franklin was worried about a tendency toward monarchy. The threat today, imminent and real, is a state of affairs in which money itself is King.

One of the central problems exposed by the campaign-finance revelations has to do with the distinction we make between illegal conduct and improper conduct in public life, and the standards we use to judge such conduct. To this day some prominent elected officials contend that most of the scandals of 1996 involved violations of laws already on the books, and that therefore the appropriate response is simply tougher punishment and tougher enforcement. The reality is otherwise. Most of the sleazy behavior that characterized those elections was legal. The blatant skirting of limits on individual contributions; the subversion of restrictions on presidential candidates who receive public funds; the conversion of supposedly nonpartisan, tax-exempt groups into political agents; the fact that unions and corporations funneled millions of dollars into the two parties despite the law's absolute ban on their involvement in national campaigns—all these acts compromised the integrity of our elections and our government, and all plainly violate the spirit of our laws. Yet all of them also appear to be legal.

In effect, then, what the law permitted in 1996 was as outrageous as any crime that was committed. This point is enormously significant, not just in terms of gauging the import of this scandal but also for determining the steps we should take to repair our broken campaign-finance system. It may be that enforcement of various kinds will curb some of the illegal activities that occurred during the 1996 elections. Yet we can make no similar statement about the wide range of corrosive activities that continue to be legal. In fact, just the opposite is true; it is certain that these behaviors will persist unless we make them illegal.

It is not only the political system that has been compromised and corrupted; so have the values and standards of those who operate within it. In politics as in many segments of our society today, from professional-sports leagues that wink at the shocking behavior of big stars to TV talk-show producers who achieve new lows in degradation and exploitation every day, the bottom line in raising money has too often become the dominant line. Basic differences between right and wrong have become blurred. The moral standard for campaigns today is not what is unassailably proper but what is technically legal.

Plugging the most egregious loopholes to make the clearly improper clearly illegal will deter some future wrongdoing, which is sufficient reason to plug them. But these changes won't be enough. The law serves as an expression of our values. It can stake out ethical boundaries, point us in the right direction, and punish actions that are wrong, but it cannot compel moral behavior. We cannot fully write into law what citizens have a right to expect from their representatives: that those who wish to write the rules for the nation will themselves respect the rules, rather than searching high and low for ways to evade legal requirements and eviscerate their intent; that those who have sworn to abide by the Constitution will honor the trust and responsibilities the Constitution places in their hands, rather than catering to the special interests depositing soft money in their pockets. For our democracy to function, we must rely on a common core of values beyond what the law requires, a system of moral checks and balances comparable to the ones built into the Constitution. But over the past several years the pressure to raise huge amounts of money has eroded those values among politicians, has "defined deviancy down" and left them prey to their baser instincts.

The 1996 elections provided ample evidence of the threat that political money-scrounging poses to the legitimacy of our government. Although it has yet to be proved that any U.S. policy, foreign or domestic, was altered by any of the hustlers and opportunists who bought access to some of our top leaders, we cannot deny that the potential existed for this kind of purchase. Nor can we ignore the dangers inherent in the simple appearance of influence peddling. Consider some of the comments volunteered by the unsavory characters who sought to buy their way into our political system. Johnny Chung: "I see the White House as like a subway you have to put in coins to open the gates." Roger Tamraz, explaining how money bought him political access that had been denied him through other channels: "If they kicked me from the door, I will come through the window."

Hearing these comments, the average American would have every reason to suspect the worst about the government and those who are running it, and to question just whose interests are being served. This may be the gravest consequence of the moral breakdown that our politics has suffered. Take away the Johnny Chungs and the Roger Tamrazes and the other shakedown artists, and we are still left with a system that bends over backward to indulge big donors and their special interests, a system that suggests to the public that power will be exercised chiefly in behalf of those who pay top dollar.

The breakdown in our political values is akin to a broader problem in our society, the sense that popular culture has disoriented our moral compass. In the intense competition for higher television ratings or more record sales, many good people working at great and honorable companies have debased themselves by conveying images of extreme violence, sexual promiscuity, and vulgarity into our children's minds. By extension they have debased us all. And they have defended their behavior by waving the First Amendment as if it were some kind of constitutional hall pass, whereby the right to speak freely justifies any and all behavior exercised under that right, no matter who is hurt.

What has happened within our culture is strikingly similar to what has happened within our polity. Both arenas are plagued by enormous competitive pressures, the powerful temptation of big money, and a reflexive reliance on the right of free speech to shield the unseemly and the corrosive. In Hollywood the thinking goes, If I can say it or portray it and people will pay, then I must indeed say it and portray it, because then I will succeed. In Washington the analogue is, If the law does not clearly prohibit me from doing it, then I must do it or I will lose.

Our experience in the so-called culture wars tells us that it is unrealistic to expect politicians to change their behavior and elevate their standards voluntarily. It is imperative to change the way our political process works to suppress the temptation to stray from core values. And the only way to accomplish this is to reduce the unrelenting pressure to raise vast sums of money. The most promising step would be to close the soft-money loophole through which corporate and labor-union money floods, making a mockery of the rules that bar those very entities from contributing to campaigns. A further step would be to prohibit presidential candidates who accept public money from raising any other money. Other steps might be to eliminate fake "issue ads" broadcast by political parties and independent groups and to encourage voluntary limits on campaign spending.

The mistrust and alienation that many Americans feel toward their government and their elected leaders are reflected over and over again in polls. A Gallup poll after the 1996 elections found that just 32 percent of the public trusts in government to "do what is right" most of the time. A survey done by Peter Hart and Robert Teeter for the Council for Excellence in Government found that when asked whether elected officials have honesty and integrity, nearly three quarters of the respondents said no.

One powerful indicator of the public's lack of confidence is its reaction to campaign-finance reform. When asked whether they believed that major changes in the laws could reduce the corrupting influence of big money in politics, nearly 60 percent of the respondents said that special interests will always find a way to maintain their power in Washington, no matter what laws we pass.

Such hopelessness is undoubtedly why the public has not been demanding campaign-finance reform. The first task for reformers in both parties is to raise the level of trust to the point where people believe that reform can make a difference, so that they will demand it from their representatives. Without that demand reform will not happen. The responsibility falls on us all, in and out of public life. We no longer have the luxury of waiting idly for others to take the lead.

Issue 10
News Media

INTRODUCTION

Few events have helped to define more clearly the present-day fault lines running between politics, culture, and the media than the Clinton-Lewinsky scandal. Like an earthquake rumbling through the political landscape, the scandal has dislocated old relationships and revealed new ones. As the aftershocks fade, the institutions of government may seem to function as before. However, beneath the surface of politics, the scandal and its aftermath of impeachment have ruptured old understandings of the relationship between private morality and public life. Whatever we may think of President Clinton's and Ms. Lewinsky's behavior as a private matter, its public—and even constitutional—consequences force us to rethink both the meaning of public service and the particular requirements that we, as voters, place upon candidates for public office.

In addition to its impact on public institutions, the scandal has also focused attention on the role of the media in politics. Publicity is the very oxygen of scandal. Without it, the flames of titillation and outrage subside into the dying embers of lust or greed. The news media of today—newspapers, radio, television, and newer outlets like the Internet—style themselves as a "fourth branch" of government: an indispensable resource for an informed citizenry and a watchdog against government misbehavior. At the same time, however, the media represent businesses with their own need to make a profit, to package news in a way that also caters to the entertainment desires of a prurient public. The media not only report on scandals but also give life to them through their very reporting, at times pandering to the worst instincts of the public that the media profess to serve. Scandal may have public consequences, but scandal also sells. The ongoing need to balance the conflicting goals of public service and private profit shape the media's own participation in political life.

This conflict between objectivity and entertainment is a relatively recent problem for the news media. For most of the nineteenth century, newspapers were merely extensions of, and mouthpieces for, party politics. The separation between news reporting and editorializing did not exist. By the end of that century, however, two trends took hold that changed the significance of the news media in American life. The first trend was the development of the "yellow" press, associated with such publishers as Hearst and Pulitzer, which marketed sensationalist reporting to a mass audience. Although these publishers had political agendas, their newspaper empires operated independently of political parties and on an explicitly commercial basis.

The second trend was a strengthening norm of journalistic objectivity. Symbolized by the rise of the *New York Times* under the editorship of Adolph Ochs as the national newspaper of record, serious journalism increasingly viewed its role in politics and society as a dispassionate chronicler of events and neutral source of information for an educated public. The new ideal for journalism was to be above politics—at least in its news-gathering operations. This ideal found reinforcement not only in the civic ideals of the Progressive Era but also in Supreme Court rulings that elevated First Amendment rights to free speech to a canonical status. Indeed, by the twentieth century, journalism itself was increasingly seen as a profession with its own special schools and credentials, instead of as a rough education in the seamy side of life dominated by amateur scribblers and bourbon-soaked hacks.

Despite this ideal of objectivity, journalists still exercised considerable discretion over what they would or would not publish. Journalists might be objective in how they wrote, but what they wrote about itself reflected value judgments concerning which topics did or did not belong in the public eye. Topics that remained beyond the public eye included politicians' personal lives. For example, President John F. Kennedy's priapic indulgences remained a private matter. The result was a certain cosiness between journalists and politicians. Both pursued their crafts according to well-understood but unstated ground rules. Both used each other for their own ends.

This state of affairs changed with the Watergate scandal and the role of investigative journalism in driving President Nixon from office in 1974. Thanks to the stunning success of Bob Woodward and Carl Bernstein at the *Washington Post,* journalists increasingly took a skeptical and adversarial stance towards public officials as a matter of professional duty (and ambition). The enhanced prestige of journalism led its practitioners to imagine themselves as guardians of the public trust. After presidential candidate Gary Hart challenged the press in 1987 to pursue his personal life, with disastrous results for him, journalists and their colleagues within the wider media began to regard all aspects of a candidate's life as newsworthy. With the ever-present pressure of commercial competition sharpened by the emergence of cable television and the Internet as alternative sources of news, the media have abandoned old inhibitions about investigating politicians' personal lives. For better or for worse, public appearance and private reality have become intertwined as never before.

The following selections cast a critical eye towards the media's performance during the Clinton-Lewinsky scandal. Todd Gitlin's biting critique of the national media alleges that, far from upholding standards of journalistic objectivity, the media have abetted a partisan attack on the president by Kenneth Starr and his right-wing allies. Despite the liberal reputation of the national media, Gitlin contends that the media have shown snobbish hostility towards Clinton. In their eyes, according to Gitlin, Clinton's worst fault has been that he simply does not take the media as seriously as they do themselves. An outsider to the Washington scene, Clinton never stroked the egos and agendas of a journalistic elite whose sense of self-importance and professional arrogance have led it to abandon any sense of proportion and fairness regarding the president's indiscretions.

Michael Bader looks beyond the pretensions of the media to consider the social psychology of scandal itself. In his view, the national obsession with the Clinton-Lewinsky scandal reflects a broader trend within the media—particularly within the tabloid format of "trash-TV" talk shows like Jerry Springer's—towards voyeuristic identification with the transgressor of social norms. In this sense, Bader argues, Clinton's mistakes have been magnified all out of proportion to their actual significance. As with the mesmerizing effect of the botched lives on the Jerry Springer show, we are drawn to Clinton's imperfections, even as we condemn them out of a need to purge and even deny our own weaknesses. In Bader's words, "We're horrified that Clinton is so sick, but we continue to deny our common flawed humanity."

As you read the articles, consider the following questions.

Discussion Questions

1. Not only do the news media engage in adversarial journalism, but they revel in scandalous details (regarding Clinton, for instance) quite like the material shown on the *Jerry Springer Show*. Are the media just selling entertainment in the guise of news?

2. Even if the Lewinsky scandal is entertaining, the media certainly didn't make it up. Why should the media come under critical scrutiny, when after all it was Clinton's behavior that produced this scandal in the first place?

3. Bader argues that media coverage of the Lewinsky scandal expresses something important about American society. Compare the media coverage of this scandal with its extensive treatment of John F. Kennedy, Jr.'s recent death in a plane crash. What made this event newsworthy?

4. A common criticism of the national news media holds that they are biased in favor of liberal causes and opinions. Do you believe this criticism is correct, or not?

For more information on this topic, visit the following websites:

`http://www.aim.org`
Accuracy in Media

`http://www.fair.org`
FAIR (Fairness and Accuracy in Reporting)

`http://www.freedomforum.org`
Freedom Forum

`http://www.accuracy.org`
Institute for Public Accuracy

The Clinton-Lewinsky Obsession:
How the Press Made a Scandal of Itself

TODD GITLIN

To derail his presidency, a thrill-seeking president had to come into the sights of a prosecutor with virtually unbridled powers, married to an omnivorous press. How did the news business, also known (when it is giving itself awards) as the profession of journalism, turn into a nonstop strip-search? How to account for the sheer volume of the scandal coverage, and the gloating tone of much of it, the gleeful obsession, the overkill and wallowing that seized hold of journalism in these United States?

BARKING HEADS

Start with the Sunday morning barking heads, the high church that certifies each week what the political class is and ought to be talking about, issuing self-fulfilling prophecies for inside dopesters. Consider especially ABC's "This Week," where Cokie Roberts declared, on Jan. 25, 1998, with the Lewinsky story four days old, "There's only one real question that's being asked in Washington this week, and that is, can President Clinton survive?" Along the Potomac, among the knowing, it was thunderously clear what was real—and it was not the fate of women without childcare, or children without doctors.

One function of the Sunday shows is to make certain notions thinkable. Between his Sunday punditry and nightly reports, no one bulldogs America's political conversation more than ABC's Sam Donaldson. Donaldson's repute rests not on his reporting, not on his preparation, but on his leather lungs, his selective bullying and his bellow. He jeers the big cheese in charge, whoever it is, because ideology matters less than attitude. On "This Week," the emphatic Donaldson makes George Will look thoughtful, the studious boy who does his homework as opposed to the loudmouth pumped up on attitude. Here was Donaldson on Jan. 25:

Todd Gitlin is a professor of culture, journalism, and sociology at New York University, and a 1998–99 fellow at the Media Studies Center. He is the author of *The Sixties: Years of Hope, Days of Rage and the Twilight of Common Dreams: Why America Is Wracked by Culture Wars*. Carl Bromley and Jennifer Kelley provided research assistance for this article.

Reprinted by permission. *Washington Monthly*, Dec. 1998. Vol. 30, Issue 12, p. 13.

"If he's not telling the truth, I think his presidency is numbered in days. This isn't going to drag out. We're not going to be here three months from now talking about this."

Of course more than nine months later Donaldson, Roberts, Will & Co. were still talking about "this." But Donaldson, Roberts, Will, Tim Russert and the rest matter not because of their acumen, let alone their accuracy, but because powerful people think that what they say matters—because official Washington and its eavesdroppers watch the Sunday shows in order to know what they had better take into account as they plot their own moves. Like prosecutors talking about "this case" as if they were observers from the far reaches of outer space, journalists like to talk as though "this story" had a life of its own, as if it landed and stayed on front pages and Sunday morning shows by itself. Already, on Jan. 25, Donaldson was declaring, "I'm amazed at the speed with which this story is going." Of course it all depends what the meaning of "this story" is. On Jan. 21, the day the Monica story broke, it was Donaldson—not "this story"—who, at the White House press briefing, asked whether Clinton would cooperate with an impeachment inquiry.

The ardor of the barking heads even makes straight news people squeamish at times. Chris Vlasto, an ABC News producer who, as we shall see, cannot be accused of excessive tenderness toward the White House, told me: "The night Jackie [Judd] and I broke the story, Jan. 21, impeachment never crossed our minds. It only came up that Sunday on 'This Week.' I think it's unfair that the talking heads on MSNBC, on our own network and the rest, have stoked the flames."

THE RUSH BACK FROM HAVANA

The thrill of a breaking story, any breaking story, is easy to understand, and so is the dynamic that keeps CNN and MSNBC, the 24-hour news channels, along with the tabloids, scraping the bottoms of all accessible barrels for cigar butts. The word of words is competition, and not only for bottom-line purposes. News organizations live for the frenzy of getting "there" first, getting "the story," getting the "get," getting the Big Creep. Recall that on Jan. 21, all three network anchors were in Havana to cover the Pope's visit—all in a position, American news media being what they are, to certify to the American public that Cuba exists and that what happens there might be newsworthy. All three promptly picked themselves up and flew back to Washington to cover (or rather, witness the wreckage from) Hurricane Monica. Dan Rather seems to have been most reluctant to go, later telling Jeff Greenfield on CNN: "If you want to stay in the anchoring business, you have two choices. You can get back to Washington and cover this big breaking story, or you ask for asylum in Cuba . . . If one [anchor] had made the decision to stay, one of the three over-the-air national anchor people, I think he'd have gotten killed in the press. He'd have gotten killed by his bosses internally. I just don't think it was practical to say no." In March, receiving a career excellence award at Harvard, Rather picked up this theme again: "If I really deserved this award, I'd have stayed behind in Havana to cover the Pope's visit," instead of returning to "lurid innuendo, sex, and sensationalism and smirking and winking . . . I wish I'd had the guts but I chickened out." Rather's confession might have made a nice story for some major paper, or *TV Guide* or *People*, but it didn't rate.

As it was, on Jan. 21, CBS delayed 26 precious minutes before going to the president's Jim Lehrer interview denying entanglement with Lewinsky. For lagging behind ABC, NBC, CNN, and Fox, CBS got tweaked in the papers. "After months of chanting hard news, hard news," crowed Eric Mink in the *New York Daily News*, "CBS News blew it with the pressure on." No one rushed to defend CBS for its principled foot-dragging. It was lost on no one that the one network executive who didn't go live to the death and transfiguration of the people's princess in 1997, Lane Venardos, was soon demoted from his position overseeing hard news.

Did CNN, MSNBC, and the Internet force Rather's hand? Cable and on-line news are too easy to blame for pressing the once-respectable organs ever downward. True, a TV monitor stays tuned to CNN in every newsroom, and on MSNBC, where the soap-opera format glided seamlessly from All-OJ to All-Diana to All-Monica, many a media personage has tied his success to the rising Starr. Instant stars have no incentive to see the scandal with any sense of proportion. Chris Matthews' nightly rant, "Hardball," swelled from 30 to 60 minutes last March, and when the Clinton video was released, MSNBC ratings shot up seven times higher than average. The absolute numbers are still small—CNN and MSNBC between them average less than three-quarters of a million viewers in prime time—but the increment is most attractive. Media analysts tune to these channels and are inclined to blame them—along with Internet news—for driving the hunt for scoops, stripping away inhibitions.

"We felt the drumbeat of CNN from the beginning," one top CBS news executive told me. "The picture of Monica in the beret. All the repetition elevated the importance of the story, made us feel that we'd better put more resources into it." But the competition CBS cares about most comes from ABC and NBC, not cable. It's ABC's Jackie Judd who runs CBS a merry race. In print, too, the drive toward scoops can never be underestimated. The *Times*, still smarting from the *Post*'s Watergate coup, jumped the gun with Whitewater, and since then, leaping from gate to gate, neither the *Times* nor the *Post* has looked back.

FROM WOODWARD & BERNSTEIN TO ISIKOFF

Newsweek's Michael Isikoff, who dogged the Clinton sex story for months and finally got the scoop of scoops, got his journalistic start working for the Capitol Hill News Service, a Nader-funded operation. Was he, as reported, inspired by Robert Woodward and Carl Bernstein? "In the general way that anybody of my age probably was," he told me. Such is the cunning of history. Woodward and Bernstein rounded out the Sixties by bringing down a government steeped in lies not about sex but about burglary, assault, and war. Whereupon investigative reporters were knighted by an invigorated establishment press. At the *Post*, self-mythologizing took over. In TV news, attitude became the norm: insouciance, snideness, and badgering, easily—but falsely—mistaken for ideological opposition. Something similar happened in print, leading Woodward to speak of the press last year, even before the Lewinsky uproar, as "prisoners of Watergate"—trapped in the assumption that behind a scatter of facts and allegations, as in the murk of Whitewater, lies a grand plot.

Whitewater and all the other "-gates" (Travel-, File-, et al.) have been pounced on as instances of Watergate Lite, a matter of moral passion applied indiscriminately. Sex tales matter vastly more than the bombing of a pharmaceutical plant in Khartoum. Follow the money or the intern. Politics is reduced to criminality. Dirty land deals and stained dresses are easy to insinuate about. To cover them, as Joe Klein put it in an interview with Tim Russert, "You don't have to know anything." But the traverse from Woodward and Bernstein to Isikoff required another element too. "The personal is political" is no simple feminist slogan; it has evolved into a legal norm and a journalistic axiom. In the late 1960s and into the 1970s, the phrase meant that childcare and housework should be equalized, that women had the right to orgasm and not to be beaten. As politicians became more suspect and journalists more suspicious, "the personal is political" evolved into 1987's question of Gary Hart, "Have you ever committed adultery?" After Hart's crash and burn came the live TV spectacle of Anita Hill's testimony against Clarence Thomas, when the Senate Judiciary Committee in its majesty decided that charges of sexual harassment were vastly more relevant to the question of his fitness for a court position than Thomas' claim that he had never discussed *Roe v. Wade*. The spreading inquisition into sexual conduct in the workplace led not only to the right-wing mobilization behind Paula Jones but to the principle that a man's prior sexual conduct was admissible in civil sex-harassment cases when a woman's was not—which led, in turn, to Clinton's decision to give his enemies a mighty sword at his deposition in Paula Jones' lawsuit. In a hard-breathing political culture, the spirit of moral absolutism had attached itself to the cause of women.

For years now, in other words, the firestorm of the culture wars has been burning up the oxygen of political dispute. Clinton was ripe for the picking. "One of the reasons this story exploded in January," *Los Angeles Times* Washington bureau chief Doyle McManus told me, "is that when the story first came up, every investigative reporter had a boxful of related stories" about Clinton's dalliances. Still, one might think the media's relentlessness a bit much for an aggregation of individuals not especially renowned for highfalutin family morals. In recent years, at least three editors of major newspapers have left their wives of twenty-plus years without public disgrace. But of course they did not, so far as is known, lie or fudge under oath. They did not (usually) dally with employees. No special prosecutor prosecuted them. So with a lot of huffing and puffing about public morality, they could ready the pillories in good conscience. And so the vigilantes of Washington bent over backwards for months, professing to be shocked, shocked by office sex, deal-making, and corner-cutting.

WHY BITE THE HAND THAT LEAKS?

Since the maiden issue of *Brill's Content*, there can be no rational doubt that Starr and his deputies were the main unattributed sources who kept Clinton reeling for the better part of a year. Brill made a few trivial mistakes, but he was right on the main point—that Starr's office leaked from the start. Whether Starr violated the law, as seems obvious, will in the end depend upon the meaning of words like "information" and "release." But the press, as leakee, colluded, and the collusion begins long before Lewinsky. The watchdogs dutifully carried Starr's leaks about indicting Hillary Rodham Clinton over Whitewater matters. They lifted no eyebrows when Starr's Little Rock grand jury folded last May without indicting Hillary. While Federal Judge Norma Holloway Johnson was investigating White House charges that Starr's office illegally leaked, that investigation was not especially interesting to the press. When this fall she found prima facie evidence of illegal leaks to ABC, CBS, NBC, CNN, the *Times*, the *Post* and *Newsweek*—against secrecy rules encompassing not only "the direct revelation of grand jury transcripts" but also prosecutors' disclosure of "the identities of witnesses or jurors, the substance of testimony, [or] the strategy or direction of the investigation," the story landed on page A9 of the *Times*, albeit with a tease on page A1. We have come a long way from the time when Jack Newfield could call

White House reporters "stenographers with amnesia." The stenographers moved on to the Office of the Independent Counsel.

Starr mastered the press in ways that any big-city prosecutor would envy—or perhaps mastery is not the right concept, common interest being the point. Leaking away, the prosecutor set traps for potential witnesses and polluted his Washington grand jury for months, not incidentally grabbing the attention of the House of Representatives that is, in effect, the grandest jury of all. While editors occasionally denied, for public consumption, that they were stalking Watergate II, the magnitude and the intensity of their coverage suggests that they thought they had in their sights another president fairly begging to be brought down. One reason most of the press volunteered as Starr's echo chamber is that he offered a lot of the stuff Washington reporters crave. "The story was about Starr launching an investigation," Isikoff told me. "At some point, you're acting as a censor if you say we're not going to pursue credible allegations," meaning Starr's.

Remember the infamous "talking points," much bruited about at the beginning of the scandal? Here lies one egregious example of the media running unquestioningly with the OIC's leaks. *Newsweek* on Jan. 22 had Starr doubting, given the legalistic prose, that Lewinsky was the sole author of the document. Virtually every major news outlet leaped to speculate that the fine hand of Vernon Jordan or Bruce Lindsay or another lawyer in the White House cabal was detectable. A tattoo of repetition made the speculation seem a no-brainer, an assumption that reached its zenith when Chris Matthews crowed on CNBC that "Monica is not protecting Bruce Lindsey, and not Bob Bennett, and not Vernon Jordan, but the person who gave her the talking points may in fact have been . . . the President." No fewer than four versions of the "official" memo surfaced in the fray. While the media hyped this document as a "smoking gun," the final Starr report referred to it all of twice. It never made the list of possible grounds for impeachment, nor was it used as evidence in the charge of obstruction of justice.

Of course, once Starr's report had arrived at the House, on the Internet, and everywhere else, Starr was no longer useful to the media. All his Monica data were presumably now in plain view. Now—only now—did Starr himself become a subject for independent investigation. The *Times'* Oct. 4 front-page investigation of Starr's methods, by Don van Natta, Jr., and Jill Abramson, was the bellwether. The wind was changing. Even *Newsweek* got into the new act with a coy cover, Sept. 28, clucking, "How Low Can It Go?" over a simulated supermarket tabloid, "The Starr"—the same *Newsweek* that, back in January, had agreed to hold back Isikoff's first story at the behest of Starr deputy Jackie Bennett, Jr., because Starr was working a sting against Monica Lewinsky with the connivance of Linda Tripp.

BUT THE LIBERAL MEDIA!

The anti-Clinton animus of the bluntly right-wing media requires no special explanation. One expects the Rev. Sun Myung Moon's Washington Times, Rupert Murdoch's Weekly Standard, George Will and William Kristol (on a single show, yet!) to hammer away at the dope-non-inhaling, draft-dodging adulterer—not only because they sniff a whiff of the 1960s they despise, but because they hate the Clintonians for their success in borrowing some of the conservative program. It is not remarkable that Republican flasks carry corrosive acid.

The more interesting question is, How to understand the venom of the *New York Times'* editorial page editor Howell Raines, once closely aligned with the civil rights movement, who on Sept. 22, after months of relentless attacks and Clinton's repeated apologies after he finally 'fessed up, could still write: "President Clinton continues to demand that we, as a people, endorse his lying." This editorial Ahab (as Joan Didion rightly says) of the Clintonian white whale has made the nice judgment that Starr is guilty of "legal klutziness" while declaring that "whatever Mr. Starr's failings, they will never achieve the grand malignancy of Mr. Clinton's folly and miscalculations." Klutziness! Where was Raines' equivalent outrage when grand jury testimony was leaked and leaked again and finally released on-line to a leering world? How to explain the ferocity of pundits like Tim Russert and Chris Matthews?

In 1987, when Ronald Reagan insisted that there was no arms-for-hostages deal, and repeatedly couldn't recall details, pundits and editorialists did not leap to their drums to pound away for impeachment. They did not speculate about resignation from day one when a president they knew to be either rampantly deceitful or incipiently senile told them the sun was shining when they had their own umbrellas out. Reporters regularly overestimated Reagan's popularity. His famous Teflon wasn't born, it was sprayed—by politicians and journalists.

By contrast, some left-of-center reporters despise Clinton because he repeatedly sided with the New Democrats. He took the Democratic Leadership Council's advice on welfare. Even reporters like Joe Klein who approved centrist policies and had been swept off their feet by Clinton in '92 turned against him with the fury of scorned lovers. They saw a lot of character not to like. But more important is what Jefferson Morley of the *Washington Post* calls "a conservative bias of liberal media . . . They bend over backwards to prove that they're not liberal." Backwards indeed. Ronald Reagan certainly benefited from this self-spin. The Washington press corps, styling itself rambunctious, was in fact gullible. They frequently disliked Reagan's politics but harbored a sense of him as the nation's benign paterfamilias. The establishment press believed it had brought down Johnson and Nixon, dragged down America's image with

them, and with America struggling to stand tall after a decade of humili-
ations, damned if they were going to be responsible for another regicide.
As *Post* reporter Lou Cannon said in 1983, "Everybody wants our president to be up on a pedestal a little."

But not Billick Willie, Bubba, the slob who eats off other people's
plates, or the Good Old Boy cannot be mistaken for any reporter's dad.
Rather, he's everybody's brother, a bumbler to boot, and with his Big
Macs and Gennifer Flowers it has been hard to imagine him on any
pedestal. From the start, he inspired not only affection but suspicion,
and little awe. He was Southern, like Jimmy Carter, another scorned in-
terloper—an out-of-towner surrounded by out-of-towners (read hicks)
and kids. Southerners like Howell Raines must be embarrassed by Clinton as much as Hollywood loves him. If his back-country ways weren't
bad enough, he didn't romance reporters or their employers—at least not
as much as they thought their due. He was suspicious of them—were
they not overplaying Whitewater? He offended them in little ways and
big. They took umbrage.

The consummate hedonist, Clinton also reminded his agemates of
what troubled them about themselves. As Joe Klein put it to Tim
Russert on CNBC (Sept. 19), "The things that we are most upset with
Bill Clinton about are the things that I think we're most upset with ourselves about. And there are three counts in . . . this kind of spiritual impeachment. One, he put marketing over substance, which is something
that we in the media are very, very, very conscious of . . . Count number
two, the sexual revolution . . . Most of us who have lived through the
last 30 years, including a lot of the people who are writing these
pompous editorials, have done things that we are not proud of, and by
casting out Bill Clinton, maybe we cast out some of our own demons.
But the third thing . . . is in some ways . . . the saddest and . . . the most
profound, and that is there's a sense in Bill Clinton's generation, our
generation, that we skated, that we cut corners, that we got off easy, and
man, if there was ever a guy who skated and cut corners and fudged and
got off easy, it was Bill Clinton." Purge him.

CATCH A RISING STARR

Ken Starr was something else again—the counter-Sixties incarnate. And
the *Post* in particular hitched itself to him. Journalists are frequently
squires in search of knights. There's nothing especially odd or sinister
about their symbiosis with sources: Careers are routinely made by attaching oneself to newsworthy subjects. This can be done negatively—
the way Dan Rather was cast as Richard Nixon's nemesis. But it can also
be done positively, by placing one's journalistic organ at the service of

information providers. Prosecutors are particularly serviceable. And by conspicuous contrast with Bill Clinton, ever since his appointment as independent prosecutor in August 1994, Kenneth Starr has been a master of media. "Starr assiduously courted the media in Washington," says freelance writer Mollie Dickenson. "He developed friends there, particularly Susan Schmidt of *The Washington Post.*" Reportorial coziness with Starr extends far beyond the usual backscratching. According to Howard Kurtz, White House reporters "liked Starr and his prosecutors and tended to give them the benefit of the doubt."

Outside easy public view, Starr even received an unusual testimonial from one journalist whose role in reporting the rolling scandal since Whitewater has been substantial. Whitewater promoter Jim McDougal and ABC News producer Chris Vlasto became friends during Vlasto's Whitewater investigations. In *Arkansas Mischief,* his memoir with the *Boston Globe*'s Curtis Wilkie, McDougal recounted how, in 1996, he was awaiting sentencing after having been indicted on 18 felony counts by Starr's Little Rock grand jury. Depressed, he told Vlasto he was afraid of dying in jail. "'Listen, Jim,' Chris said, 'you don't have to go out this way. If you walk in to see Ken Starr, he'll greet you with open arms.' He recommended that I at least talk with the independent counsel." I asked Vlasto whether McDougal's account was accurate. "In general, absolutely," he told me. "The gist of the story is true."

Vlasto, who is Jackie Judd's producer on the ABC Evening News and also produces for "Nightline," has been relentless in his pursuit of White House scandals. This does not, of course, mean that there is anything wrong with his fact-finding. The fact that he has written for the *Wall Street Journal* is not necessarily here or there. Neither is the fact that the organ in which he profiled Jim McDougal is the conservative *Weekly Standard.* Vlasto is entitled to his opinions, and entitled to advise a friend. I asked him whether he had become part of the story by virtue of his conversations with McDougal, in particular his advice. After a very long pause, he said: "I was acting as a journalist. It was a matter of my relation with my sources."

A STARR-STRUCK ESTABLISHMENT

Leakworthiness is not the only reason the media establishment liked Starr—Judge Starr, as he was called. Starr's Washington reputation for probity was prime. In a city that monitors the rise and fall of reputation as attentively as others monitor pork bellies, a reputation for honor is worth a lot. To Starr's non-Republican friends in high places, it surely was not irrelevant that Clinton is both trailer park and Oxford—a class pincer that cuts Georgetown from both sides. The Clintons, like the Carters before them, didn't play proper court. Sally Quinn, partygiver extraordinaire, wrote scornfully of a president who "is not of this town and who will be gone in less than three years, if that . . . The establishment rallies to preserve its institutions against interlopers who might corrode or undermine them." On "60 Minutes," she sniffed that the Clintons didn't even own their own home. As recently as Nov. 2, the day before the election, Quinn wrote at length in the *Post* that Establishment Washington—"they," she calls them—have been "outraged by the president's behavior. They feel Washington has been brought into disrepute by the actions of the president"— not by those of Judge Starr. In their eyes, in a contrast Quinn does not make, Reagan did not bring Washington into disrepute when he lied about Iran-contra, nor did Bush when, on Christmas Eve, 1992, he pardoned six high administration officials, four of whom had already been convicted of perjury and withholding information from Congress. Quinn quotes *Post* columnist David Broder: Clinton "came in here and he trashed the place, and it's not his place." Quinn leaves no doubt as to whose place she and her friends believe it to be.

Meanwhile, how did Starr secure his comfort level? In 1991, the sociologist Michael Schudson, interviewing Bob Woodward, was surprised when Woodward told him that, as a watershed in the history of journalism, Watergate was less important than a 1987 Court of Appeals decision in a libel suit involving the *Washington Post*. The suit in question was filed against the paper by Mobil Oil CEO William P. Tavoulareas and his son, and the Court of Appeals, reversing an earlier decision by a three-judge Court of Appeals panel, found for the *Post* in April 1987. Two months later, that decision was upheld by the Supreme Court in what *Post* Executive Editor Ben Bradlee hailed as a great "victory for responsible journalism." The author of the Court of Appeals decision, as the reader will by now have guessed, was Judge Kenneth W. Starr.

The reader had to guess, most likely, because reporting of this fact has been next to nonexistent in publications for non-specialists. In February 1998, Mollie Dickenson noted it in *Salon*, adding that Ben Bradlee had spoken effusively of Starr in public. I found a C-SPAN tape of an American Bar Association meeting on February 7, 1997. There, pre-Monica, commenting on what he called the "swamp" of Whitewater, which he thought quite unlike Watergate in either clarity or gravity, Bradlee added about Judge Starr: "He's a man for whom *The Washington Post* has this tremendous respect because he finally got rid of a $2 million libel suit against the *Post*, and as far as I'm concerned he can do no wrong." To be sure, Bradlee, a Whitewater skeptic, went on to say: "They could get an indictment against anyone they wanted, I think, and they haven't got it. It isn't there." Nonetheless, the matter of Starr's decision in the Tavoulareas case has never been reported in a general-interest national medium. It suggests an atmosphere. Bradlee told me that now, as for Starr, "I don't know if I have any [opinion] or not," and that as for Clinton, "I don't think he should be hung at midnight."

Bradlee's longtime presumption in favor of the judicious Judge Starr was representative. On Nov. 2, after Judge Johnson had found prima-facie evidence of Starr's illegal leaks, Bradlee's wife, Sally Quinn, could still write: "Starr is not seen by many Washington insiders as an out-of-control prudish crusader. Starr is a Washington insider, too. He has lived and worked here for years. He had a reputation as a fair and honest judge. He has many friends in both parties. Their wives are friendly with one another and their children go to the same schools. He is seen as someone who is operating under a legal statute."

THERE GOES THE EASTERN SEABOARD

Consistently, since January, roughly 60 percent of the polled public has said that Clinton lied, but that Starr was unfair, that the press dwelt too much on the scandal and was wrong to rely on anonymous sources. This remarkable stability in public opinion can't be reduced to partisanship, since more people think the press unfair to Clinton than voted for him. In a Media Studies Center poll conducted Sept. 25 to Oct. 1, only 18 percent rated the ethical standards of newspaper reporters "high" or "very high"—tied with lawyers and corporate executives.

Faced with disgruntlement on this scale, media statesmen are thrown back on defensive mantras: The story is taking place "out there." Don't blame the storyteller. Don't shoot the messenger. If the public is fed up, that testifies to the press' professionalism, as a patient's wince tells the doctor that he's poked the right place. There is also the resort to high-minded hauteur: Sooner or later, the people will wise up and follow their opinion leaders—they'd better. Professionals have responsibilities, after all. Does the surgeon ask the patient where to cut? If people hate them, this must be hypocrisy (the great unwashed who say they want to scrub out our mouths are watching and reading our stuff) or tribute (we tell people what they need to know, and the hell with the consequences).

But sooner has turned to later and the public remains steadfastly unimpressed. Americans, who revel in smarm as much as anyone retain a grip on their sense of proportion. Of course there are enough viewers and page-turners to kick circulation up. *Newsweek*'s Jan. 26 issue, Lewinsky I, more than doubled the magazine's average newsstand sales to 350,000. Yet on the whole, the public seems to know the difference between the delectation they feel as consumers of spectacle and the gravitas they know should be brought to bear on matters of state. They know, at least some of the time, the difference between what they delight in knowing (or clucking over) and what they need to know to govern themselves. Barry Goldwater, were he alive, would bask in prophetic glory. In 1961, he proposed to chop off the Eastern Seaboard. Today, no axe would be required, for the Washington–New York media brain stem has cut itself loose from the rest of the country by its own hand. For the better part of a year, watchdogs and pundits have nipped at the presidential underwear, exposed it, analyzed it, and in the process stained themselves. The Washington news establishment's investment in the tawdry story has contributed to the nation's disinvestment in them—disgust, anger, and a limp feeling that the national weal has been abducted by aliens.

Public anger at the press is the good news—the only good news during the months of this miserable spectacle that brought back the pillory and the stocks as instruments of jurisprudence, permitted a Javertian prosecutor to paralyze democratic government, and turned American politics and journalism into an international joke, or worse.

RECESSIONAL

The day before the House Judiciary Committee voted to pursue impeachment hearings, I passed near the Vietnam Memorial on the Washington Mall in a taxi. Over the radio, some congressman was blaring on about how the moral fabric of the country is worn thin by lies. Over at the Capitol, scorched-earth moralists were hard at work on their slow-motion coup d'etat. I stared at the wall of some 58,000 names, thought of three million Vietnamese names not engraved anywhere, thought of the presidential evasions, misleadings, and outright lies that produced that catastrophe, thought of the Congresses that voted again and again to finance a war as devastating as it was undeclared. I thought about lies and lies, lies of consequence and lies of adultery, lethal lies and sex-covering lies. I thought of the press as a scandal of its own. For the hundredth time during these miserable months, I thought of attorney Joseph Welch's question to Senator Joseph McCarthy: "Have you no sense of decency?"

High Crimes & Jerry Springer:
The Psychopathology of a Public Hanging

MICHAEL BADER

Watching the Clinton/Lewinsky scandal unfold is like watching the Jerry Springer show. At first, we're compelled to watch, then we feel horrified and vaguely soiled, and finally we want to run away. The formula is the same: someone exposes highly intimate behavior and fantasies—usually of a sexual nature—to public scrutiny and ridicule. The talk show guest reveals that she slept with her daughter's boyfriend; the audience is outraged. Bill Clinton involuntarily reveals that he likes phone sex; we're all appalled. There is almost an obligatory quality to our condemnation. Even liberals who want to fight back against the cruel right-wing essence of the Starr report have to preface their political critiques with moral critiques of Clinton. This morality holds that Clinton's behavior is sordid, inappropriate, besmirches the dignity of his office, and/or is just plain "sick." This is a valid position on its face, of course. But since such compulsive infidelity is actually so ordinary in our culture and the sexual behavior reported is so bland and prosaic, the sources of the widespread moral outrage and shock have to be more complex.

Michael Lerner is correct when he argues that the cynical nature of both Clinton's sexual behavior and his coverup is a very faint reflection of his more fundamental cynicism about and betrayal of the promise of a 1960s idealism. But I think that the intimate nature of Starr's revelations also has evoked in many of us an experience of vicarious humiliation that has its own special dynamics. When we watch someone embarrass himself in public, we tend to feel a great need to distance ourselves at the same time that we are transfixed by the spectacle. We're transfixed because it is our worst nightmare come true; we want to run away for the same reason.

We all work hard to avoid feelings of shameful self-disclosure: to keep private those thoughts, feelings, and actions that we think will be critically judged by others. The revelations about Clinton's sexcapades—like those of Jerry Springer's guests—actualize the very situation that we're psychically working to avoid all of the time. We all have experiences and fantasies that we are convinced would repel others if they were exposed. Bob Dylan once wrote, "If my thought-dreams could be seen, they'd probably put my head in a guillotine." This is particularly true when it comes to sexual fantasies. We have desires for all sorts of

Reprinted by permission. *Tikkun*, Nov.–Dec. 1998. Vol. 13, No. 6, p. 8.

sex with all sorts of people. We don't all act on all of these wishes, although many of us do act on at least some of them. For complicated psychological and social reasons, we feel tremendously guilty and ashamed of these sexual impulses. We feel almost as guilty about the thoughts and wishes as we do the actions. That's why we keep them private, secret even to ourselves. We're afraid of being humiliated and punished, or of humiliating and hurting others if these feelings come to the surface. When someone like Clinton is forced to publicly reveal his peccadilloes, we vicariously experience his shame. We feel exposed and humiliated on his behalf.

But only for a moment. We immediately try to master these feelings or to get rid of them. One way we deal with this vicarious humiliation is to purge ourselves of any similar feelings by projecting them onto others and becoming morally outraged at "them." We do this with Jerry Springer's guest who reveals her sexual interest in her daughter's boyfriends on television, and we do it with Clinton. We then can enjoy the imaginary feeling of camaraderie and anonymity offered by our spectator status. As spectators to "their" depravity, we feel connected to each other and to some clean moral community. We judge "them" and feel ourselves subtly superior. There is an "us" who would never be so sleazy and who, if we were to be so sleazy (we self-righteously claim), would sure as hell be smarter about it! We can't get over how outrageous that woman on Jerry Springer was, or how repulsive Clinton's cigar fetish appears to be. At the moment we're feeling this, we're pretending that we can put ourselves outside what Freud called the "psychopathology of everyday life," the tragically conflicted, anxiety-ridden dimension of human existence—at least human existence in this alienated culture of ours. We feel as if he or she "out there" is wounded—and we're not.

Secretly we know that we are, though, that we're wounded and handicapped just like Clinton and those freaky people on TV. But we have no place to talk about it, except to our therapists. There is no place in the public world where people can talk about their pain EXCEPT on these terrible TV and radio shows, and there only in the most bizarre form. Eventually, "we" give up on "them" as hopelessly screwed up, but we never have to face or work through the shame we feel about our own very personal versions of these stories. Our own shame about being messed-up remains intact. We're horrified that Clinton is so sick, but continue to deny our common flawed humanity.

This is most evident, of course, in the sanctimonious judgments of Clinton that we hear from the politicians and pundits, from Orrin Hatch to Sam Donaldson. These are people on whose consciences must lie "crimes and misdemeanors" so high as to make Clinton's cigar look like rosary beads. One (almost) wants to ask them: How do they like to "do it"? How many of them have always been faithful? How many opponents or competitors have they destroyed, or feelings have they hurt? How much do they treat others as made in the image of God? What are they ashamed will some day come to light? Do they ever feel guilty about their impulses? Their pious attacks on Clinton's "repulsive" behavior sound like the self-righteous outrage that Jerry or Jenny or Geraldo or Montel whip up in their audiences in response to the pathetic sociopaths and perverts that appear on their (wildly popular) shows.

In these moments of moral indignation we see the results of a process—sometimes consciously calculated and other times involuntary—of projection and externalization that is very familiar to psychoanalysts. We re-experience internal conflicts as if they were external ones. We desperately wish we were better people, that we didn't have problems to be ashamed of, thoughts and feelings that invite the critical judgment of others. We wish we were above and beyond reproach, that we were, in a sense, perfect. We're not. We wish others were perfect, and they're not. The shame over this failure is severe. In this case, it has taken the form of an exaggerated disgust with the public disclosures of Clinton's sexual behavior.

The answer is not to give everyone a free pass. Compassion and empathy toward ourselves and others, however, is a crucial step in the process of change. Without it, we can't tolerate our own moral failings enough to understand where they come from and how they prevent us from realizing our highest ideals. But we have to maintain a tilt toward goodness, toward health and transcendence. In this case, for instance, we can't turn away from holding Clinton accountable for using his power over Lewinsky for selfish sexual gain. Similarly, Monica Lewinsky's struggles with her own self-esteem which led to a sexualized idealization of and dependency on a powerful man reflect a damaged psyche. This is a problem that she actively re-enacts; she is not a passive victim and we need to confront the fact that this pathology leads her to hurt herself and others.

Tilting toward goodness means that while we condemn the right-wing agenda behind Starr's attack on Clinton, we might also use the moral and psychological failings of these two people to start a national dialogue about how men and women can hurt and use each other and devalue themselves in our society. We might be better able to see that these processes exist in some form in most of us, not just in "them." If we're going to lay a moral hammer on Clinton, let's do it for the right reason. The political cynicism that Clinton has embodied as president is what should be attacked, not Bill Clinton as a person. While the man's politics might be founded on lies and so be worthy of our condemnation, we need to be caring toward him as a person, and not act out our own self-criticisms and disappointments on such a grand and dangerous scale.

PART IV
Government Institutions

Issue 11
Congress

INTRODUCTION

Congress is where representation of the American people takes place. A representative democracy like the United States faces a constant trade-off between the needs of legislative efficiency and popular legitimacy. On the one hand, efficiency matters because in the everyday sense, government is about getting things done. Being efficient means that we know what we want to do and how to do it. The first requires proper deliberation, the second requires proper technique. Each may be difficult, but rational people hold out for the possibility that there exists, somewhere, one best way of doing both. Political legitimacy, on the other hand, is a very different thing. There is no one best way to gain it. For a voting public, politics can be legitimate, in two senses. We give our consent to both its processes and its outcomes.

First, we may like an outcome (a vote, a policy) yet not care overly much how we got to it. Second, we may not like the outcome yet give it our obedience nonetheless, precisely because we do respect the process by which we got to it. Legitimacy in this second, processual, sense is far more important than it is in the first sense, for believing in the process of democracy itself holds out the possibility that people will accept votes and policies even if they don't agree with them.

A working representative democracy thus requires both rules and respect for rules. It takes rules to decide how elected officials will represent their constituents. These rules determine how elections take place. Respect for these rules shows in how candidates campaign and in how citizens vote. A candidate who appeals to the basest instincts of the voters shows contempt for the rules, just as voters who stay away from the polls express their disillusionment with them. It also takes rules to decide how those officials who, once elected, will deliberate and how the outcomes of their deliberations can be rendered as workable expressions of popular sovereignty.

These rules determine how Congress goes about its complicated daily business of committee meetings, hearings, and votes. Congressmen show contempt for these rules through their lack of comity and their willingness to be bought off by one special interest or another. Citizens, for their part, demonstrate their disaffection with these rules in the only way possible, namely by simply not obeying the laws that these rules produce.

The question of whether Congress, and particularly the House of Representatives, is an efficient or a legitimate institution is a perennial focus of reformers. In the following selections, two political scientists cast a critical eye on the workings of this institution. As the premier lawmaking body of Congress, does the House do what it's supposed to do? Arend Lijphart argues that the House faces a threefold problem of legitimacy. First, by following a "winner-take-all" rule that gives electoral victory to that candidate with the majority or even a mere plurality of votes, the House falls short in its duty to represent the full range of opinion existing in the electorate. Significant minorities in the population find their views unrepresented. Second, the low rate of voter turnout in the House's biannual elections reinforces their unrepresentative character. Finally, the relatively small size of the House—435 members representing a population of 270 million—suggests that House members can't do a good job of representing large and diverse populations of voters even if they wanted to. To correct these legitimacy problems, Lijphart suggests three "moderately radical" proposals: replace winner-take-all with proportional representation, lengthen representatives' terms to four years, and increase the number of representatives to match ratios of lawmakers to voters that commonly prevail in other democracies.

Professors C. Lawrence Evans and Walter Oleszek counter that the House's problems are not with legitimacy but rather with efficiency. If anything, representatives are too concerned with the needs of their constituents. Indeed, the original reason for limiting representatives' terms to two years was to keep them responsive to the preferences of voters. Frequent elections would provide the electorate with a recurring opportunity to pronounce their judgment on sitting officials; lengthening their terms would only dilute their accountability to the electorate. Expanding the number of representatives would disrupt the operations of the House by decreasing the likelihood that members would know, respect, and trust one another. In a political atmosphere that is increasingly partisan and ideological, comity is at a premium. Rather than change election rules, Evans and Oleszek propose more modest, procedural reforms that would lessen representatives' workloads and rationalize the allocation of the committee work that lies at the heart of the House's everyday activities.

As you read the articles, consider the following questions.

Discussion Questions

1. Like Michael Lind (Issue Eight), Arend Lijphart prefers some version of proportional representation over the current American system. How otherwise do their analyses compare?
2. In what ways do the competing reform proposals presented below reflect differing ideas about what makes a democracy healthy?
3. Ultimately, any reform proposal must have in mind some conception of the public interest. What idea of the public interest do these reform proposals have in mind? What do you think public interest is?
4. American government may have many virtues, but efficiency is not often one of them. Why is our government inefficient? Is it possible to have a government that is too efficient?

For more information on this topic, visit the following websites:

`http://thomas.loc.gov/`
U.S. Library of Congress

`http://www.capweb.net/`
The Internet Guide to the U.S. Congress

`http://www.cbo.gov/`
The Congressional Budget Office

`http://www.brookings.org`
The Brookings Institution

Reforming the House:

Three Moderately Radical Proposals

AREND LIJPHART

Most observers of the United States House of Representatives undoubtedly agree that in many respects, large and small, the House does not perform its representative function very well. Not being an expert on the details and intricacies of House operations, I shall leave the smaller matters—such as incremental steps to reform the financing of election campaigns—to the specialists. Let me focus instead on three major characteristics that make the House insufficiently representative: (1) its election by plurality, which does not provide adequate representation for minorities and minority views; (2) its election by an unrepresentative electorate, especially in midterm elections when only about one-third of the eligible voters make use of their right to vote; and (3) its comparatively small size of only 435 members.

Three reforms that would greatly alleviate these defects are the introduction of proportional representation (PR) for House elections, adoption of a four-year term for Representatives, and enlargement of the House by about 50% to roughly 650 members. Many political scientists and other informed observers would regard these proposals as quite radical. I call them only moderately radical for two reasons. One is that I can think of considerably more drastic proposals which I believe also would improve the representative quality of the House, such as a shift from our presidential system to a parliamentary form of government. Second, my three proposals may look radical from a purely national point of view but, in comparative terms, they are not radical at all: they would merely bring the U.S. House in line with the lower (or only) houses in most of the established democracies.

Arend Lijphart is research professor of political science at the University of California, San Diego. A specialist in comparative politics, he is the author of more than a dozen books, including *Democracies: Patterns of Majoritarian and Consensus Government in Twenty-One Countries* (1984) and *Parliamentary versus Presidential Government* (1992). Lijphart served as president of the APSA in 1996.
Reprinted by permission: *PS: Political Science & Politics*, March 1998. Vol. 31, No. 1, p. 10.

PROPORTIONAL REPRESENTATION

That PR provides more accurate representation than majoritarian election methods is not controversial. What opponents of PR fear, however,
is that this advantage is outweighed by serious disadvantages, particularly the fragmentation of the party system. I agree that this concern is
valid in presidential systems. Scott Mainwaring (1993) called the combination of presidentialism and multipartism—common in Latin American democracies—"the difficult combination" because multipartism
increases the likelihood that the president's party will not have a
congressional majority and, hence, also the likelihood of executive-
legislative deadlock.

On the other hand, political scientists also have found that, in presidential systems, the use of PR for congressional elections tends not to
lead to a high degree of fragmentation of the party system under two
conditions: the election of the president by plurality instead of majority
run-off and the concurrence of presidential and congressional elections
(Shugart and Carey 1992, 226–58; Jones 1995, 88–118). The reason is that
plurality in presidential elections discourages minor parties from participating and advantages the larger, especially the two largest, parties, and
that this advantage for the largest parties spills over into congressional
elections if these are held simultaneously. Both of these conditions are
fulfilled in the United States in presidential election years. The Electoral
College method for presidential elections is a rough functional equivalent of the plurality method, and both presidential and congressional
elections take place at the same time in early November. This means
that, while the adoption of PR for House elections might well lead to the
end of our almost pure two-party system, it would be unlikely to lead to
excessive fragmentation.

Another important consideration, of course, is the type of PR that
would be adopted. PR comes in a multitude of forms that have an effect
on the number of parties. Of particular importance is the so-called district magnitude, that is, the number of representatives elected in the
election district: the smaller the districts, the more difficult it is for
small parties to gain representation, and the less fragmented the party
system is likely to be (Taagepera and Shugart 1989, 112–25; Lijphart
1994). On the assumption of the most straightforward kind of PR system
in which the 50 states would serve as the election districts for House
elections, the average district magnitude would be only 8.7 (435 divided
by 50). This is a relatively low number by comparative standards, and is
not likely to produce extreme multipartism.

Another way to look at the restrictive effect of district magnitude
is to calculate what the equivalent electoral threshold would be. Thresholds are often used in PR systems to deny representation to very small

parties. District magnitudes and electoral thresholds, therefore, can be seen as two sides of the same coin, and a reasonable approximation of their relationship, suggested by Rein Taagepera, is

$$T = 75\%/(M + 1)$$

in which T is the threshold and M the average district magnitude (Lijphart 1994, 182–83). The average magnitude of 8.7 Representatives per district calculated for House elections above, then, is the equivalent of an electoral threshold of about 7.7%—indicating that parties receiving less than about 7.7% of the nationwide vote in a House election will be disadvantaged seriously, if not barred altogether. Such a 7.7% threshold is considerably higher than the legal threshold of 4–5% applied in many European PR systems.

In short, while the combination of PR and presidentialism may be a "difficult combination" in other countries, it is highly unlikely to lead to major problems in the United States.

FOUR-YEAR TERMS

One qualification needs to be added at once to the above conclusion, insofar as it is based on the concurrent election of President and House: It applies only to presidential election years since midterm congressional elections are not concurrent elections. In order to make all House elections concurrent, the term of office of U.S. Representatives would have to be increased from two to four years (or, of course, presidential terms would have to be decreased from four to two years, but I think that the latter possibility does not need to be seriously considered). If PR is to be introduced for House elections, it should ideally be combined with a shift to four-year terms for House members.

However, four-year terms are worth adopting even in the absence of PR. The reason is that voter turnout in House elections in presidential election years is considerably better—or, more accurately, considerably less poor—than in midterm congressional elections. Raising voter participation from about one-third of the eligible voters, typical of midterm elections, to about one-half in recent presidential elections means an increase of about 50%. Generally speaking, more privileged voters—those with higher incomes, greater wealth, and better education—turn out to vote in greater numbers than less advantaged citizens, and the lower the turnout, the greater this difference tends to become. Unequal turnout results in unequal representation and unequal influence. Four-year terms, coinciding with the four-year presidential terms, would therefore make the House appreciably more representative. It also should be pointed out that four-year terms are close to the norm for lower or only houses in the established democracies. There are only a few countries with three-year terms, like Australia and New Zealand, and most democracies use four-year or five-year terms. In parliamentary systems, these terms are maximum rather than fixed terms, but the average actual legislative term of office in the established democracies is still close to four years.

The above argument in favor of four-year terms is based on the desirability of making the House more representative by raising the turnout in House elections and, thereby, making turnout more equal. This advantage can be achieved by establishing four-year terms without making any other changes in the system, such as the introduction of PR. However, another advantage of adopting both PR and four-year terms is that PR also has the effect of raising turnout—by roughly 10 percentage points (Blais and Carty 1990). Other measures that can boost turnout include automatic registration and especially, as I have argued at length elsewhere, compulsory voting (Lijphart 1997).

ENLARGING THE HOUSE

Finally, the House of Representatives could be made more representative if its membership were enlarged. The general pattern in democracies is for the size of lower (or only) houses to increase with population size: small countries tend to have smaller legislatures than large countries. As Rein Taagepera (1972) discovered, this pattern can be expressed in a neat formula: the size of a country's national assembly tends to approximate the cube root of its population size. According to this norm, the U.S. House, with its 435 members, is unusually small for a country with a population of about 270 million people; it "should" have a membership of about 650. (The exact cube root of 270 million is 646.) The fact that both the United Kingdom and Germany have lower houses of approximately this size shows that a membership of 650 is not too large for the effective operation of a legislature.

Having 650 Representatives would improve representation in two major ways. First, increasing the membership of the House by about 50% entails a decrease in the population size of the average congressional district by about 50%, which would lessen the distance between voters and their legislators. Second, assuming that plurality elections would be maintained, smaller congressional districts make it easier to draw these districts in such a way as to provide representation for geographically concentrated minorities without having to fashion the outrageously shaped districts that the Supreme Court dislikes.

If the 650 Representatives were elected by PR under the conditions outlined above (that is, in districts coinciding with the 50 states), the average district magnitude would go up from 8.7 to 13 and the equivalent electoral threshold would go down from about 7.7% to about 5.4%. This change could be considered an advantage in that it would increase the proportionality of the election results; it would probably also reduce the number of very small states with only one Representative—and hence necessarily without PR, because PR requires two or more seats per district. Moreover, a threshold of 5.4% is still higher than the 4–5% threshold used in many European PR systems. On the other hand, if the new district magnitudes were regarded as too permissive for small parties, a legal threshold of, say, 6–7% could be imposed.

FEASIBILITY

I am well aware of the political science law that the probability of reform varies inversely with the magnitude of the proposed reform. Therefore, even though I consider the above proposals only moderately radical, I am not overly optimistic that they have an excellent chance of being adopted in the foreseeable future. At the same time, the most radical—or the least moderate—of my three proposals, the adoption of PR, together with the enlargement of the House, may actually have a somewhat better chance than the less drastic proposal to shift from two-year to four-year terms. For one thing, four-year terms for Representatives would require a constitutional amendment whereas PR, as well as increasing the size of the House, can be accomplished by law.

Second, the three proposals differ in the degree to which they can be introduced step-by-step. It is hard to see how a four-year term could be adopted incrementally. Could terms be extended, for instance, at first for some Representatives but not for others? Or could all terms be initially increased to three years, and later extended to four years? At a minimum, a three-year term would aggravate the problem of non-concurrence between House elections and presidential elections. However, both the enlargement of the House and the adoption of PR could be implemented incrementally. This is very obvious in the case of the former proposal, although for practical reasons increases in membership would have to coincide with decennial reapportionments; as a result, unless relatively large increases were adopted every ten years, it would take a long time to reach the goal of 650 House members.

As far as the gradual adoption of PR is concerned, the United States is unusual among western democracies in having a tradition in which different jurisdictions may elect their Representatives by different election methods. For instance, most states in the United States currently use plurality single member districts for electing their Representatives, but majority-runoff elections are used in Louisiana (where the first round of the election is referred to as the "non-partisan primary") and were used in Georgia until recently; moreover, until 1970, several states had at-large instead of single member district elections, or elected one at-large Representative in addition to Representatives chosen in single member districts. The elimination of the legal requirement mandating single member districts, as Rep. Cynthia McKinney (D-GA) has proposed, would enable some states to adopt proportional or semi-proportional systems while others could retain plurality single member district elections while waiting and seeing how the PR or semi-proportional experiments worked out.

In the final analysis, major reforms may be less, perhaps much less, likely than minor ones, but they also have the potential of improving the House a great deal more. It would be a pity, therefore, if we believed in the political science law stated above to such an extent that we would not even think seriously about major reforms like the three proposed in this article—thereby making this pessimistic law into a self-fulfilling prophecy.

REFERENCES

Blais, Andre, and R. K. Carty. 1990. "Does Proportional Representation Foster Voter Turnout?" European Journal of Political Research 18(2): 167–81.

Jones, Mark. 1995. Electoral Laws and the Survival of Presidential Democracies. Notre Dame: University of Notre Dame Press.

Lijphart, Arend. 1994. Electoral Systems and Party Systems: A Study of Twenty-Seven Democracies, 1945–1990. New Haven: Yale University Press.

———. 1997. "Unequal Participation: Democracy's Unresolved Dilemma." American Political Science Review 91(1): 1–14.

Mainwaring, Scott. 1993. "Presidentialism, Multipartism, and Democracy: The Difficult Combination." Comparative Political Studies 26(2): 198–228.

Shugart, Matthew Soberg, and John M. Carey. 1992. Presidents and Assemblies: Constitutional Design and Electoral Dynamics. Cambridge: Cambridge University Press.

Taagepera, Rein. 1972. "The Size of National Assemblies." Social Science Research 1(4): 385–401.

———, and Matthew Soberg Shugart. 1989. Seats and Votes: The Effects and Determinants of Electoral Systems. New Haven: Yale University Press.

If It Ain't Broke Bad, Don't Fix It a Lot

C. LAWRENCE EVANS AND WALTER J. OLESZEK

The House of Representatives is one of the most dynamic of governmental institutions. Formally and informally, the House regularly revises its rules, procedures, practices, and structures to adapt and adjust to, among other things, membership and workload changes. Absent its capacities for reform, the House would soon find itself unable to meet the diverse challenges of the day. Generally, the House's reorganization imperative is driven by the constant influx of new lawmakers who bring fresh perspectives on how the House should work; typically, they want to make changes in the status quo.

House reform is also triggered by a wide variety of other forces. For instance, when the House is dissatisfied with some aspect of its structure or procedures, a critical mass may unite to establish a select reorganization panel to address the problems. Times of transition and turbulence often produce legislative reform movements whose members may seek to modernize the House or to redistribute internal power from those who have it to those who want it. Public anger at the institution— the House "bank" scandal of the early 1990s is an example—also provokes introspective reviews of institutional operations. Party leaders, too, may take the lead in procedural and organizational transformations.

Change and reform, in short, are common phenomena on Capitol Hill. Worth noting is the difference between the two terms. Reform is a "plan to do things differently, often so as to embody change; change is the result of new developments" (Jones 1994). The electoral earthquake of November 1994 certainly produced a "change" in the majority composition of the House. This new development also triggered action on a purposeful plan to "reform" the structures (committee, subcommittee, and committee staff reductions, for instance) and procedures (more authority lodged in the Speakership, for example) of the House. Although reform can be a "tricky" word, as former President and House GOP

C. Lawrence Evans is associate professor of government at the College of William and Mary. Author of *Leadership in Committee* (University of Michigan, 1991) and coauthor of *Congress Under Fire* (Houghton Mifflin, 1997), he served in 1992–93 on the staff of the Joint Committee on the Organization of Congress. Walter J. Oleszek is a senior specialist in the legislative process at the Congressional Research Service. He has served as a professional staff member of numerous congressional reform panels, including in 1993 as a policy director of the Joint Committee on the Organization of Congress. He is the author of several books on Congress.

Reprinted by permission. *PS: Political Science & Politics*, March 1998. Vol. 31, No. 1, p. 24.

Leader Gerald Ford once said, our common sense understanding is that congressional reform means that things will improve and get better (quoted in McInnis 1966, xii).

In this article, we want to make the point that legislative reforms should at least try to fix something in House operations that is plainly broken. Several "semi-radical" reforms seem to address imaginary problems with unnecessary solutions. To us, semi-radical reforms include those intended to transform the basic structure, membership, or procedures of the contemporary House. To wit, this includes such ideas as instituting proportional representation for the House, enlarging its size from 435 to 650, or increasing the term of representatives from two to four years.[1] Accordingly, we first examine several semi-radical ideas and then outline our reform objectives for the contemporary House.

PROPORTIONAL REPRESENTATION FOR HOUSE ELECTIONS

Compared to the "winner-take-all" electoral system employed for House elections—where the candidate winning the most votes represents a distinct geographic area—proportional representation is used by many European democracies. Under some versions of proportional representation, candidates run on party slates in multi-member districts; a party that receives a certain percentage of the popular vote elects its candidates. Other parties that receive a certain threshold vote elect the remaining officeholders. The argument for proportional representation is that it more accurately reflects voter preferences. Under the winner take all system, a plurality winner may attract the most votes but not represent the real majoritarian preference. In a three-way race, for example, a conservative may end up the winner with less than 50% of the vote because most of the electorate split their ballots between two liberal candidates. On the other hand, proportional representation for House elections is likely to undermine America's traditional two-party system by encouraging the formation of numerous splinter parties. In a 650-seat House, for instance, California would be entitled to 78 seats based on 1990 census figures; so many targets of opportunity would provide incentives for splinter groups to vie for some of those seats.

Some champions of this reform argue for proportional representation on the theory that House members do not represent the diversity of their constituencies very well. In fact, the reverse argument is more accurate: House members are often too responsive to constituency sentiments. Most lawmakers travel every weekend to their districts; the House's work is compressed into a Tuesday–Thursday time frame to accommodate their weekend visits; many personal staff aides now work full-time in districts to maintain a constant constituency-service presence; when in Washington, lawmakers beam daily messages to the home folks; faxes, polls, and e-mails from constituents bombard Capitol Hill offices. Today's lawmakers appear to be at risk of becoming almost full-time ombudsmen for their constituents. Proportional representation would further encourage this tendency and, thus, divert members' attention away from their lawmaking and oversight responsibilities.

FOUR-YEAR TERMS FOR HOUSE MEMBERS

The idea of extending the terms of House members from two to four years is an old one. In 1966, President Lyndon Johnson recommended a four-year term in his State of the Union message. The arguments for extending House terms are well-known: longer terms would enable lawmakers to spend more time on the job addressing complex issues; representatives must currently focus inordinate attention on the campaign "money chase"; off-year elections, with their relatively low levels of turnout, are unrepresentative of the country's sentiments; concurrent four-year terms for House members and the president would strengthen legislative-executive party unity.[2]

These are all interesting notions, but they are not as compelling as those for maintaining the two-year term for representatives. The Framers deliberately chose the compromise (between 1 year and 3 years) of two-year terms to foster, as James Madison said, "an immediate dependence on, and an intimate sympathy with the people." Why should voters have to wait four years to oust a lawmaker whom they believe is not doing a good job? Second, the issue of campaigning can be addressed without constitutional tinkering with the electoral term of House members. Third, mid-term elections provide attentive voters an opportunity to express a judgment on what the Congress and the president have accomplished—or not accomplished. Mid-term elections provide an important electoral "safety valve" for our diverse society. Finally, four-year House terms concurrent with the president's might alter our "checks and balances" system by making representatives somewhat more susceptible both to his blandishments and "coattails." In sum, why fundamentally change an electoral arrangement that has stood the test of time?

INCREASING THE SIZE OF THE HOUSE

The Constitution provides for the minimum and the maximum size of the House. It can be as small as 50 members (one per state) or as large as about 8,300 (one member per 30,000 persons using 1990 census figures).

Today, the size is statutorily fixed at 435, but some suggest that House membership should be increased to 650 lawmakers. The argument for a larger House is that it would ease the constituency burdens of lawmakers by changing the population ratio per member, provide greater opportunities for the underrepresented to win House seats, and facilitate closer ties between the representatives and the represented. Periodically, proposals are made in the House to increase its membership; sometimes measures are introduced to reduce its size. Our contention is that a 650-seat House would produce far more negative than positive consequences. First, members hardly know each other. As House Democratic Leader Richard Gephardt (MO) once said: "Members are islands. They're very busy, and they don't often have the time to get to know one another" (quoted in Doubrava 1985). Contemplate what it might be like with 650 lawmakers interacting as "strangers" in a partisan environment where the incentives are to go for the political jugular. Second, the job of coalition-building would certainly be more difficult, as party and other leaders strove to make the compromises and adjustments needed to pass legislation. Delays and stalemates would multiply with a 650-member chamber even though the "majority rule" principle undergirds House operations. Finally, there are a host of practical issues including providing more space and staff for the new lawmakers, reconfiguring the House chamber, increasing the number of committees and/or committee sizes, and revising House rules to accommodate the membership increase. Maybe 435 is not the right size for today's House, but 650 seems too large.

REFORM OBJECTIVES FOR IMPROVING THE HOUSE

There are many reforms that would improve the organization and operations of the House. Five reorganization categories are briefly listed below in no special order. Whether adopted singly or in combination, each recommendation, in our view, has merit in its own right. These ideas are illustrative of the types of reforms that appear to us to be practical, focused on the realistic concerns of lawmakers, and, under the right conditions, capable of adoption.[3]

1. *Strengthen Deliberation.* Scholars have recently identified a significant dropoff in the quality of deliberation in the House. Increasingly, "the House floor is a processor of bills rather than an arena of deliberation" (Connor and Oppenheimer 1993, 318). The decline of deliberation stems from at least three factors: lack of timely information during floor debate, lack of member time to attend debates, and lack of institutional structures to encourage debate. To address the first, we propose that the

House consider revising its rules to permit lawmakers to use personal laptop computers on the floor so they can instantly access policy-specific information and analysis. Broader and more informed participation in floor debate might increase as rank-and-file members employ their laptops to acquire data and analysis previously available only to committee members. Use of the laptops would be governed by rules and regulations promulgated by the House Oversight Committee.

Second, to alleviate at least some time pressures, the current ban on proxy voting in committee and subcommittee could be restricted to the reporting stage. The prohibition on proxy voting, intended to increase committee attendance and participation, has not worked in practice. Instead, members now sprint back and forth from committees to the floor (or between committees marking up measures concurrently) to cast their votes with minimal opportunity to participate in debates. Third, the House should undertake a major reexamination of ways to enhance deliberation through means such as wider use of Oxford Union–style debates, which were used on a trial basis in the 103rd Congress. Improvements in scheduling the House's business could also strengthen deliberation, especially if the current "Tuesday–Thursday" workweek is expanded to allow members longer and more concentrated time periods in which to debate the issues of the day. A four-day workweek with alternating two-day and four-day weekends is an option that merits consideration by the party leadership.

2. *Promote Civility.* The House today is a meaner-spirited institution than it has been for several decades. The lack of civility makes negotiation more difficult and causes more time to be spent on unproductive personal and partisan attacks rather than on constructive lawmaking and debate. Part of the incivility results from trends in the broader society as well as other changes, such as heightened partisanship (Uslaner 1993). The rise of incivility in the House even led to a March 1997 "Civility Retreat" in Hershey, Pennsylvania, where lawmakers were encouraged to get to know each other and to relate to one another as colleagues instead of partisan adversaries or enemies. Much more needs to be done to promote civility on Capitol Hill, including stricter enforcement of the rules against unparliamentary language (Jamieson 1997). For example, we suggest that if the Speaker rules that a lawmaker has used unparliamentary language during debate, he/she would lose the right to speak on the floor not just for the remainder of that day (the current practice) but for several consecutive days or for a legislative week.

3. *Adjustments to the Committee System.* Because committees are the "workshops" of the House, where many of the most important decisions are made, it is essential that they be as representative and efficient as possible. At present, important policy areas are divided across

several committees, making comprehensive approaches difficult; further, committees sometimes fail to represent a sufficiently wide range of interests. To address these shortcomings, the House should restructure its committees so that both broad and competing substantive areas (energy and environment, for example) are incorporated as completely as practicable within the jurisdictional mandate of a single committee. Unrepresentative committees filled with advocates for specific interests are unlikely to serve the broader deliberative and policy interests of the House. As the 1973–74 Bolling Committee (named for the late Rep. Richard Bolling, [D-MO]) phrased it: "Committees should be able to attract a broadly representative membership and embrace a variety of viewpoints on the questions within their jurisdiction" (U.S. Congress 1974, 19).

4. *Reduction in Workload.* Today, each lawmaker represents almost 600,000 constituents, compared to a little more than 400,000 in the 1960s. Moreover, demands from constituents have increased and the complexity of policy has become far greater. Yet, the House has not systematically examined how it might reduce some of its current workload since passage of the Legislative Reorganization Act of 1946. The 1946 LRA delegated certain of Congress's responsibilities (the settlement of private claims against the Government, for instance) to other federal entities. Given increases in the complexity of the House's workload, it may be time for another major review of whether some matters could be handled by other public or private entities. We suggest, for instance, that the House revisit the idea of establishing a congressional ombudsman to assist representatives in handling their burgeoning constituent service (or "casework").

5. *Public Understanding of the House.* Today, scores of individuals can watch gavel-to-gavel floor coverage of House (and Senate) proceedings over C-SPAN; they can also tune in to many televised committee hearings. Despite being in the "electronic gallery," a large percentage of the public fails to understand or appreciate how Congress works. As two scholars point out, people have a "patently unrealistic" view of the legislative process (Hibbing and Thiess-Morse 1997, 147).[4] In short, the challenge of explaining Congress to the public remains an unfinished assignment. We have two proposals for promoting public understanding. First, during "dead time" (votes, quorum calls, etc.), C-SPAN might, on a regular basis, explain to viewers what is actually happening on the floor. Parliamentary language is often arcane and ornate and interpretative explanations would likely be informative to the viewing public. Second, the House's rulebook is written for parliamentarians and not the general lay person. A readable, widely distributed (over the Internet, for instance), and easy-to-use manual should be developed (and kept

updated) to accompany the formal rulebook. This manual—perhaps with an accompanying videotape of floor illustrations—would explain the basic operating procedures and practices of the House.

In conclusion, the House is not an overly "creaky institution" that cannot reform itself incrementally. Institutionally-minded lawmakers— probably fewer today than in previous years—regularly strive to put "the House in order." Where we differ with some analysts is on the kind of reforms that will ostensibly enhance the House's governing capacities. We tilt toward revisions that track the House's long-standing reform tradition. We are unsupportive of reforms that, while appealing in their broad sweep, are unlikely to work in the real world of Capitol Hill politics and policymaking. In matters of House reform, said Rep. John Dingell (D-MI), the great and wise counsel of the shade tree mechanic needs to be observed: "If it ain't broke, don't fix it" (U.S. Congress 1993, 186).

NOTES

The authors thank Ron Rapoport for his helpful review of this article.

1. A "radical" reform would be replacing our congressional-presidential system with parliamentary government.
2. Needless to say, there are other election options with different implications beside concurrent, such as in the off-years or split between the two, as with the Senate.
3. To be sure, there are many other reform issues that merit review, such as ethics, budgeting, oversight, party leadership, or congressional campaign costs.
4. For further information about congressional reforms, see Thomas E. Mann and Norman J. Ornstein (1993).

REFERENCES

Connor, George E., and Bruce I. Oppenheimer. 1993. "Deliberation: An Untimed Value in a Time Game." In *Congress Reconsidered*, 5th ed., ed. Lawrence C. Dodd and Bruce I. Oppenheimer. Washington, DC: CO Press.

Doubrava, Dave. 1985. "House Democrats Huddle Over Plans." *The Washington Times*, March 1, A4.

Hibbing, John R., and Elizabeth Thiess-Morse. 1995. *Congress as Public Enemy.* New York: Cambridge University Press,

Jamieson, Kathleen Hall. 1997. *Civility in the House of Representatives: A Background Report.* Philadelphia: Annenberg Public Policy Center, University of Pennsylvania.

Jones, Charles O. 1994. "Radical Change in Makeup of Congress Will Occur Regardless of Reform Efforts." *Roll Call*, August 8, 30.

Mann, Thomas E., and Norman J. Ornstein. 1993. *Renewing Congress, A Second Report.* Washington, DC: The American Enterprise Institute and the Brookings Institution.

McInnis, Mary, ed. 1966. *We Propose: A Modern Congress.* New York: McGraw-Hill.

U.S. Congress. House of Representatives. 1974. Committee Reform Amendments of 1974. 93rd Cong, 2d sess., H. Rept. 916, pt. II.

U.S. Congress. Joint Committee on the Organization of Congress. 1993. Committee Structure. 103rd Cong., 1st sess, April 29.

Uslaner, Eric. 1993. *The Decline of Comity in Congress.* Ann Arbor: University of Michigan Press.

Issue 12
The Presidency

INTRODUCTION

The impeachment and attempted removal of William Jefferson Clinton from office has struck not only at a sitting president but also at the office of the presidency itself. Presidents enter office with two sets of resources: those that arise from their previous experiences or personal talents, and those that inhere in the presidency as an institutional branch of government. Some of the institutional resources of the presidency derive from those familiar powers explicitly granted to the office by Article II of the Constitution. These include the power to veto acts of Congress, appoint various officials, and lead the nation into war as commander in chief. Other institutional resources derive instead from certain implied powers that the office enjoys. Over time, these powers have threatened to tip the balance of power that exists between the executive and the legislative branches of government.

Suspicious of kingly pretensions, the writers of the Constitution originally envisioned a government in which the legislative branch would dominate the new national government. This attitude was encapsulated in the curious device of the electoral college, so obscure to modern Americans, which sought to prevent presidential aspirants from treating their elections as a mandate from the people. The electoral college was to help guarantee that the executive branch, apart from its explicit powers, would be essentially limited by its duty to "faithfully execute" the laws passed by Congress. In this view, the president would merely do what Congress told him to.

This vision of congressional dominance persisted essentially unchanged for the country's first hundred years. Indeed, in 1885 the political scientist (and later President) Woodrow Wilson would give the title *Congressional Government* to his famous analysis of national politics. True, some presidents enjoyed more influence than others, thanks to either personal qualities or national emergency. Andrew Jackson introduced the nation into a new era of mass democratic politics, whereas Abraham Lincoln led the union against a rebellion that threatened the very existence of the nation. Still, after these personalities or events passed away, national politics returned to its normal equilibrium of legislative dominance.

Even as this dominance reasserted itself, however, longer-term changes slowly undermined the structural basis of congressional supremacy. As early as the Jacksonian era, the use of national party conventions for choosing presidential candidates promoted the idea that presidents were national figures with some independence from Congress. New technologies of travel and communication, beginning with the railroad and the telegraph, made it easier for a single politician to campaign across a far-flung nation. The expansion of national government functions, beginning in the 1890s but gaining speed during the New Deal of the 1930s, disproportionately benefited the executive branch. Although it is always Congress that creates new federal responsibilities, the statutory role of the president in executing the law means that Congress has delegated to the president increasing authority as to how new responsibilities will be met. In practice, this authority has taken the form of administrative discretion over how Congress's general legislation will be put into effect by the growing executive bureaucracy. Finally, the expansion of the president's implied powers has been reinforced by his power to conduct foreign policy. As the United States emerged out of its continental isolation to become a world power after 1945, authority over international relations passed easily to the presidency. The fragmented nature of congressional power and the parochial concerns of the average legislator meant that responsibility for global strategies of national security was more competently managed by a unified executive branch.

Within this new equilibrium of executive-branch influence, the success of modern presidents still depends on their peculiar mix of personal qualities and institutional resources. The Watergate scandal of the Nixon era energized the media into habits of adversarial journalism that have dimmed the prestige of national politicians. Other Watergate-era innovations like the War Powers Act and the Office of Independent Counsel represent Congress's desire to take back some of the power enjoyed by modern presidents. In addition, the end of the Cold War has diminished Congress's willingness to grant presidents unfettered discretion in foreign policy. More broadly, the rise of conservative philosophies of governance such as represented by the Republican Party invariably undercut the pretensions of a strong presidency: A government that recognizes limits to its power also restrains the executive branch from asserting new responsibilities.

As a Democratic president, Bill Clinton has confronted these structural limits to the power of his office, even as his own behavior in the Lewinsky scandal will shape the freedom of action available to future presidents. Clinton's impeachment and the attempt to remove him from office stand as both a personal and a national humiliation. Yet how might this scandal affect the institutional powers of the presidency? *The Economist* stresses the constraints imposed by the post-Watergate emergence of an intrusive press. The "gotcha journalism" of the national news media and its defining down of journalistic standards of propriety now subject the personal and public lives of national figures to relentless scrutiny. Ironically, Clinton's very attempts to conceal his behavior have placed new constraints on presidential power. Thanks to the Paula Jones sexual harassment suit, there is now a precedent for suing a sitting president. The investigations conducted by Independent Counsel Kenneth Starr have resulted in Supreme Court rulings that further narrow the grounds for future presidents to invoke the doctrine of "Executive Privilege" to maintain secrecy.

Wilson McWilliams focuses not on the structural constraints on executive power but on the public consequences of investigating the president's private life. Much as the national government deregulates and privatizes its operations, the Lewinsky scandal seems to herald a blending of presidents' public and private lives. The Lewinsky scandal may well represent "an anecdote without a punchline." At the very least, however, future presidents must be prepared more than ever to open their private lives to public scrutiny.

As you read the articles, consider the following questions.

Discussion Questions

1. Despite his shortcomings as president and as a man, Bill Clinton is distinct from the institution of the presidency. What features of the modern presidency suggest that the office will remain powerful, despite the misbehavior of its recent occupant?
2. What developments, either in domestic American politics or in the wider realm of international relations, might serve to alter the power of the president relative to the other branches of government?
3. In a vague but nonetheless real way, the power of the modern presidency relies upon the pomp and majesty of the office. Has Bill Clinton undermined the office of the presidency simply by placing himself in a humiliating situation?
4. Even if Clinton himself became involved in scandal, modern presidents, as well as candidates for the office, have increasingly cultivated closer connections with the mass of voters by revealing personal details about their lives. In this way, public figures hope to appear as 'just plain folks' who are attuned to the aspirations of ordinary people. Seen from this view, does the Lewinsky scandal really hurt the office of the presidency, or is the possibility of such bad publicity merely a price that modern presidents sometimes must pay for the prerogatives of the office?

    For more on this topic, visit the following websites:

    http://www.thepresidency.org
    Center for the Study of the Presidency

    http://www.interlink-café.com/uspresidents
    The American Presidency—Selected Resources

    http://www.thomas.loc.gov/icreport
    The Starr Report

What Clinton Hath Wrought

EDITORS OF *THE ECONOMIST*

At first sight, the Lewinsky scandal has weakened America's leaders. In the longer run, the opposite may be true. America is a model of political continuity: its constitution has been in force for longer than any other written constitution in the world. Nonetheless, the history of American government is marked by turning-points, times when the constitution's workings have shifted in big ways. The Civil War of 1861–65 strengthened the federal government at the expense of the states; the New Deal strengthened the presidency at the expense of the judiciary and Congress; Watergate weakened the presidency again. For all its tawdry pathos, the crisis now engulfing Bill Clinton may mark some kind of watershed. It may turn out to be, as Senator Daniel Patrick Moynihan has proclaimed it, "a crisis in the regime."

If so, how will the regime change? At first sight, the answer is that the power of the presidency will be diminished, and therefore that the prestige of rival branches of government will rise. After Watergate, the previous big presidential scandal, Congress passed a number of measures to limit presidential ambitions. Something similar happened after the impeachment of Andrew Johnson in 1868. Congress entered a period of successful self-assertion, even claiming the right to veto the president's dismissal of members of his own cabinet (which had been the ground for Johnson's impeachment); and the next eight occupants of the White House, spanning the period until the inauguration in 1901 of the feisty Teddy Roosevelt, made little impression on the land.

In some ways, a repeat of this pattern seems likely, though for reasons subtly different from those that mattered in the past. In the late 19th century, the party barons who dominated Congress also dominated the smoke-filled rooms in which presidential nominees were selected, and so the run of weak characters in the White House was no coincidence. In these days of primary elections, however, there is no mechanism to ensure their weakness.

For the moment, the favourites to succeed Mr Clinton are more competent than inspiring: on the Democratic side, the front-runner remains the vice-president, Al Gore, though he has been weakened by a campaign-finance scandal; on the Republican side, the line-up is led by Governor George Bush of Texas, son and namesake of the former president. But these are early days, and some powerful new figure may yet emerge to join the fray.

Reprinted by permission. *The Economist*; Sept. 19, 1998. Vol. 348, Issue 8086, p. 27.

After Watergate, the presidency was weakened because Congress asserted itself. A repeat of this seems more likely than a run of weak characters in the White House. Impeachment, or even just talk of it, has a way of making Congress remember its constitutional weight. Over the past fortnight or so, Senator Joe Lieberman, the Democrat who greatly added to the tide of opinion now running against Mr Clinton, has reminded the country of the moral force of a speech delivered from the Senate floor. The House, now charged with assessing Kenneth Starr's report on Mr Clinton's wrongdoings, may find that this exercise brings back a lost sense of its importance. Over the past week, a humbled president has been grovelling to Congress for forgiveness; and congressmen have savoured the gravity of their responsibility, entrusted to them by the country's founders, for deciding the president's fate.

Moreover, Mr Clinton's disgrace may lead to Republican gains in November's mid-term elections. The party stands to pick up half a dozen seats in the House, adding a margin of comfort to its present 21-vote majority. It will probably also do well in the Senate, where it currently holds 55 seats out of 100; it may even gain the five seats it needs to secure a filibuster-proof majority. Fortified by these gains, Republican leaders may be able to spend less time worrying about party feuds that threaten their grip on Congress, and more time on policy. This, along with the talk of impeachment, may restore to Congress some of the initiative usually held by the White House.

THE JOURNALISTS GO TO WORK

As well as the threat of an assertive Congress, the presidency faces the challenge of an increasingly intrusive press. This is, to a large extent, the creation of Watergate. Until that scandal, press assaults on presidents were muted. Top journalists were often friends of the president and his entourage, and did not want to jeopardise this access: they knew of John Kennedy's affairs and Lyndon Johnson's tantrums, but they kept the public in the dark. During Watergate, when the *Washington Post* published a series of scoops discrediting Nixon, the newspaper was widely criticised. But the scoops proved accurate, and Hollywood made heroes out of the *Post's* reporters, Carl Bernstein and Bob Woodward.

As a result, the status of journalists, and their appetite for felling presidents, swelled mightily. They were not only prepared to publish embarrassing facts about public figures; they were prepared to seek out such facts, including personal ones. In 1987 another *Washington Post* journalist demanded to know, in the middle of a press conference, whether Gary Hart had committed adultery; Mr Hart's presidential candidacy was soon at an end.

With the Lewinsky scandal, "gotcha journalism" has gone electronic. A profusion of cable television stations have served up relays of pundits who attack the president with all the force of Messrs Bernstein and Woodward, but often with less research. The pressure to be first on air with the news, or first on the Internet with it, drives the attack onwards. Matt Drudge, who runs an Internet tip sheet, has, unlike the heroes of Watergate, no "deep throat" source inside the White House. He merely retails political gossip. But, because many of the salacious rumours about Mr Clinton have now been substantiated, the Drudge style of journalism has acquired some respectability, much as Watergate made deep-throat journalism acceptable. As a result of the Lewinsky scandal, the journalists' assault on future presidents may conceivably be fiercer than any America has yet seen.

In contrast to Watergate and to Johnson's impeachment, however, the biggest threat to the power of the presidency now comes from the judicial branch. During the Watergate business, Nixon was able to fire his prosecutor, Archibald Cox, at the cost of making himself even more unpopular. This time, Mr Clinton's accuser is protected by the independent-counsel statute, passed in 1978 by Congress as part of its post-Watergate efforts to constrain the presidency.

SHOOTING STARRS

Since that law was passed, a score of independent prosecutors have been appointed to investigate presidents and cabinet officials: seven under Ronald Reagan, four during George Bush's single term in office, seven so far under Mr Clinton, with the imminent possibility of two more. Moreover, the appointment of all these prosecutors has created a kind of ratchet effect. Each time one of them asserts his authority by new legal expedients, he creates a precedent that may be followed by whoever is appointed next.

As he has delved into the Lewinsky scandal, Mr Starr has done more than any other independent prosecutor to tighten this ratchet. He has insisted on the right to interrogate presidential advisers under oath, considerably narrowing the president's zone of privacy. In May, Mr Starr won a court case securing the right to question Sidney Blumenthal, a White House strategist, defeating White House arguments that Mr Blumenthal should be protected from Mr Starr's subpoenas because of "executive privilege" (meaning, in this case, the president's right to have confidential conversations with close aides).

Next, Mr Starr won a case in which he claimed the right to question the president's legal advisers. The White House retorted that these should be immune from Mr Starr's subpoena because of "attorney-client privilege," which protects ordinary lawyers from being made to testify against their clients; but the courts decided this privilege did not apply to White House lawyers, who are on the public payroll. And then Mr Starr sought and won the right to interrogate the secret servicemen who guard the president from assassins.

THE PAULA JONES EFFECT

On top of these precedents, the Lewinsky scandal has weakened the presidency by demonstrating its vulnerability to private lawsuits. The scandal came to light because of a sexual-harassment suit filed against Mr Clinton by Paula Jones. The judge in this case eventually dismissed the suit. But the political consequences of the Jones suit, from the point of view of Mr Clinton's enemies, turned out to be boundless. It gave Mrs Jones's legal team power to compel testimony from other women about their relations with the president: and one of these women was Monica Lewinsky. The resulting damage to Mr Clinton has been so spectacular that future enemies of future presidents will doubtless do their utmost to file suits against them too.

This is all the more likely because, last year, the Supreme Court affirmed the legitimacy of such suits. Fearing the political distractions arising from the Jones suit, the White House argued that it should be delayed until the president left office. But the Supreme Court ruled that the Jones case should proceed immediately, setting a precedent that clears the way for more such suits in future. And the effectiveness of civil suits is greatly enhanced by the existence of the independent counsel. Once a civil suit uncovers the first signs of presidential wrongdoing, the heavy work of following through with the investigation can be passed on to the special prosecutor, armed with awesome powers to compel testimony from the top man's friends.

It would not be surprising, or even necessarily worrying, if the presidency did indeed emerge weakened from the Lewinsky scandal. The power of the office has waxed and waned since its founding. Wars and economic crises have expanded the appetite for firm leadership. The Civil War created the circumstances for Lincoln's strong presidency; the dislocation wrought by mass immigration and rapid industrialisation ushered in Theodore Roosevelt and Woodrow Wilson; the Depression brought Franklin Roosevelt; the turmoil of Vietnam and civil rights brought Lyndon Johnson. But the appetite for a strong presidency has never become permanent. After Lincoln, Congress reasserted itself by impeaching Andrew Johnson. After Roosevelt and Wilson came Harding and Coolidge and Hoover, forgettable figures every one.

These cycles have done as much as scandals to affect the power of the presidency. In the 1970s, it was not just the Watergate burglary that ushered in a period of new constraints on the White House. It was a feeling that the presidency had grown too imperial anyway, and that it was time to rein it in. The independent-counsel law was a direct response to Nixon's dismissal of his Watergate prosecutor. But the passage of the War Powers Act, asserting that Congress must approve a president's military adventures, was a response to Vietnam.

Equally, if the presidency is now weakened for a time, it will be for reasons that reach beyond Mr Clinton's sex life. In times of peace and relative prosperity, Americans often profess indifference towards presidential leadership. Journalists assail public figures because they believe the public wants to know their dark secrets; courts support Mr Starr's penetration of presidential privacy because, indirectly, they too reflect the national mood.

In a time of crisis, both media and judiciary might behave differently. During the second world war, for example, the courts upheld Roosevelt's internment of Japanese-Americans, even though this was later regarded as an egregious violation of civil liberties. It can even be argued that, in time of crisis, the Supreme Court, sensitive to the danger of weakening the executive, might have sided with the White House in the Paula Jones case, requiring that her suit be shelved until the end of Mr Clinton's term.

And yet, despite the court's decision, and despite the media assault on the presidency, it is not clear that America really is in a period of indifference to executive power. The Lewinsky scandal may come to be seen, a few years from now, as a special case. The extension of post-Watergate checks on the presidency—new powers for the independent counsel, and journalism's new electronic reach—may produce a backlash, and a demand to limit the activities of prosecutors and journalists.

TIDES DO TURN

Many Americans, if you look at the opinion polls, feel queasy about the inquisitorial culture that unearthed the Lewinsky scandal. They do not want their president to be above the law. But they are conscious that few ordinary citizens would be subjected to $40m-worth of hostile scrutiny from an independent counsel. They feel dismay at the president's conduct, and at his efforts to conceal it. But, until now at least, they do not agree with Mr Starr that these constitute grounds for impeachment.

Over the next week or so, the mood may swing against the president, vindicating the labours of his inquisitors. But, if it does not, the drive to curb future inquisitions may take several forms. The Supreme

Court's Paula Jones verdict could, in theory, be overturned by act of Congress: the court's contention that the suit could go ahead without distracting the president from the tasks of government has proved manifestly false. Equally, the lower-court rulings requiring White House lawyers and secret servicemen to testify before Mr Starr might be overturned, either in Congress or on appeal to the Supreme Court. But the likeliest kind of anti-inquisitorial backlash concerns the independent counsel himself.

The law authorising the appointment of independent counsels expires next year, and the betting is that it will not be renewed in its current form. Republicans have long disliked the law, regarding it as an excessive check on the presidency; thanks to Mr Starr, Democrats too have come to dislike it. Both sides complain that independent counsels are appointed too frequently and that, once appointed, they can expand their investigations too easily—as Mr Starr did, ranging from obscure Arkansas land deals to Oval Office sex.

This has been so widely criticised that future presidential prosecutors are likely to find their responsibilities more narrowly delineated. They may be told to investigate a particular allegation, rather than to embark on a general search for information embarrassing to their target; their time and budget may be limited. By defanging the main judicial challenge to the presidency, this would make America's executive stronger than it was before the Lewinsky scandal.

It may even be possible, to some degree, to defang "gotcha" journalism. For all its competitive aggression, the press is capable of restraint if it thinks the public (or even the White House) demands it: there has been almost no coverage, for example, of how the unfortunate Chelsea Clinton is handling her father's behaviour. And almost any journalist is sensitive to the possibility that too much cynicism may cause him to lose touch with his audience.

Even if invasive journalism proves enduring—and, given the competitive pressure exerted by cable television and the Internet, it may well do—its impact on presidential power may wane. Americans may continue to watch talk shows that air embarrassing personal facts about their presidents; but they may be decreasingly moved by them. From the start of the Lewinsky scandal, journalists have assailed the president, but their audiences have been reluctant to pass judgment on him. It may turn out that the post-Watergate drive to expose the truth about public figures has, after the first brave hope that this would produce better leaders, simply deepened the voters' tolerance of imperfection.

In sum, the Lewinsky scandal may indeed mark a watershed in American politics, but not the one that seems most obvious now. Rather than weakening the presidency, it may represent a softening of the standards by which presidents are judged. Rather than extending Watergate's inquisitorial culture, it may represent the end of the idealism on which that culture was based. After Nixon's fall, Americans hoped that a vigilant press and a determined prosecutor could prevent presidential wrongdoing, and thereby ensure that the country would be blessed with virtuous leaders. But perhaps no amount of vigilance and prosecutorial energy is able to cleanse politics, and even Americans may give up hoping that it can.

The Presidency at Risk:

We Need a Grown-Up

WILSON CAREY McWILLIAMS

Politically, the president is in pretty good shape. Vulnerable, Bill Clinton surely is: the voters aren't much inclined to believe what he says, and they respect him even less. Renewed charges that Chinese campaign contributions influenced national security policy also could hurt badly. Just as bad, the Middle East negotiations are stalled, India and Pakistan are building nuclear arsenals, and, around the world, one economy or another always seems to be teetering on the edge of disaster. But Clinton's good luck still hasn't deserted him. Monica Lewinsky is back in the headlines, but Paula Jones is more or less off the board, tales of the president's amorous escapades are having little effect on voters, and Special Prosecutor Kenneth Starr has not become any more lovable, even with the help of professional image-brighteners. The economy is still turning out good numbers. For the moment, there is even hope for Ireland. And with the Clintons' approval ratings high and the president himself a limping lame duck, Republican strategists—concerned to keep their House majority—have been focusing more of their attacks on the Democrats as a party, turning to Clinton stories only to get a laugh. It's the presidency that's in trouble, and in that story, the public plays as big a role as its leaders.

Wilson Carey McWilliams, a longtime *Commonweal* contributor, teaches political science at Rutgers University.
Reprinted by permission. Commonweal, July 17, 1998. Vol. 125, No. 13, p. 11.

At least intuitively, the majority of Americans understand the case for executive power as Alexander Hamilton set it down in *The Federalist*. Constitutional government exists by convention, through agreements and institutions that create a domesticated public space in which the law can rule. But outside and underneath the hedge of the laws is a fundamental lawlessness that always threatens forms and proprieties, especially through the sort of change that renders old laws at least temporarily inadequate or obsolete. Even John Locke, that paladin of liberal constitutionalism, argued that government requires some element of "prerogative," the capacity to act without, or sometimes against, legal rules. After all, when citizens act as rulers, they can't be merely law-abiding; they have to evaluate laws and policies, standing outside and above legality. For most of us, however, this exercise of sovereignty happens only in moments, chiefly in imagination or in the voting booth. On a day-to-day basis, the buck, as Harry Truman famously observed, stops with the president.

Presidents, Americans recognize, need the skill and constitutional power to deal with knaves and villains; we can't afford a president who is too honorable or tied to convention. The most conspicuously decent occupants of the presidency in recent years—Gerald Ford and Jimmy Carter—are commonly regarded as failures. In recent elections, American voters have showed a decided preference for supple rascality over hampered rectitude; Clinton's very reputation for impropriety may have helped establish him as the candidate better able to build a "bridge to the future."

Nobody needs to tell us that this is a dangerous world, full of threatening presences, in which life is being reordered with scant regard for old ways and certitudes. Increasingly, technology and markets are transforming families, shattering communities, and undermining our older ideas of citizenship and self-government. Civic life seems less able to govern the forces of the time, and also less necessary. And as political community appears to afford us less support for our pride and dignity, we offer it less of ourselves. Americans feel more and more "unencumbered" (the term is political philosopher Michael Sandel's), allowed to follow an ethic of personal liberation which, in turn, encourages tolerance for the president's "private life."

In the same spirit, public life is becoming privatized, not only through deregulation and government downsizing, but through a politics in which money and lawsuits, administrative hearings and "rights talk" replace the effort to persuade and organize majorities. We are more apt to think of political leaders, including the president, as lawyers or advocates, people we hire for essentially private purposes. Bill Clinton, in these terms, is doing a good job: we put him in as CEO to fix the economy, and his character is irrelevant unless it shows up in the bottom line. If you were O. J. Simpson, would you care about the state of Johnny Cochrane's soul? And it follows, as in the popular recent thriller, *Air Force One*, that presidents also put private motives first, which is O.K., the movie teaches, so long as the Soviet general gets killed in the end.

Other problems aside, however, political leaders may—especially in times of great transformation—have to ask us to do things that cost or hurt, that trouble the existing order, or that challenge the way we see ourselves and our country. In this respect, the privatized view of the presidency, and Clinton's conduct in office, seem more and more like an anecdote without a punch line, or more charitably, an episode of "Seinfeld." As *New York Times* columnist Frank Rich wrote, the swirl of scandal has served to distract attention from the "hollowness of Mr. Clinton's second term," just as his approval ratings often seem to serve no purpose other than "deflecting an impeachment proceeding."

The authority to do great things requires a stronger relation between people and president, one in which we give our allegiance and our willingness to sacrifice, but in which we receive moral assurance and personal responsibility from those who lead us into new ways and times. Presidents, acting for us—he took power, FDR said, "in the spirit of the gift"—mediate between convention and nature, the laws and the divine. Able to dispense mercy, presidents can bring down the apocalypse; at bottom, the presidency is hierophantic and tinted with regality, a truth partly captured in FDR's hyperbolic likening of his administration to Christ's driving the moneychangers from the temple. But the public price of that dangerous authority is the president's willingness to sacrifice his or her private self while in office, assuming a wholly public persona: In great monarchies, like the papacy, rulers often surrender their private names, just as high kings must be willing to die or to offer up those they love.

In liberal republics, the price of office, like its authority, is ordinarily not so steep. Still, if our rulers want to be taken seriously, they have to give up most of the liberty they would enjoy as private citizens. Above all, they have to show personal respect for the forms, for the very conventions and laws that a president's extra-legal public power may have to repair or reform.

At the beginning of American national life, there were strayings among the Framers. Assuming that all the charges against Clinton are true, Alexander Hamilton—"a sexual libertine," John Adams called him—was probably his match, though certainly more graceful in his predations. But when Hamilton was accused of winking at or collaborating in the corrupt schemes of his paramour's husband in order to cover up the affair, he chose to publish a self-reviling confession, sacrificing his private character to preserve the honor of his public conduct and policy.

It's an example the current president has so far been unable to appreciate, let alone follow.

Bill Clinton is genuinely engaging, and even his misdeeds suggest a Tom Sawyerish kind of mischief, the sometimes very hurtful frivolities of a basically good kid. But kings who are children have always been bad omens, and the presidency of the United States is cut to an adult's measure. We will need to do better next time.

Issue 13
The Judiciary

INTRODUCTION

The judiciary—and above all, the Supreme Court—presents a paradox. On the one hand, it enjoys a degree of prestige and popular respect that the other two branches can only dream of. Its deliberations are shielded from public view; its public proceedings drip with pomp and ceremony. By and large, we trust the court system as a dispassionate (if not impartial) arbiter of the law and of the Constitution. It acts for the good of the nation, we think, whereas too frequently the president and Congress act for selfish—even libidinal—reasons. On the other hand, the judiciary is the most undemocratic of the branches. Judges at the federal level are appointed for life terms and can be removed only through a laborious process of impeachment (assassination is illegal).

This paradox is grounded in the institutional powers of our highest court. On the one hand, the Supreme Court, ever since the celebrated cases *Marbury v. Madison* (1803) and *Fletcher v. Peck* (1810), wields the power of judicial review that has enabled it to declare unconstitutional laws at the national and state levels. The other two branches enjoy nothing like this privilege. On the other hand, the judiciary's freedom of action is constrained in many important ways by the other branches. Federal judges are appointed by the president, but with congressional approval; they may be removed, their number changed, and their jurisdictions altered. Congress may even attempt to undo a judicial decision with retaliatory legislation. Above all, rulings of the Supreme Court may simply be ignored by the other branches. The Supreme Court depends on the other branches to enforce its rulings; if enforcement does not occur, then the Court is an impotent body.

The broad outline of American constitutional history is marked by the continual attempt by the Supreme Court to negotiate this paradox. Although it is given the power to interpret the Constitution, the Court can never go too far ahead (or fall too far behind) the public's sense of the national interest. As a matter of convention, observers of the judicial system distinguish between two judicial philosophies. The first philosophy, judicial restraint, asserts that judges should interpret not only statutes but also the Constitution itself as far as possible with reference to the original intent of their authors. The second, judicial activism, allows that judges may interpret statutory and fundamental law with reference to the changed circumstances and perceived needs of contemporary society. These philosophies correspond generally, although hardly always, to political conservatism and liberalism.

At its best, the Court leads the nation in a direction that it ought to go. In the case of the civil rights movement, the Court's decision in *Brown v. Board of Education* (1954) pushed the nation in the direction of greater racial understanding and tolerance, even when the other branches of government lacked the courage to take the lead. Only ten years later did Congress begin passing the landmark civil rights legislation that has deepened the meaning of "equal protection." Certainly there are limits to the public's acceptance of civil rights, as illustrated by the disputes over school busing for integration and affirmative action. Nonetheless, as far as the core of the civil rights movement goes, the Court has served as the conscience of the nation.

In contrast, the Supreme Court's defense of abortion rights has enjoyed no such popular consensus. In *Roe v. Wade* (1973), state laws against abortion were struck down as unconstitutional. However, unlike civil rights, a woman's alleged "right to privacy" has not acquired complete legitimacy. Some critics question the very idea of a federally protected "right to privacy" as an illegitimate encroachment on the powers of state governments; others consider abortion to be murder and thus regard the Court's decision as profoundly immoral. Whatever one thinks about abortion, clearly American society has not entirely accepted *Roe v. Wade.* In retrospect, the Court's ruling took an issue prematurely out of the public debate and attempted to impose a nationwide solution that has awakened passionate opposition.

As a result, the Court's authority has been diminished in subtle ways. Judicial appointments are far more contested and politicized than they used to be. Also, critics have become quicker to interpret the Court's behavior as reflecting a liberal (or conservative) political agenda. In part, this perception may reflect deeper ideological divides within society at large. However, *Roe v. Wade* did not help the Court in its continual effort to remain aloof from, yet influential over, the important public debates of the day. Presently, a Democratic president and a Republican Congress have engaged in a veritable standoff over judicial appointments, as Congress has almost routinely refused to approve the president's nominations to federal judgeships.

In these selections, Robert George and Ramesh Ponnuru argue that the court system is biased in a way that goes beyond any ideological commitment to activist philosophies. Instead, they contend that the very idea of judicial supremacy must be challenged in order to restore to democratic publics their ability to control their own destinies without judicial interference. The problem, in George's and Ponnuru's view, is not merely that courts render obnoxious rulings. Rather, the accepted interpretation of judicial review itself reflects a long-standing bias towards judicial activism. Why, the authors ask in the spirit of the old-style doctrine of "nullification," should the court system have the last word on what the Constitution means? Courts are unelected institutions that coexist uneasily with American traditions of democratic participation.

Herman Schwartz counters that activism and restraint are really in the eyes of the beholder. When conservatives criticize the judicial system for indulging in activism, what they really dislike is that the courts are delivering rulings that go against conservative causes. Far more important, to Schwartz, is maintaining the judiciary's independence. Judicial appointments may never be free from partisanship. However, after some point, the principle of judicial independence must be respected by all sides. To Schwartz, the attempt by Republicans to subject all appointments to an ideological test amounts to "gumming up the works" in a way that damages the judiciary for the sake of partisan gain.

As you read the articles, consider the following questions.

Discussion Questions

1. Given that the judiciary is the least democratic branch of our national government, why not limit judges' terms of office, or even make them elected officials? After all, many states already do this. How might this change judicial politics in this country, as well as the character of the judiciary itself?
2. Given that, in some ways, the judiciary is also the weakest branch of our national governement, what might be done to further strengthen the judicial branch, and insulate it even further from pressure from the other two branches of government?
3. George and Ponnuru question the very idea of judicial review. How would relations between states and the national government change if states shared the power to interpret the constitution?
4. In Issue two, you were introduced to the distinction between judicial activism and judicial restraint. Do you think that Schwartz is correct in regarding this distinction as merely opportunistic? In what ways might a conservative support judicial activism, and a liberal support judicial restraint?

For more on this topic, visit the following websites:

http://www.findlaw.com
FindLaw

http://supct.law.cornell.edu/supct
Cornell University's Legal Information Institute—Supreme Court Collection

http://www.uscourts.gov
The Federal Judiciary Homepage

Courting Trouble:

*Only a Frontal Assault on the Power of the Courts Can
Restore America's Constitutional Balance*

ROBERT P. GEORGE AND RAMESH PONNURU

The campaign to combat judicial usurpation seems to be fizzling. While
conservatives have talked about ambitious projects like impeaching out-
of-control judges or amending the Constitution to require judges to hew
to the original understanding of its provisions, they have been unable
even to slow down the Senate's assembly-line confirmation of Clinton
judicial nominees. True, Republicans have shot down easy targets like
Frederica Massiah-Jackson, whose outlandishly pro-criminal-defense
record embarrassed even liberals. But overall, the Republican Senate is
confirming judges faster than an earlier Republican Senate confirmed
President Reagan's nominees.

Republicans appear simply to lack the will to take on the courts.
And who can blame them? The public isn't up in arms about judicial imperialism. The issue isn't easy to publicize either, especially through a
hostile media. Despite what is now a long history of abuses, federal
judges in general are respected (even though they stand at the intersec-
tion of lawyers and politicians). Finally, politicians often don't mind
having their powers usurped when it relieves them of responsibility for
controversial matters.

But Republicans duck the issue at their peril. All the supposed conservative judicial triumphs of recent years, from rolling back racial preferences to restoring federalism, have been won by narrow majorities;
with three Supreme Court appointments likely in the next five to seven
years, all of them could be reversed. Already, only a few circuits practice
self-restraint. And as President Clinton appoints more judges, the courts
will grow increasingly effective in blocking Republican public-policy initiatives.

If Republicans don't care about constitutional considerations, they
should consider civic and political ones. Courts have struck down state
partial-birth–abortion bans on grounds stretching from the specious to
the ludicrous. Thus, the "compromise" position that has endlessly been
urged on pro-lifers—leave the abortion license in place, and settle for restrictions at the margin—is not permitted; even infanticide can't be

Robert P. George is a professor of politics at Princeton University. Ramesh Ponnuru
is National Review's national reporter.

Reprinted by permission. *National Review*, Aug. 17, 1998. Vol. 50, No. 15, p. 33(2).

banned. Pro-lifers will just have to go back to the arduous task of passing a constitutional amendment to undo the courts' handiwork. As the courts move leftward, this will not be the only constitutional amendment conservatives will have to demand.

And that is the optimistic view. If the rules are going to be changed to their systematic disadvantage, why should conservatives participate in normal politics at all? Some social conservatives will be tempted to retreat from politics; others, to resort to an unproductive and morally wrong-headed extremism or even to extra-constitutional resistance. Since social conservatives are the single largest portion of the GOP's base, either reaction would threaten its political health.

Self-interest, then, should move Republicans to act—and more effectively than in the past. They have tried to combat judicial usurpation by appointing originalist judges and by proposing constitutional amendments. Neither strategy has worked. That's not surprising: the courts' excessive power is a structural problem not amenable to piecemeal solutions. The problem, that is, is less that liberals sit on the bench and make bad decisions than that they have a largely unchecked power to do so.

Any proposed remedy should both be educational (and thus of value even if the campaign for it fails) and solve the core problem (in case it succeeds). Some of the institutional fixes conservatives have proposed— e.g., term limits for judges—may or may not have merit, but aren't focused enough to meet these tests. Again, these proposals fail to challenge judicial imperialism at its root: the courts' claim always to have the last, authoritative word on constitutional interpretation.

Constitutional amendments to overturn particular judicial decisions don't challenge it either; indeed, they arguably also concede the courts' reading of the unamended Constitution.

But the Founders never intended to give the federal courts a monopoly over the interpretation of the Constitution. *Marbury v. Madison*, often cited in support of a monopoly, actually stands for a far more modest claim, namely that courts must apply the Constitution; nowhere does it deny that the other branches must do the same according to their own best lights. It stands, in other words, for constitutional supremacy, not judicial supremacy.

Abraham Lincoln, often reckoned the most profound student of the Founding in our political history, also challenged the idea of judicial supremacy over constitutional interpretation. Faced with an outrageous usurpation of democratic authority by the Supreme Court in *Dred Scott v. Sandford*, Lincoln said in his first inaugural that while court decisions must be respected in particular cases, they need not be considered binding as policy on other branches of government. His words are still apt: "If the policy of the government upon vital questions, affecting the whole people, is to be irrevocably fixed by decisions of the Supreme Court, ... the people will have ceased to be their own rulers, having, to that extent, practically resigned their government into the hands of that eminent tribunal." From time to time, the people themselves must resolve a constitutional question by the political act of supporting one branch's interpretation over another's. There is no scandal in this, since the Constitution, by its own understanding, derives its authority from the will of the people.

In our own time, many conservatives accept judicial supremacy, merely caviling at this or that decision. Some, especially libertarians, even accept the courts' self-presentation as the guarantor of our freedoms, and would worry about the safety of liberty if the courts were forced to retrench. If, for example, Congress were to exercise its power under Article III, Section 2 of the Constitution to eliminate the federal courts' jurisdiction over, say, term limits, many conservatives would worry that this structural check on the courts could itself be abused; correct court decisions could be overturned by a majority vote.

These fears are well founded. Any power can be abused, as conservatives have always insisted. But it is also true, as Justice Felix Frankfurter repeatedly warned, that the only ultimate protection for our rights is a general public commitment to them—a commitment eroded when the task of protection is entrusted solely to an unelected elite. Many legislators today don't think about the constitutionality of their bills, despite their oaths of office, because they rely on the courts to sort it out. Nor has judicial supremacy proved a reliable ally of the individual rights we actually possess: consider, for starters, the right to life.

Congress, however, now has an opportunity to begin returning the judiciary to its constitutional dimensions. One year ago, the Supreme Court struck down the Religious Freedom Restoration Act. RFRA was a response to an earlier Supreme Court decision holding that the free exercise of religion does not exempt believers from laws that incidentally impede the practice of their faith. RFRA attempted to restore those exemptions, so that, e.g., the Native American Church's sacramental use of peyote would not run afoul of drug laws. The Court held that Congress had impermissibly second-guessed it.

Conservatives were split, some supporting the law and others the Court. NR found itself in a lonely position, opposed to both. The Justices' decision to strike down RFRA aggrandized the courts—but so did RFRA, by giving them a sweeping, indeed conceptually boundless, discretion to grant exemptions from laws. What was worthwhile about RFRA was one of the features that got it struck down: it was the first significant attempt by Congress in decades to assert its power to "enforce" the Fourteenth Amendment, granted in its fifth section. (In this context, "enforce" can be understood only as "give meaning to.")

Now one group of social conservatives is pushing Congress to re-enact RFRA with an accompanying resolution denouncing the Court's decision as wrong and usurpative. Another group supports Rep. Charles Canady's (R., Fla.) Religious Liberty Protection Act, which is essentially RFRA II. This time, however, Congress is said to have authority for the bill under a combination of the commerce clause and the spending power. Thus the bill jettisons RFRA's strong point—its challenge to the courts—while implicitly going along with the post–New Deal loose view of the commerce clause (just when the courts are recovering the older one). So conservatives who usually work together now find themselves in conflict.

Whatever the merits of these proposals, a seemingly unrelated bill before Congress offers conservatives a chance to unite in an important strike against judicial usurpation. Freshman Rep. Robert Aderholt (R., Ala.) has sponsored, and Gary Bauer's Family Research Council promoted, a little-noticed bill called the Ten Commandments Defense Act. It would erect a "federalism shield" allowing state officials to display the Decalogue. (A controversy has arisen over Alabama judge Roy Moore's so doing in his courtroom.) Invoking its own authority to interpret the Tenth Amendment, Congress would declare that such display is a power reserved to the states.

Some commentators say that the congressional action proposed in the Aderholt bill is merely "declaratory" and thus of no legal effect. But this criticism presupposes the very judicial supremacy that the federalism-shield law challenges. Moreover, the bill may prove popular: an earlier Aderholt resolution in favor of allowing the public display of the Commandments passed the House 295 to 125. And it would plant in the law and the political culture a profoundly important principle. It would be a small way for Congress to regain some of the authority it has ceded to the judiciary.

The judges are likely to strike the bill down for that very reason. But raising the temperature of judicial politics is not a bad thing. By their actions, the judges have put themselves squarely in the political arena, and until they withdraw they are the proper subject of political battles. The goal of conservatives should be to provoke a constitutional crisis—or, more accurately, to expose the one that judicial usurpation has already created.

One Man's Activist:

What Republicans Really Mean When They Condemn Judicial Activism (GOP lawmakers, Bob Barr, Orrin G. Hatch, and Majority Whip Tom DeLay attack judicial activism)

HERMAN SCHWARTZ

Judges, watch your backs: The Congressional Republicans have officially declared war on "judicial activists," judges who go beyond interpreting the law into the realm of what GOP lawmakers consider "making" the law. Rep. Bob Barr of Georgia is but one of several Republicans to denounce the current crop of jurists for "assuming for themselves the powers and responsibilities of legislators or executives"—an offense those on the right say must not be treated lightly. They have been particularly incensed over a few recent decisions setting aside death sentences, excluding evidence in a drug case, and blocking the implementation of the California referendum ending affirmative action programs. This May, Barr joined Majority Whip Tom DeLay of Texas in calling for the impeachment of judges as a "proper tool" for "political offenses," with an impeachable offense defined by DeLay as "whatever a majority of the House of Representatives considers it to be at a given moment in history." Their stated goal, according to DeLay: "The judges need to be intimidated."

With an eye toward weeding out future judicial activists, GOP senators have virtually hijacked the appointment process. Judiciary Committee Chairman Orrin Hatch has declared he will not "stand by to see judicial activists named to the federal bench." To this end, Hatch and his fellow Republicans have instituted a massive slowdown on judicial appointments. According to political scientist Sheldon Goldman of the University of Massachusetts, who has been studying the nomination process for 40 years, the Republicans are engaged in an effort "unprecedented in its scope . . . to deny the Clinton administration as many nominations as possible."

Among their favorite tactics is the imposition of increasingly intrusive requests for the nominee's opinions. For example, last year Margaret Morrow, the first woman to serve as president of the California Bar Association, was unanimously approved by the Senate Judiciary Committee. Because of Republican foot-dragging, however, Morrow's nomination didn't come up for a floor vote during the 1996 session. Moreover,

Herman Schwartz is the author of *Packing the Courts: The Conservative Campaign to Reunite the Constitution.*

Reprinted by permission. *Washington Monthly,* Nov. 1997. Vol. 29, No. 11, p. 10.

when the Senate reconvened this year, Republican Charles Grassley of Iowa demanded Morrow's position on every one of 160 California initiatives in the last 10 years. (Grassley eventually scaled back his demands—after all, how much intimidation is necessary?)

Other GOP legislators have pushed for even more direct action to keep "activists" off the bench. Sen. Slade Gorton of Washington tried unsuccessfully to have Congress cut into the president's nominating power by requiring the president to get advance approval for a judicial candidate's ideology from the senators representing the circuit to which the candidate would be nominated. For his part, Sen. Phil Gramm of Texas pledged to block a Clinton nominee on the basis that the person had been "politically active."

Such delaying tactics have already borne fruit. In all of 1996, the Senate let through only 17 trial judges and no appellate judges, an unprecedentedly small number. This year's Congress seems to be following the same route: As of September 30, the Senate had confirmed just 18 judges, leaving 96 vacancies on the federal bench—including around 30 that the Administrative Office of the United States Courts calls "judicial emergencies," judgeships unfilled for more than 18 months. Some slots have been vacant since 1994. For a while, President Clinton provided the Republicans with a convenient excuse for the outrageous number of vacancies by sending up very few nominations. However, this cover is no longer available, as the president has now nominated some 70 judges, many originally sent up during the last Congress.

The conservative crusade against activist judges has been even more effective on the state level, where elective judges who voted in ways displeasing to Republicans have been denied re-election by organized electoral campaigns. In Tennessee, for example, Judge Penny J. White heard only one death penalty case in her 19 months on the state Supreme Court. In that case, she voted with her colleagues to order a new death-sentence hearing for a convicted murderer. Less than two months later, she was denied reappointment in a routine retention election, the victim of a Tennessee Republican Party campaign against her. Likewise, Nebraska Supreme Court Justice David Lanphier was ousted last November for having voted against a term-limits law and in favor of a retrial for some defendants convicted of second-degree murder.

The result of the conservative campaign is a massive pile-up in the federal courts. On the West Coast, oral arguments in some 600 cases were canceled last year, and the Second Circuit in New York has had to cancel sittings as well. One trial judge in Illinois put all of his civil cases on hold and went an entire year hearing only criminal cases, while a San Diego district court holds only about 10 civil trials a year.

The Republicans justify themselves by arguing that the damage they're inflicting is all in the name of defending the constitutional separation of powers against judicial activism. But oddly enough, Republican crusaders seem to have overlooked an important point: Some of the worst "activist" offenders on the bench today are the conservative members of the Supreme Court.

ACTION PACKED

Despite DeLay and company's condemnation of judges who they say "have thrown out the Constitution" in favor of their own wisdom, over the years, it is the Supreme Court's conservatives who have frequently done just that.

For example, in the 1976 case *Nat'l League of Cities v. Usery*, Chief Justice William Rehnquist (then an associate justice) succeeded in coalescing a majority to overturn federal legislation requiring state and local governments to meet the minimum-wage and maximum-hours provisions of the Fair Labor Standards Act. Unable to rely on any constitutional text, Rehnquist invoked vague notions of "state sovereignty."

More recently, this June the five conservative justices on the court overturned the Brady Gun Control bill because it required local sheriffs to do a background check on a prospective gun purchaser. As in the *Nat'l League of Cities* case, the conservative justices conceded that they could not actually derive any limitations on federal power from the text of the 10th Amendment, which simply "reserves" to the states the "powers not delegated to the United States." As Justice O'Connor admitted, this is "essentially a tautology," because the amendment says nothing about what powers are in fact reserved. Instead, the justices relied solely on their own conception of what "state sovereignty" and "the federal structure" entail.

In some cases, the conservative majority has gone so far as to openly rewrite constitutional text. The 11th Amendment to the Constitution explicitly excludes from the federal judicial power only suits "against one of the United States by citizens of another State." Nevertheless, two years ago the court's conservatives rewrote the amendment to also exclude suits against a state by its own citizens—in the process overruling a recent precedent, and overturning a federal statute. And just this year, the court overturned the Religious Freedom Restoration Act, a law passed unanimously in the House and by a 97–3 vote in the Senate, which sought to expand protection for religious freedom, particularly for minority sects.

Of course, in the current antigovernment climate, the argument that the justices are simply curtailing federal power in order to honor states' rights is a popular one. It is also flawed. Take the issue of affirmative action: Since 1978, when the Bakke case involving the University of California's decision to set aside 16 out of 100 places for minorities at the Davis School of Medicine was decided, conservatives have voted to strike down virtually every affirmative action plan to come before the court, regardless of whether the plan was adopted by state or federal legislators or officials. Until 1989, they failed except with respect to employee layoffs. With the arrival of Justice Kennedy in 1988, however, the balance shifted, and with its ruling on the 1989 Richmond, Va., case, the Supreme Court struck down some 236 state and local affirmative action plans.

Another example of this indifference to states' rights is the area of criminal justice. Since the Nixon appointees took over in 1972, the conservative majority has steadily cut into the Warren Court decisions establishing rights for the accused. Disregarding its long-standing policy not to hear state cases involving federal constitutional questions if those cases could be decided under state law, the court has reached out to overturn decisions of more liberal state courts.

What becomes increasingly clear from the court's record is that conservative justices are not so much concerned with strict adherence to the Constitution as with promoting conservative values. In none of the aforementioned cases, or numerous others like them, has the conservatives' purported zeal for judicial restraint or states' rights prevented them from riding roughshod over state and local legislation or court rulings that they disagreed with. And although the court's liberals have joined conservatives in some of their most controversial rulings, like overturning the Religious Freedom Restoration Act, even Clint Bolick's Institute for Justice has admitted that the court's conservatives are more inclined to strike down both federal and state laws than Clinton's two appointees, Ruth Bader Ginsburg and Stephen Breyer.

So why aren't Messrs. Hatch, DeLay, Barr, and their friends threatening to impeach the high Court's most active "activists"? Simple: Like their conservative counterparts on the courts, congressional Republicans don't object to "judicial activism" per se. They simply oppose "liberal judicial activism." As one federal judge put it, "The Republicans define 'activist' according to their political agenda. It's OK to be an activist if you're striking down affirmative action and gun-free school laws." Or, as American Bar Association President and staunch conservative N. Lee Cooper puts it: "Activism [is] a phrase that, like beauty, seems to be in the eye of the beholder. It is fair to say that for the most vocal critics in today's debate, judicial activism is conveniently tossed around as a means of condemning any position that doesn't fit the critic's ideological mold."

In fact, the political debate over "judicial activism" has undergone a 180-degree turn in the last 70 years. During Franklin Roosevelt's administration, when the largely conservative Supreme Court was striking down New Deal legislation, liberals were up in arms about jurists' overstepping their constitutional bounds. And upon being named to the court, FDR appointee Justice Felix Frankfurter adhered to a strict policy of judicial restraint, reflecting his belief that the court should, whenever possible, defer to the will of the people as expressed through the legislature.

Today, of course, it's the conservatives who are up in arms. Their current campaign against "liberal judicial activists" is part of an ideological struggle that began in earnest as a reaction to the transformation of American life that started in the 1950s: the increased openness and freedom; the refusal of those outside the favored circle of power and privilege—women, blacks, homosexuals—to stay in their place; the ever-more powerful role of government in social and economic matters, and concomitant with that, the implicit devaluation of the rugged, Darwinian individualist. The federal courts were crucial to these changes, making them a natural target for the backlash. The "Impeach Earl Warren" signs that went up all over the South in the wake of the *Brown* school desegregation decision were among the first expressions of that reaction.

With the Reagan Revolution of 1981, the anti-court forces went into high gear. After numerous legislative failures, Edwin Meese and other die-hard conservatives decided that the only way to radically change American law was by tilting the federal bench sharply to the right. They went at it systematically, focusing on the Supreme Court and intermediate appellate levels where federal law is made. Men (and an occasional woman) from the far right of the judicial spectrum were appointed en masse. Such well-known and not-so-well-known conservatives as Sandra Day O'Connor, Anthony Kennedy, Antonin Scalia, Clarence Thomas, Robert Bork, Richard Posner, and Kenneth Starr were appointed—without objection, in all but a few cases. Two notable exceptions are Bork's and Thomas's appointments to the Supreme Court—though not their appointments to the circuit court.) Potential nominees were asked their views on abortion, school prayer, unions, and other controversial matters. Moderates like Republican Judith Whittaker, who made the mistake of supporting the Equal Rights Amendment; and Philip Lacovara, one of Washington's most distinguished attorneys who, though a Goldwater supporter, joined a lawyers' civil rights group, were vetoed. Independents like Deputy Solicitor General Andrew Frey, who had given $25 to a gun-control group, were also rejected.

The result was a transformation of the federal judiciary as 12 years of Reagan-Bush appointees put solid conservative majorities on almost all the federal courts. The only court that remained relatively free of conservative domination for much of this period was the Supreme Court, because Justice Lewis Powell—most of the time a conservative vote—not infrequently swung over to the liberal side on key issues like affirmative action. That came to an end with the arrival of Anthony Kennedy who, with a few notable exceptions, has consistently voted with the Rehnquist-Scalia-Thomas-O'Connor bloc.

Bill Clinton's victory in 1992 and a Democratic Senate gave liberal Democrats a chance to restore some balance to the federal courts. The Republicans, though in the minority in 1993–94, threatened to challenge nominees they considered too liberal. Clinton's response was to avoid nominating judges who could be labeled as clearly liberal. As a result, a recent study by three political scientists found that the Clinton judges are less liberal than President Jimmy Carter's and quite similar to those of President George Bush, except that there are more minorities and women among the Clinton group.

Then came the Republican takeover of the Senate in 1994. Now, Clinton's judicial nominees and appointees alike find themselves under attack for their "liberal activism"—despite the fact that conservative activists like Clint Bolick have conceded that Clinton's nominees have been "moderate."

HANDS OFF THE COURTS

Truth be told, all judges are "activist." They have to be, particularly in constitutional cases. To last more than a few years, a constitution must be written in what Chief Justice John Marshall called "great outlines" that specify only "its important objects," outlines that must be filled in by judges. This is particularly true of our Constitution, written over 200 years ago by people whose vision was shaped by an America very different from the one in which we live today. After all, *Brown v. Board of Education* was one of the most "activist" decisions in our history. Would we have wanted it to come out differently?

Moreover, all constitutions and most statutes are the product of compromises, many of which are deliberately ambiguous in order to paper over differences that cannot be bridged, only bypassed. When these deliberately ambiguous texts come to the courts, the latter have no choice but to "make" the law.

Activism can, of course, go too far—though what is "too far" is often disputable and usually depends on who wins or loses. It is generally agreed that the pre–New Deal conservative judges were too aggressive, and these days a vociferous minority of our population believes that the *Roe v. Wade* court was as well. By and large, however, the system has managed to keep this activism within accepted limits. Many of the liberal activist "horrors" cited by DeLay et al., for example, were reversed by higher courts, rightly or wrongly. And if the mainstream of the nation believes the courts have gone too far, history shows that sooner or later the offending rulings will be modified or overruled.

The important thing is to maintain judicial independence. For that, we must try to keep the judiciary as free as possible from the partisanship to which it has recently been subjected. The House Judiciary Committee, for instance, has held hearings on a proposed constitutional amendment to eliminate the life tenure for federal judges that is the precondition for their independence. And Judge Robert Bork shocked even his allies with a proposal to allow a majority of either house of Congress to overrule federal or state court decisions.

Of course, some partisanship is inevitable, especially at the Supreme Court level. A conservative president can naturally be expected to nominate somewhat conservative judges, and vice-versa. What has kept the system running smoothly in the past has been the understanding that it is the president's prerogative to nominate any jurist he feels has the intellectual mettle to do the job well. And by and large, Democrats went along with the Reagan-Bush appointments. (In fact, during Bush's final year in the White House, the Democrat-controlled Senate approved 66 judicial appointments.) In order for an ideological balance to be maintained in the courts, the Congress must respect the will of the people—as expressed through their elected president—where judicial appointments are concerned. That's the way the system is supposed to work. By trying to win the whole game, the Republicans are gumming up the works. It is they, in fact, and not the judges they are attacking, who are betraying our constitutional heritage "in order to advance their own political views."

PART V
Issues in Public Policy

Issue 14
Economic Policy

INTRODUCTION

Taxes don't lie. Whatever the promises and half-truths of politicians, taxes determine what goes into a government's coffers. Although projections of tax revenues may be unrealistic or even manipulated, they often express the bottom line of political life.

We typically judge the character of public policy by how the government spends its funds. Yet it is equally illuminating to consider where those funds come from. The nation's tax system expresses its own set of policy priorities. Who bears the tax burden reflects the distribution of power as well as the notions of equity that animate the political system. These twin poles of power and principle are held together by the prevailing rules of the political game. As American history shows, these rules change over time. Originally, the Constitution forbade the national government from collecting "direct taxes," and it was not until 1913 that a constitutional amendment legitimated the income tax as a revenue source. As a result, throughout the nineteenth century, most government revenue came from an extensive patchwork of tariffs (taxes on imports paid indirectly by American consumers and producers) and selective levies such as the excise tax on whiskey. Since tariffs placed measurable burdens on some domestic interests but offered economic protection to others, the tariff schedules remained the center of congressional politics for most of the century. Each interest group measured its power by its ability to influence the outcome of tariff legislation.

With the introduction of the federal income tax (followed by direct payroll deductions during World War II), the dynamics of tax policy, as well as the burden of government, shifted decisively. Generally, taxes on income and capital gains have shifted more of the burden onto richer Americans. Moreover, an income-tax-based system has transformed the policy significance of taxation. Whereas in the nineteenth century, tariff politics was Congress-centered and expressed the shifting balance of interests between Congressional constituencies, in the twentieth century, the income tax has become the centerpiece of a new, executive-centered regulatory politics that implements policy through targeted adjustments of the tax code. Above all, the mechanism of payroll deductions itself has assured the national government a stream of revenue whose size and regularity have made possible the growth of government during the twentieth century.

Although Americans no longer fight over tariffs as an issue of tax policy, the underlying conflict over taxes remains ongoing. What is the optimal form or level of taxation for the United States? Expressing the interests of wealthier Americans, the Republican party has consistently stood for lower income and capital gains taxes, whereas Democratic constituencies see tax cuts as a threat to social programs. At the same time, each party justifies its preferences in terms of larger values. For Republicans, tax cuts not only benefit their supporters but also help shrink the size of government—itself a good thing, in their view. In addition, they claim, lower taxes spur economic growth by giving the wealthy greater incentives to invest their surpluses in productive enterprise. For their part, Democrats distrust such tax cuts because they shift the burden of government onto poorer people; at the same time, a smaller government implies fewer resources spent on the poor. Despite these differences, both parties do agree on one thing: The tax code remains a legitimate and convenient policy tool for structuring the behavior of citizens.

One recent expression of this ongoing conflict can be found in the debate over the "flat tax." Championed by presidential hopeful Steven Forbes and others, the flat tax combines the traditional Republican devotion to smaller government with a conviction that the ever more complex tax code distorts behavior in unproductive ways and reduces the code's legitimacy in the eyes of exasperated taxpayers. As politicians tinker with a system riddled by exemptions and credits, taxpayers experience the burdens of citizenship as an irksome and wasteful game of tax avoidance. In the first article, House Majority Leader Richard Armey explains that the flat tax would sweep away the current system in favor of a single rate for all taxpayers. The arresting simplicity of this plan is justified by a commonsense appeal to equity, namely, that each citizen should, in fairness, pay the percentage of his or her income to the government. Yet for all the virtues of simplicity, analyst William Gale cautions that the flat tax might cause more problems than it solves. Any tax system, according to Gale, must balance the benefits of simplicity, efficiency, and fairness. In view of Congress's temptation to complicate the tax code with favors to powerful interests, it may be unrealistic to expect that a flat tax would remain simple—or flat—for long.

As you read the articles, consider the following questions.

Discussion Questions

1. To be legitimate, a tax system must be at least somewhat fair. But what is fairness? Contrast the ideal of a single tax rate for everyone with the idea that richer people ought to pay proportionally more as a percentage of their income, or what is called a "progressive" tax system. Which tax system—flat or progressive—appears to be more just?
2. Representative Armey envisions many benefits flowing from the flat tax. Which benefits are the most important to him? How does Gale respond to these assertions?
3. According to Gale, a flat tax is not an income tax, but a "consumption tax." What does he mean? What are the differences between an income tax and a consumption tax?
4. Most of the complexity of our current tax code arises from the desire by Congress to encourage certain kinds of behavior and to discourage others. Think of some common examples of how the tax code is used in this fashion. Should the tax code be used to change people's behavior, or should it be used only to raise revenue?

For more on this topic, visit the following websites:

`http://www.policy.com`
The Policy News and Information Service

`http://www.atr.org`
Americans for Tax Reform

`http://www.ctj.org`
Citizens for Tax Justice

`http://www.ntu.com`
National Taxpayers Union

After Years of Abuse, Americans Deserve a Flat-Tax Break Today

RICHARD K. ARMEY

Americans are crying out for relief from the current oppressive federal tax code. It's easy to see why: We have a system that's too complicated, unfair and hinders economic growth.

The tax code is so complex that when *Money* magazine asked 45 tax professionals to prepare a return for a fictional family, no two came up with the same tax total.

This complicated code fosters not only resentment toward the government, but toward our fellow citizens. One reason is that our nation's capital is dominated by 67,000 lobbyists who seek to advance the agenda of special interests rather than the broader public interest. Not surprisingly, more lobbyists work on taxes than any other issue.

The result is that each year, Americans spend more than 5.4 billion hours complying with the tax code—that's more time than it takes to make every car, truck and van in the United States.

Taxpayers are fed up. Two out of three Americans say that overhauling the nation's tax system is very important to them, according to a recent *Washington Post* poll.

The Republican Party is responding. We've been leading the charge on fundamental tax reform, which is the best issue conservatives have had since the Reagan tax revolution of 1981. The tax-reform movement is sweeping the nation.

Republican Rep. Billy Tauzin of Louisiana and I have been traveling the country since last October to make our case for comprehensive tax reform and debate the merits of Tauzin's national sales tax and my 17 percent flat-rate income tax. On Aug. 18, we will bring the "scrap the code" tour to Kansas City and Chicago, marking our 30th public debate. The response has been stunning.

In Atlanta, for example, one of the tour's first stops, the 1,000 seat auditorium and the overflow room were filled to capacity. Hundreds more spilled over into the convention-center foyer to view the debate on closed-circuit television. At an impromptu rally after the debate, hundreds of emotionally charged taxpayers shouted their support for our reform efforts. The mood was electric. Jim Miller, former Reagan budget director

Republican Richard K. Armey of Texas is the majority leader of the U.S. House of Representatives.

Insight on the News, Aug. 17, 1998. Vol. 14, No. 30, p. 29(1).

and counselor for the Citizens for a Sound Economy Foundation, the sponsor of the tax tour, remarked, "I haven't witnessed such a display of enthusiasm over a public-policy issue since my days with Reagan."

Atlanta is not unique. In cities and towns all across America, taxpayers no longer accept today's corrupt, destructive tax code. They are demanding that their leaders scrap it and replace it with a code that is simple and fair. That's why my flat-tax legislation is so popular. It would scrap the current tax code and replace it with a 17 percent tax on all income. You could file your return on a 10-line postcard. There are no loopholes or tax breaks for special interests. And it would lead to an economic boom and higher wages. In coffee shops, around kitchen tables across America and on the Internet—my flat-tax World Wide Web site (www.flattax.gov) receives about 100,000 hits each month—people enthusiastically are embracing the tax-reform movement.

So powerful, in fact, is the growing tax-reform movement that many reform opponents find they no longer can defend the status quo and are discovering creative ways to jump on the tax-reform bandwagon. For example, following last fall's Senate hearings that exposed an IRS run amok, President Clinton went from an unapologetic defender of the status quo to a reluctant supporter of the Republican-led, bipartisan IRS reform legislation. According to the *New York Times*, Clinton was prodded into reversing course out of fear that Republicans could use the issue against Democrats in the 1998 elections to gain the upper hand on an array of tax-related issues.

Public discontent with the current tax code has made possible what was before unthinkable—a Clinton signature on a real IRS reform bill. As a result, the American people will have some measure of protection against tax-collection abuses until we can pass comprehensive tax reform.

In addition, just a few weeks ago, the House of Representatives passed a revolutionary bill that would terminate the current IRS code by 2002. Such measures, although destined for a Clinton veto, help to elevate the tax-reform debate which pits reformers against the defenders of the status quo. As a result, I strongly believe that all serious candidates for the GOP presidential nomination in 2000 will have to make tax reform a centerpiece of their campaign.

Now more than ever, comprehensive tax reform is a realistic and achievable goal. When I began drafting flat-tax legislation in 1994, I wanted a bill that was radical enough to yank the entire tax debate away from half-measures and tinkering.

I knew that there would be ferocious opposition from the establishment. For example, Washington's $8.4 billion lobbying industry employs more than 67,000 people. Many of these people make very good livings securing and defending special tax breaks and loopholes for their powerful clients. Then there is the Clinton administration and its class warriors and income redistributors at the Treasury Department. I knew that they would oppose any tax plan that treats all taxpayers the same. (There is no gentle way to scrap the tax code and shift power from Washington to Main Street without angering those who are wedded to the status quo.)

In 1994, I said that the flat tax would be enacted into law when America beat Washington. At that time I believed that passing the flat tax would be a 10-year project. But today I believe that it can be achieved sooner.

Like any campaign of this magnitude, the opposition will be fierce and there will be many obstacles to success. But when the dust settles, it will be the flat tax that comes out on top.

Simple, Efficient, Fair. Or Is It?

WILLIAM G. GALE

The U.S. tax system remains continually, and deservedly, under attack. Many people find taxes too complex. Analysts blame the tax system for depressing saving, entrepreneurship, and economic growth. Few people believe it to be entirely fair or transparent.

Members of both political parties have put forth plans to overhaul the current tax system. The best known is the "flat tax." Conceived by Stanford economist Robert Hall and political scientist Alvin Rabushka in the early 1980s, the flat tax has been given legislative form in the past few years by Rep. Richard Armey (R-TX) and Sen. Richard Shelby (R-AL).

The flat tax would replace taxes on personal and corporate income and estates. Households would pay taxes on wages and pension income in excess of substantial personal and child allowances. Businesses would pay taxes on their sales less their wage and pension payments, input costs, and capital purchases. No other income would be taxed, no other deductions allowed. Businesses and individuals would face the same flat tax rate.

William G. Gale is a senior fellow in the Brookings Economic Studies program. He is the author, with Henry J. Aaron, of a forthcoming Brookings book on tax policy.

Reprinted by permission. *Brookings Review*, Summer 1998. Vol. 16, Issue 3, p. 40, 5p.

Proponents have made strong claims for the flat tax. It would be so simple that the tax form could fit on a postcard; it would take tax considerations out of people's economic decisionmaking, thereby increasing efficiency and revitalizing the economy; it is a fair and airtight system.

In theory, the flat tax is, indeed, a clever, principled approach to changing the nature of federal taxation. Whether it could satisfactorily meet the competing demands placed on the tax system—fairness, simplicity, growth—and the transition to the real world is an open question.

JUST WHAT IS THE FLAT TAX??

The flat tax is not an income tax, but a consumption tax. The simplest form of consumption tax is a tax on retail sales. If we switch to a consumption tax, why not just adopt the simplest?

Implementing a national retail sales tax would be problematic for several reasons. First, it would be regressive. Poor households consume a much greater share of their income than do other households. Taxing their total consumption would be a large burden, especially compared with the current income tax system, which channels money to many poor working households via the earned income tax credit. In addition, as the sales taxes that now exist in 45 states have shown, it is often hard to distinguish business-to-business sales from business-to-household sales. But if each sale from business to business is taxed, the eventual product is taxed several times, resulting in "cascading," a problem that encourages firms to integrate vertically and also creates capricious redistributions of tax-burdens across goods and people. Most important, though, a retail sales tax with a rate high enough—well over 30 percent—to replace existing federal taxes would be very hard to enforce. European countries that have tried to raise significant revenue by retail sales taxes have found that they become unadministrable at rates as low as 10–12 percent. They have therefore shifted to a different form of consumption tax, a value-added tax (VAT).

A sales tax and a VAT differ in the point at which they are exacted: a sales tax, on the final sale price; a VAT, at each stage of production. Under a VAT, each business pays a tax on the difference between gross revenues from all sales (including business-to-business sales) and the cost of materials, including capital goods. Thus it pays taxes on wages, interest, and profits, the sum of which represents the value added by the firm in providing goods and services.

The VAT avoids cascading because sales between businesses wash out. The baker who sells bread to the grocer pays VAT on the sale, but the grocer deducts the purchase in calculating his VAT. The VAT is also easier to enforce. One reason is that the seller, in trying to decide whether to report a transaction to the tax authorities, knows that the buyer will file the transaction with the tax authorities to claim the deduction for funds spent.

Like the sales tax, however, the VAT is regressive. Governments can address that problem by exempting from taxation, say, the first $20,000 of consumption by sending each family a check for $5,000 (assuming a 25 percent tax rate). But financing such transfers requires higher tax rates. Targeting the transfers to the poor would mean that rates would not have to be raised as much, but it would require all households to file information on income, thus sacrificing some of the simplicity gain.

The flat tax is a VAT, with two adjustments that help address the regressivity problem. First, businesses deduct wages and pensions, along with materials costs and capital investments. Second, the wages and pensions that businesses deduct are taxed at the individual (or household) level above a specified exemption. Dividing the VAT into two parts, one for businesses and one for households, makes possible the family exemptions that can ease the burden of the consumption tax for lower-income households.

HOW DOES THE FLAT TAX DIFFER FROM THE CURRENT SYSTEM?

Today's federal "income" tax is actually a hybrid between an income and a consumption tax. A pure income tax would tax all labor earnings and capital income, whether realized in cash, in kind, or accrued. But the current system does not tax certain forms of income, such as employer-provided health insurance or accrued gains on unsold assets. And it taxes some income more than once: in the case of corporate earnings, once at the corporate level and again at the individual level when distributed as dividends. It also taxes some items not properly considered income, such as the inflationary components of interest payments and realized capital gains. The flat tax would not tax capital income—such as interest, dividends, and capital gains—at the household level, or financial flows at any level. On the other hand, most saving—in pensions, IRAs, and so forth—is already taxed as it would be under a consumption tax.

Unlike the flat tax, the current income tax also permits dozens of allowances, credits, exclusions, and deductions. Taken together these "loopholes" reduced personal tax collections by some $1.3 trillion in 1993, about 50 percent of the actual tax base. Eliminating them all would make it possible to reduce tax rates across the board, or set rates as low as 13.5 percent.

The income tax is graduated: its six rates—0, 15, 28, 31, 36, and 39.6 percent—rise with taxable income. Multiple tax rates increase progressivity, but raise compliance and administrative costs and the importance of the deductions. A deduction that matters little when the tax rate is 10 percent is of much more consequence when the rate is 40 percent.

But the biggest differences between the existing system and the flat tax arise not because of large inherent differences in the underlying tax base. In fact, if the flat tax allowed firms to deduct investment expenditures over time, in accordance with the economic depreciation of their assets, instead of allowing them to deduct all investment expenses the year they are made, the flat tax would then be a flat income tax.

Rather, the key point is that the differences arise because, in response to a variety of political pressures, the existing tax system has strayed from a pure income tax structure. Indeed, perhaps the crucial question about the flat tax is how it would respond to those same pressures if it were to move from idea to reality.

The Armey-Shelby flat tax proposal features a $31,400 exemption for a family of four and a 20 percent tax rate. After two years the exemption would rise to $33,300 and the rate would fall to 17 percent. (The low tax rate is possible because the proposal is not "revenue neutral"; that is, it combines tax reform with a tax cut.)

But in recent years, different variants of the flat tax have begun to take on some features of today's income tax. Sen. Arlen Spector's (R-PA) proposal would reinstate the mortgage and charity deductions. So would Pat Buchanan's, which would also tax at least some capital income at the household level. The Kemp Commission favored deductions for payroll taxes and for mortgage interest and charity. Robert Dole voiced a wish to protect deductions for mortgages, charity, and state and local taxes.

These cracks in the flat tax armor, appearing long before serious legislative action takes place, suggest that the pressures that led to an impure income tax are likely to affect the flat tax as well.

POLITICAL AND ECONOMIC DILEMMAS TAX REFORM

Richard Armey, like some other advocates of the flat tax, candidly links his proposal to big tax cuts (although he does not specify how he would cut government spending to make up for the lost revenue). Because it is misleading to compare a plan that simultaneously reforms the tax structure and cuts taxes with the existing system, I will lay out the issues raised by the flat tax without the confounding effects of tax reduction.

Tax reform that collects the same amount of revenue in a new way will necessarily redistribute tax burdens among taxpayers. Those who stand to lose often try to prevent reform or to secure "transition relief" to avoid or delay the full brunt of the new law. The flat tax embodies this problem in stark form, because it proposes a single rate on businesses and on household money wages above a threshold, with no deductions and no transition relief.

The biggest transition problem for the flat tax involves business. Under the current system, businesses may deduct depreciation, the loss of value of capital assets over their useful lives, in computing taxable business income. Under the flat tax, businesses can deduct the full value of the asset the year it is purchased. The practical problem is what to do about assets that have not been fully depreciated when the new tax takes effect.

The pure flat tax would allow no deductions for depreciation on existing assets. But companies that lose their existing depreciation deductions will claim unfair treatment. And the stakes are high. In 1993, corporations claimed $363 billion in depreciation deductions, unincorporated businesses about one-third that.

Similarly, under the current system many businesses have net operating losses that they can carry forward as offsets against future profits. And businesses' interest payments are deductible because they are a cost of earning income. The flat tax would disallow both the carryforwards and the deduction for interest payments. Firms that depend on those provisions will press for transition relief under the flat tax.

Flat tax advocates have already acknowledged the need for transition relief. The Kemp Commission, for example, recommended that policymakers "take care to protect the existing savings, investment, and other assets" during a transition to a new tax system. But these political concessions carry a big price tag. Transition relief will reduce the size of the tax base and therefore require higher tax rates on the rest of the base. Policymakers will have to choose: the more transitional relief they provide, the less efficient the new tax system.

WHAT ABOUT THE EXISTING DEDUCTIONS?

Many prominent features of the income tax have long been a part of American economic life. The original (1913) income tax allowed deductions for mortgage interest and for state and local income and property taxes. Deductions for charity and employer-financed health insurance followed by 1918.

A pure flat tax would scrap these longstanding provisions. Without question, doing so would hurt the affected sectors of the economy. That, after all, is one of the points of tax reform: using the tax code to subsidize these sectors has channeled too many of society's resources to them. Removing the subsidy would make for a more efficient overall allocation of resources across sectors. But the affected groups are not likely to see things that way.

Under current tax law, for example, owner-occupied housing enjoys big advantages over other investments.

Homeowners may deduct mortgage interest and property taxes without being required to report the imputed rental income they receive as owners. These deductions increase demand for owner-occupied housing and boost the price of housing and land. By treating owner-occupied housing and other assets alike, the flat tax would reduce the relative price of housing. Estimates of how much range widely, but even declines as low as 5–10 percent would hurt homeowners and could affect lending institutions through increased defaults.

Confronted with these realities, is Congress likely to end the tax advantages of owner-occupied housing? Perhaps not. But retaining the mortgage interest deduction means that tax rates would have to be higher to replace revenue lost from the deduction.

The same story would unfold with each of the other long-standing deductions. Under the flat tax, health insurance would no longer be deductible by businesses and would become taxable at the flat tax rate. Jonathan Gruber and James Poterba calculate that the change would boost the price of health insurance by an average of 21 percent and reduce the number of people who are insured by between 5.5 million and 14.3 million people. Pressure to keep the deduction would be strong. But if Congress were to retain it, the flat tax base would shrink, and rates would have to rise to maintain revenues.

Likewise, terminating the charitable contributions deduction would reduce charitable giving—and at a time when cuts in government spending are being justified on the grounds that private philanthropy should pick up the slack. But retaining the deduction means a higher tax rate to maintain revenues.

FLAT TAX TRADE-OFFS: HOW MUCH?

In short, the flat tax is unlikely to be adopted in its pure form. What are the budget implications of various policy changes to the pure flat tax structure?

By my calculations, the Armey-Shelby plan with a 17 percent rate would have raised $138 billion less in 1996 than the current system. Even a 20 percent rate, which Jack Kemp referred to as the maximum acceptable flat tax rate in press conferences after the Kemp Commission report was released, would result in a shortfall of $29 billion. Allowing businesses to grandfather existing depreciation deductions—one form of transition relief—would raise the required rate to 23.1 percent. Allowing deductions for mortgage interest payments, as well as transition relief, would raise the required rate to 24.4 percent. If the deduction for employer-provided health insurance were also retained, the rate would rise to 26.5 percent. Adding in deductions for charitable contributions, individual deductions of state and local income and property tax payments, and the earned income tax credit would raise the rate to 29 percent. With all these adjustments, a tax rate of 20 percent would generate a revenue loss of well over $200 billion. Even with a flat tax rate of 25 percent, the revenue loss would be just over $100 billion.

Finally, retaining current payroll tax deductions for businesses would raise the required rate to 32 percent. The revenue shortfall, at a 20 percent tax rate, would be a whopping $280 billion a year. Even at a 25 percent tax rate, the revenue shortfall would be about $163 billion.

Politicians might find it hard to support a flat tax with these rates, since more than three-quarters of taxpayers now face a marginal tax rate of 15 percent or less, and less than 4 percent pay more than 28 percent on the margin. On the other hand, capping the rate at 20 percent or 25 percent would generate large losses in tax revenues that might also be hard to support.

One thing is clear. The flat tax is considered a simple tax with a relatively low rate in large part because it eliminates, on paper, deductions and exclusions that no Congress has dared touch.

THE FLAT TAX AND ECONOMIC GROWTH

Retaining existing deductions and providing transition relief will also eat into the economic growth that flat tax advocates claim the tax will spur.

The most complete economic model that generates realistic estimates of the impact of the flat tax on growth, developed by Alan Auerbach of the University of California, Laurence Kotlikoff of Boston University, and several other economists, finds that moving from the current system to a pure, flat rate, consumption tax, with no exemptions, no deductions, and no transition relief or other adjustments, would raise output, relative to what it would have been under the income tax, by 6.9 percent after the first 2 years, 9 percent after 9 years, and almost 11 percent in the long run. These are remarkably large gains, but they vanish as the tax plan becomes more realistic.

For example, if the personal exemption is set at $9,000, somewhat less than the $11,000 personal exemption in the Armey-Shelby plan, and transition relief is provided for existing depreciation deductions, the economy would grow by only 0.6 percent over 2 years, 1.8 percent after 10 years, and 3.6 percent in the long run. Adding exemptions for children (which the Armey plan now provides) would drive these estimates to zero. Adding transition relief for interest deductions and retaining the earned income credit and deductions for mortgages, health insurance, taxes paid, and charity would reduce growth further. Thus, implementing realistic versions of the flat tax could even slow economic growth.

TAX REFORM IN THE REAL WORLD

Good tax reform requires discipline. It is not hard to look at the U.S. tax code and see the need for a simpler, cleaner tax. But it is hard to look at the 1997 Taxpayer Relief Act, passed by Congress and signed by the president, and believe that the political system has the discipline to pass broad-based fundamental reform. After all, there is nothing—other than political forces and views of social equity—stopping our political leaders right now, or in any other year, from passing legislation that would broaden the tax base, close loopholes, and reduce tax rates. Those political forces and views of social equity will not vanish when the flat tax is passed. As one congressman noted, "You can't repeal politics."

The flat tax is a simple and thoughtful response to many of the problems in today's tax system. But tax reform is not a free lunch: we can't get everything we might want.

There are two ways out of this quandary. One would start with the flat tax proposals and make them less pure. For example, holding personal exemptions at about their current level would generate added revenue. And coupling the lower exemption levels with a two-tier tax rate system (similar to the 15 percent and 28 percent brackets that now apply to the vast majority of taxpayers) would raise revenue, enhance progressivity, and maintain many benefits of the flat tax.

The less radical alternative would be to start with the existing income tax system and simplify, streamlining the tax treatment of capital income, reducing the use of the tax code to run social policy, and reducing and flattening the rates. That would be an extension of the principles developed in the Tax Reform Act of 1986. Either alternative would place the resulting system somewhere between the current tax system and the flat tax on simplicity, efficiency, and equity—the three primary issues under debate.

The flat tax is an important advance in tax policy thinking and represents a thoughtful approach to several problems in the tax code and the economy. But removing the entire body of income tax law and starting over with a whole new system is a monumental task. We should approach the issue with our eyes open concerning the likely benefits, costs, and practical issues that would arise in adopting a flat tax.

Issue 15
Regulatory Policy

INTRODUCTION

Bill Gates is chairman of the Microsoft Corporation. A college dropout who, at forty-three, is hardly three years older than this PhD'd author, Mr. Gates recently had a net worth of 100 billion dollars. Thanks to his 920 million shares of Microsoft stock (which, it must be granted, do have their bad days on the market), Mr. Gates is the richest human alive. If Bill Gates were a country, he would rank somewhere between the fortieth and thirty-fifth largest economy in the world—larger than the Phillippines, but smaller than Malaysia.

Just fifteen years ago, Microsoft and Bill Gates' wealth did not exist, and Gates himself was (and perhaps still is) just another nerd with a bad haircut. The sheer eruption of Gates' wealth—so shocking yet somehow so American in its magnitude and abruptness—personifies the explosive possibilities of the computer revolution. Yet, even as this revolution transforms the ways Americans make their living, it also challenges a traditional rationale for government economic regulation. Much as Americans love winners, and celebrate Bill Gates as a folk hero, they also harbor a profound distrust of concentrated economic power. It was only with great resistance that American society in the nineteenth century came to accept the corporation—a legal but deathless person—just as Americans both admire and reviled John D. Rockefeller, Bill Gates' progenitor. The political fight against large corporations (the "Trusts") produced the Sherman and Clayton Anti-Trust acts of 1890 and 1914; anti-trust led, among other things, to the breakup of Rockefeller's Standard Oil monopoly.

In a similar way, Bill Gates' Microsoft is the target of an anti-trust suit filed by the Justice Department in 1990. While anti-trust law has evolved over the last century, the core animus against sheer bigness remains. Monopolies, it is held, are inherently bad. They raise prices and restrict consumer choices. However, as the following selections show, interpreting the Microsoft phenomenon is no simple task. With all its success, over what exactly does Microsoft wield a monopoly? Chairman Gates asserts that "we are demanding the legal right of every company to decide which features go into its own products." In contrast, John Dvorak contends that the ubiquity of Microsoft's Windows operating system (with which these introductions are written!) constitutes an "essential utility" that the government ought to regulate, if not own outright. At the very least, if there remains a case that bigness is indeed bad, then its effects in a high-technology economy where falling prices and rapid innovation are the norm force us to re-examine traditional arguments against corporate power.

As you read the articles, consider the following questions.

Discussion Questions

1. If Windows software keeps getting better and cheaper, then what's the big deal? How exactly is Microsoft alleged to have hurt the American consumer? Is Dvorak simply envious of what is a wildly-successful company?
2. How much of Microsoft's behavior appears to be just good, if ruthless, competition, as opposed to monopolistic behavior?
3. While Microsoft is a publicly-traded company, it is understandable that its fortunes and those of Bill Gates are interwined in the public mind. If Bill Gates were not so extraordinarily wealthy, would the case against Microsoft be any different? How much of Microsoft's troubles are a matter of law, versus mere public relations?
4. The case against Microsoft involves imaging what products would exist if Microsoft hadn't wielded its power. If the case against Microsoft is true, then what might this alternative future have looked like?

For more on this topic, visit the following websites:

`http://www.law.cornell.edu/topics/antitrust.html`
Cornell University's Legal Information Institute

`http://www.usdoj.gov/atr/index.html`
U.S. Department of Justice's Antitrust Division

`http://www.essential.org/antitrust/microsoft`
Ralph Nader's Essential Information

`http://www.microsoft.com/presspass`
Microsoft's Presspass

Compete, Don't Delete

BILL GATES

As a long-time admirer of *The Economist*'s stance on business and economics, I have been surprised by your recent coverage of Microsoft, and welcome this chance to set out some of the facts about our disagreement with the Justice Department.

In less than two decades, America's software industry—indeed, the entire PC industry—has become the most vibrant, innovative and competitive industry in the world. Without government regulators restricting or managing its creativity, it has grown to generate one-quarter of America's real economic growth and 8% of its national output. One element of this success is the availability of a software platform that runs on all PCs, with a common interface and numerous applications. Microsoft's Windows operating system is the most popular software platform today precisely because of its openness to developers.

Consumers, too, tell us they value our open software standard and the hugely beneficial effect it has had on the cost of computing, which has fallen by a factor of 10m since the microprocessor was invented in the early 1970s. They tell us they appreciate the fact that, thanks to the common Windows interface, they can choose from thousands of makes and models of PC, yet will always know how to use the one they opt for. And thanks to the common Windows programming environment, consumers know that virtually any PC from any manufacturer will run literally thousands of applications.

Consumers also tell us they want PC operating systems to be steadily improved with new features and functions—not an ever-increasing tangle of separate products, each with its own installation requirements, special commands and price tag.

Our development and widespread licensing of Windows have also contributed significantly to the astonishing growth of the software industry around the world. From a standing start a decade ago, the ranks of independent developers designing software for Windows have swelled to 2.2m in America, and 5m worldwide. Since 1995 alone, the PC-software industry has created 162,000 new jobs in Western Europe, and now contributes more than $15 billion a year in tax revenue for European governments.

William Gates is the CEO of Microsoft Corporation.
Reprinted by permission. *The Economist*; June 13, 1998. Vol. 347, Issue 8072, p. 19.

FOUNDED ON OPEN STANDARDS

In the American computer-services industry, more than 300,000 people work in jobs related to Microsoft software, making up an industry with $40 billion in annual revenues. There are more than twice as many opportunities for Windows-based computer-services careers in America than there are for jobs focused on the combined proprietary technologies of IBM, Novell, Oracle and Unix. Open standards are what create jobs—not regulation or the old, vertically integrated computer—industry model our competitors seek to resurrect. Open standards are the reason why PC sales have soared. . . .

The current popularity of Windows does not mean that its market position is unassailable. The potential financial reward for building the "next Windows" is so great that there will never be a shortage of new technologies seeking to challenge it. Powerful competitors such as IBM, Sun Microsystems and Oracle are spending hundreds of millions of dollars annually to develop new software aimed squarely at replacing Windows. That is one reason why we price Windows so low. If we increased prices, failed to innovate, or stopped incorporating the features consumers want (such as support for the Internet), we would rapidly lose market share.

It is often argued that Microsoft should be deemed a regulated "essential facility." This too is weak. Essential-facility law primarily applies to a physical asset or facility (such as a bridge) that a company (or companies) denies to competitors, and which cannot be duplicated by those rivals. By contrast, Windows is a piece of intellectual property whose "facilities" are totally open to partners and competitors alike. Windows' programming interfaces are published free of charge, so millions of independent software developers can make use of its built-in facilities (e.g., the user interface) in the applications they design. Those same interfaces are also provided freely to manufacturers of computer peripherals, who take similar advantage of them. And we license Windows cheaply to any PC maker that wants to use it, a strategy which has allowed computer makers such as Compaq and Dell to focus on improving their products.

Windows became a de facto standard because from the outset we adopted a low-price, high-volume business model. Your assertion that "the cost of a retail upgrade of Windows has more than doubled since 1990" is misleading: prior to Windows 95, PC buyers needed both DOS and Windows if they wanted a graphical user interface. The cost of upgrading that DOS/Windows operating system in 1990 was, at the street prices most consumers pay, much the same as today's $89 pre-order street price of a Windows 98 upgrade. This relatively stable pricing during the 1990s is in line with rival operating systems, and a fraction of the cost of Unix-based operating systems such as Sun's Solaris.

Moreover, consumers clearly think the price/value proposition of a Windows upgrade is excellent. Millions have bought upgrades, even though their PCs would continue to operate perfectly with their original operating system.

IT JUST GETS BETTER

While its price has remained relatively stable, the number of features in Windows—and its benefits to consumers and software developers—has increased dramatically, a result of our enormous investment in R&D. Windows 98 includes a new Web-like user interface, a more efficient file system, faster launching of applications, multiple-monitor support, faster 3D graphics, easier connection to peripherals (such as digital cameras) and more—all for the same low price as Windows 95. And as our Web-browsing technology was integrated into Windows 95 nearly three years ago, the launch of Windows 98 has no bearing on our competitiveness with Netscape's Navigator browser—except that Windows 98 and its integrated Web-browsing features are better than ever, and consumers are likely to respond positively to that. (Netscape's browser runs even better on Windows 98 than on Windows 95, too.)

On any measure Windows remains a bargain. For consumers paying street prices for an upgrade, the cost of using Windows 98 over three years (a conservative lifespan) will be a mere eight cents a day-cheaper than *The Economist*'s current special offer here in America. . . . For consumers who get Windows with a new PC, the cost is less than five cents a day. If you purchased separate software products to upgrade, say, Windows 3.0 to get the functionality provided by Windows 98, it would cost at least $400.

Ironically, the government's lawsuit on behalf of Netscape is attacking one of the fundamental principles that has fuelled the rapid improvement in PCs—that every company should be free to innovate and continuously improve its products on behalf of consumers, adding new features and functionality. The regulators' case centres on the claim that we integrated our Internet Explorer browsing technology into Windows in an attempt, in your words, "illegally to counter Netscape's Navigator browser." The central flaw in this allegation is that there are absolutely no laws against innovating. In fact, the law says that every company— from the smallest start-up to the largest multinational—should always work to improve its products for consumers.

Contrary to the government's central accusation, Microsoft planned the integration of Internet technology into Windows well before Netscape was even formed, and long before it shipped its first browser in

October 1994. Many Microsoft emails and memos from 1993 and early 1994 reflect this strategy.

For example, on December 7th 1993, Steve Ballmer, Microsoft's executive vice president for sales and support, sent email suggesting that it "could really help popularise" the forthcoming Windows 95 if the operating system could be positioned as "the greatest front-end to the Internet." In an email dated December 16th 1993, a Microsoft technologist noted that "Internet connectivity . . . should be an integral part of the operating system," adding that "customers will love us for providing these facilities." And in speeches made in early 1994—which were reported in the press—I too talked extensively about our plans to integrate Internet access into Windows 95.

FREE TO CHOOSE

The fact that our browser was integrated into Windows 95 from the outset did not in any way prevent consumers from choosing another browser. Windows users hardly flocked to use the early versions of Internet Explorer, and its first reviews were rather embarrassing. In August 1995 *Time* called version 1.0 "somewhat clunky," while the *Wall Street Journal*'s verdict on version 2.0 in January 1996 was that "the clear victor today is Netscape Navigator." But in the past nine months, our browsing technology has won 19 out of 20 head-to-head reviews against Netscape's, which is why we have seen more and more consumers using it. *Fortune*, for example, wrote that version 4.0 of Internet Explorer "beats Navigator hands down." I am very proud of the work our development teams have done to make it easy for Windows users to access the Internet—and we have many more improvements in the pipeline.

The regulators are trying to tell the court that Windows 98 is not one product, but two—an operating system and a separate Web browser—and that the former would work fine without the latter. This just isn't true. Windows 98 was designed from the ground up as a single product that performs a variety of functions, including Web browsing. If the software that provides Web-browsing functionality were removed from Windows 98, the operating system would fail to function in many ways.

As you observe, the government claims that Microsoft "tried to push Netscape into colluding with it" to carve up the browser market illegally during a meeting with Netscape in May 1995. The facts do not support this claim. The meeting the government seems to be referring to actually took place in June 1995, not May, and its purpose was to discuss various technologies Microsoft proposed sharing with Netscape, so that Netscape's browser could take advantage of the cool new features we were developing for Windows 95. Email sent by Marc Andreessen, one of

Netscape's founders, makes this clear, as do an agenda printed on Netscape stationery and handwritten notes taken by one of the people attending the meeting.

Shortly after the meeting, Mr Andreessen sent email to a Microsoft attendee enthusing, "Good to see you again today—we should talk more often," an odd sentiment given his supposed indignation over the meeting. And on August 24th 1995 Netscape was a featured applications developer at the Windows 95 launch event at the Microsoft campus—again, hardly consistent with the government's claim that Microsoft threatened to withhold information about Windows 95 from Netscape.

TRIAL BY SNIPPET

When you consider that Microsoft has co-operated fully with the government's investigation, and provided over a million pages of internal documents and emails, it is not surprising that the government has been able to find a handful of statements—many by relatively junior staffers—that can be taken out of context to paint a misleading picture. Once all the facts are on the table, however, we believe these misleading snippets, and the government's entire case, will be seen in a very different light.

You also refer to Microsoft's "control over the PC desktop," and suggest that the regulators' demand that we give it up is reasonable. We have made incredible investments in the Windows user interface, and when consumers buy a Windows PC this is what they expect to see. Eliminating the interface would be a step back to the old computer industry, where each machine had a unique interface and was incompatible with other computers.

PC makers already have many ways to customise the screen. They can use the open space on the Windows desktop—about 85% of the screen—to display their own branded content. They can include our competitors' software and display their icons prominently. And they can, and do, install Netscape's browser and display it "on equal terms" on the desktop—they can even make it the default browser before the PC leaves the factory. PC makers can also create their own channel on the Channel Bar, and partner with content providers to create numerous sub-channels. And consumers, with a few clicks of a mouse, can change all of the above. It is they, not Microsoft, who ultimately control the PC desktop.

Even though Netscape's browser is at most a few mouse-clicks away, the Justice Department also wants, as you note, "to make non-Microsoft browsers more available to consumers" by forcing Microsoft to include Netscape's Navigator—which the Justice Department positions as a competitor to Windows—in Windows. We have invested hundreds of millions of dollars developing and promoting Windows. We should not be forced to link Windows to software made by a competitor, whose quality we could not vouch for. It is also worth asking why Netscape, whose browser has the highest market share, should get special treatment. After all, hundreds of other software vendors offer products that compete with parts of Windows.

This goes to the heart of Microsoft's disagreement with the Justice Department: we are defending the legal right of every company to decide which features go into its own products.

The integration of innovative new ideas and products has been the path taken by almost every industry, from the auto business (which for a century has integrated new features that were once deemed "accessories") to consumer electronics (where audio, TV and movie technology are merging into all-in-one home-theatre systems). All modern computer operating systems include integrated Web browsing. And Netscape, as part of its strategy to make its browser an alternative operating system, is integrating numerous new features that are also offered separately from other software companies.

America's antitrust laws do not provide any basis for government regulators to attempt to design software products. Only last month, in a ruling granting Microsoft's motion for a stay of the preliminary injunction issued last December insofar as it applied to Windows 98, the Appeals Court stated that "the United States presented no evidence suggesting that Windows 98 was not an 'integrated product,'" as defined by the consent decree, and that, under these circumstances, any interpretation of the consent decree that would bar the distribution of Windows 98 would "put judges and juries in the unwelcome position of designing computers."

WHAT THE PEOPLE WANT

In the end, it all comes back to consumers. It is they who have benefited most from the open standards that have marked the personal-computer age. And it is they who would be harmed most if the computer industry were forced to return to the high-cost, fragmented standards that marked the age of the mainframe. Consumers tell us they want more innovation and real choice—not less innovation and choice restricted by regulators. It is free and fierce competition in the computer industry that has created innovation and choice—and consumers will continue to benefit only as long as this vibrant industry remains unfettered. It is consumers who have convinced us we are doing the right thing.

Nationalize Microsoft

JOHN C. DVORAK

Microsoft has been out of control for so long, monopolizing an entire industry and stifling competition in the name of a free market, that the best thing to do may be to let the government take over the company. The firm would never get out of court if every greedy deal in its history were admissible as evidence in the current Dept. of Justice case. Microsoft and its incredibly wealthy CEO, Bill Gates, are nevertheless among the most admired institutions in the world. Gates is a good businessman, but could better prove his worth to society in another industry. A case can be made that Windows is now an "essential utility," like gas, electricity and water, that the government should control. NASA shows that the government can design good software, despite Microsoft's complaints. An "eminent domain" confiscation might work best.

Before you accuse me of being a socialist, let me tell you I was the biggest Republican supporter of deregulation in my town. I believe in the free market and all that, but being a capitalist doesn't mean being an anarchist. There's a reason we have a government, and it's not just to run an army or spy on enemies.

It's also to keep the conniving public in line and to prevent businesses from running roughshod over everything in their paths.

I make this disclaimer to minimize letters from people who think it would be OK if Microsoft actually took over all industry worldwide and ran everything and everyone. There are too many people out there who worship lockstep at the dubious altar of no-holds-barred competition.

Microsoft has gone too long as a mad dog on the loose. Thus, the only fair thing to do is to nationalize Microsoft and let the government run it. This seems to be the only way to stop these guys from continuing their nasty habits of leveraging their monopoly.

What's going to happen to Microsoft? Most observers and even company insiders have finally realized that the government is never going to stop pursuing Microsoft until it changes its way of doing business. People who still do business with Microsoft say that it has been playing more hardball during the trial than ever before. I assume this is a reaction to the possibility of losing. Instead of being magnanimous, the company figures it should get what it can while it can and clear out of town with sacks of gold.

Reprinted by permission. *PC Magazine*, Feb. 9, 1999. p. 87.

If every tale of Microsoft's greedy behavior were told, the company would never get out of court. Have Microsoft explain, for example, how Digital Research's GEM product was derailed years ago. This early GUI product preceded Windows and had a lot of interesting characteristics. But every deal to sell GEM was queered by Microsoft in backroom deals. These early stories of Microsoft's conduct will not be heard in court, though.

Yet Microsoft is one of the most admired companies in the world, and Bill Gates is seen as a fantastic genius for accumulating an ungodly amount of money. Criticize his wealth and you're branded jealous. Within a 15-year period, Gates has accumulated more wealth than the British monarchy, which has been robbing the world and its own people since the twelfth century. And this makes sense somehow? What's wrong with you people? I don't care how great a businessman Bill Gates is, this doesn't sound right to me!

I don't begrudge Bill his money. He hasn't flipped out yet or grown long fingernails or started wearing a cloak. But there is something wrong with this picture. If Gates is such a great businessman, let's see what he can do in some other industry by starting over. Nationalize Microsoft.

There's good reason to argue that Windows has become an "essential utility" the government should control. Gas and electric companies were originally private and regulated and essentially nationalized for the good of the country. Though Microsoft likes to whine about how bad government-designed software would be, the government did quite well designing software for the space program. And Microsoft can't approach the Social Security Administration for handling volume. Besides, if you haven't noticed, Windows crashes a lot.

Because Microsoft may have gotten where it is by wrongful methods, shouldn't it simply be taken over? I wouldn't go so far as confiscating the company like a drug dealer's gaudy Mercedes, but I think something along the lines of an eminent domain confiscation would be appropriate—with the government paying fair market value for the company's assets.

The typical outcome of an antitrust case is usually some sort of consent decree with continued oversight by a court. This will not work with Microsoft, which will forever be dragged into court saying it's complying while it continues anticompetitive practices. Regulating the software industry as a whole or Microsoft specifically would be impractical. Simply using eminent domain laws to nationalize the company is the only solution and the only way to reinvigorate innovation and competition. It will level the playing field and stabilize Windows, which has yet to be debugged.

In a culture where wealth is idolized like a god and where the rich can do no wrong (and if they do, buy their way out), this move is too

gutsy and contrarian for our ethically challenged government and citizenry. But we can always hope.

If Gates is such a great businessman, let's see what he can do in
some other industry by starting over.

Issue 16
The Environment

INTRODUCTION

Everybody talks about the weather, but nobody knows quite what to do about it. This state of affairs is particularly true in the case of environmental policy-making. Two features of the relationship between politics and nature govern the making of such policy. First, many man-made changes in nature occur over such a long span of time that it is difficult either to take credit or to assign responsibility for policy actions whose consequences may emerge long after policy-makers leave office. Second, environmental policy-making is further hampered by the lack of any "natural" constituency for nature. That is to say, trees don't vote. As a result, it is difficult to incorporate some sense of nature's interests into environmental policy-making in a way that limits conflict over policy goals.

Science can investigate the effects of man-made pollution on the Earth's atmospheric temperature. If the direst predictions prove true, then progressive global warming could eventually melt the polar ice caps, resulting in a catastrophic rise in sea levels. Warming would also alter climate patterns so as fundamentally to rearrange existing patterns of world food production. Yet answers to questions such as what causes climate changes or whether certain changes are even likely, remain so conjectural that, in the absence of any definitive agreement among scientists, policy responses to the climate question will correlate with other political beliefs.

The perspectives offered in the articles that follow illustrate this correlation very well. For example, environmentalists predisposed to condemn humanity's exploitation of nature will view the accumulation of greenhouse gases, especially the carbon dioxide building up from the use of fossil fuels, as yet another indignity inflicted by man on Mother Earth out of profit-seeking greed. This is the view of the American Geophysical Union. In contrast, Patrick Michaels, of the free-market Cato Institute, accepts the exploitation of nature as the price of economic progress. According to Michaels, the problem of greenhouse gases is a false issue raised by "eco-alarmists." Hysteria about greenhouse gases merely justifies further government regulation of private property—and promotes the political aspirations of Al Gore.

At some level, pollution is a problem, since the despoiling of nature does impose costs on others. Even in a purely libertarian political order, there would be a place for environmental regulation, if only to correct for the inability of the market entirely to apportion the costs and benefits of pollution. Yet markets, like politics, work best in the short term. They discount the future in a way that unfairly bequeaths the burden of pollution to unborn (and unrepresented) generations. Within the limits of political and economic institutions, environmental policy based on good science seeks to reintroduce some sense of the long term and to represent, however imperfectly, the interests of the unborn and even the nonhuman. As Dr. Seuss's Lorax insists, someone must speak for the trees.

As you read the articles, consider the following questions.

Discussion Questions

1. If the government regulation is an inherently bad thing, as Patrick Michaels implies, then how should society go about addressing the costs of pollution?
2. The American government frequently speaks with more than one voice. How does our government sometimes aggravate and even create pollution problems through its other policies?
3. Not only do animals not vote, but they aren't even human. As a matter of public policy, should we care about animals, let alone nature itself, as creatures with moral value in and of themselves?
4. Balancing interests within the present generation involves spreading costs to match the benefits of practices like polluting. Since the future generations aren't here yet, how do we begin to go about balancing their interests against ours?

    For more on this topic, visit the following websites:

    `http://www.epa.gov/globalwarming`
    The U.S Environmental Protection Agency's Global Warming Site

    `http://www.gcrio.org/gwcc/toc.html`
    The U.S. Global Change Research Information Office

    `http://www.sierraclub.org/global-warming`
    The Sierra Club

    `http://www.cato.org/pubs/regulation`
    The Cato Review of Business and Government

Climate Change and Greenhouse Gases

COUNCIL OF THE AMERICAN GEOPHYSICAL UNION, DECEMBER 1998

Atmospheric concentrations of carbon dioxide and other greenhouse gases have substantially increased as a consequence of fossil fuel combustion and other human activities. These elevated concentrations of greenhouse gases are predicted to persist in the atmosphere for times ranging to thousands of years. Increasing concentrations of carbon dioxide and other greenhouse gases affect the Earth-atmosphere energy balance, enhancing the natural greenhouse effect and thereby exerting a warming influence at the Earth's surface.

Although greenhouse gas concentrations and their climatic influences are projected to increase, the detailed response of the system is uncertain. Principal sources of this uncertainty are the climate system's inherent complexity and natural variability. The increase in global mean surface temperatures over the past 150 years appears to be unusual in the context of the last few centuries, but it is not clearly outside the range of climate variability of the last few thousand years. The geologic record of the more distant past provides evidence of larger climate variations associated with changes in atmospheric carbon dioxide. These changes appear to be consistent with present understanding of the radiative properties of carbon dioxide and of the influence of climate on the carbon cycle. There is no known geologic precedent for the transfer of carbon from the Earth's crust to atmospheric carbon dioxide, in quantities comparable to the burning of fossil fuels, without simultaneous changes in other parts of the carbon cycle and climate system. This close coupling between atmospheric carbon dioxide and climate suggests that a change in one would in all likelihood be accompanied by a change in the other.

Present understanding of the Earth climate system provides a compelling basis for legitimate public concern over future global- and regional-scale changes resulting from increased concentrations of greenhouse gases. These changes are predicted to include increases in global mean surface temperatures, increases in global mean rates of precipitation and evaporation, rising sea levels, and changes in the biosphere. Understanding of the fundamental processes responsible for global climate change has greatly improved over the past decade, and predictive capabilities are

Reprinted by permission of the Council of the American Geophysical Union.

advancing. However, there are significant scientific uncertainties, for example, in predictions of local effects of climate change, occurrence of extreme weather events, effects of aerosols, changes in clouds, shifts in the intensity and distribution of precipitation, and changes in oceanic circulation. In view of the complexity of the Earth climate system, uncertainty in its description and in the prediction of changes will never be completely eliminated. Because of these uncertainties, there is much public debate over the extent to which increased concentrations of greenhouse gases have caused or will cause climate change, and over potential actions to limit and/or respond to climate change. It is important that public debate take into account the extent of scientific knowledge and the uncertainties. Science cannot be the sole source of guidance on how society should respond to climate issues. Nonetheless, scientific understanding based on peer-reviewed research must be central to informed decision-making. AGU calls for an enhancement of research to improve the quantification of anthropogenic influences on climate. To this end, international programs of research are essential. AGU encourages scientists worldwide to participate in such programs and in scientific assessments and policy discussions.

The world may already be committed to some degree of human-caused climate change, and further buildup of greenhouse gas concentrations may be expected to cause further change. Some of these changes may be beneficial and others damaging for different parts of the world. However, the rapidity and uneven geographic distribution of these changes could be very disruptive. AGU recommends the development and evaluation of strategies such as emissions reduction, carbon sequestration, and adaptation to the impacts of climate change. AGU believes that the present level of scientific uncertainty does not justify inaction in the mitigation of human-induced climate change and/or the adaptation to it.

Scientific Research Blows the Cover of Hard-Gore Ecoalarmists

PATRICK J. MICHAELS

Given his very bad temper, folks have been wondering when Al Gore and his environmental soul mates at the White House were going to get nasty with people who don't share their view of global warming. Well, the time is now, and it looks like another scorched-earther.

Judging by Gore's heated rhetoric lately, he sees people who disagree with him as demonic beings who will be doing the scorching. *U.S. News & World Report* quotes him as saying, "I really can't think of a clearer demonstration of the contrast between Democratic policies and Republican policies than what happened under Scar compared to what happened under Simba."

For the few of you who have not seen Disney's *The Lion King*, Scar is the evil leader who takes over the pride. A terrible drought ensues, the women are enslaved and the Circle of Life (also the name of Elton John's catchy theme song) is destroyed. For Gore, those are Republican values. When the good Simba returns after a few years away (could this be analogous to Gore at Harvard?), the rains return and balance is restored. Democrats, you see, can change the climate.

Al's worldview enthusiastically is shared by Dirk Forrister, a rock-hard Gore man who heads the White House Office of Global Climate Change. Recently he told a Washington meeting of the prestigious Energy Institute that critics who disagree with the official view of global warming are "clowns."

Half an hour later, Forrister blew up when confronted with the most recent scientific findings, which provide compelling and conclusive evidence that folks who have beaten the apocalyptic global-warming drum for the last decade have been just plain wrong.

In 1990, the U.N. Intergovernmental Panel on Climate Change, or IPCC, offered a best-estimate prediction of warming during the next century of 3.2 degrees Celsius. By 1995, thanks in part to incessant attacks by so-called skeptics, the warming estimate was lowered to 2 degrees Celsius. Three months ago Department of Commerce researcher Ed

    Patrick J. Michaels is senior fellow in environmental studies at the Cato Institute in Washington.
    Reprinted by permission. *Insight on the News*, Nov. 2, 1998. Vol. 14, No. 40, p. 30.

Dlugokenky published a paper in the scientific journal *Nature* demonstrating that atmospheric methane—an important man-made greenhouse gas—is likely to show very little change in the next century. That forces the warming estimate down to about 1.75 degrees Celsius. Forrister called this observation "frivolous."

At the same time, Norwegian researcher Gunnar Myhre discovered that the direct heating effect of carbon dioxide has been overestimated, something the skeptics had maintained had to be true because the planet has warmed so little. His work was published in *Geophysical Research Letters.* That drops the warming estimate to 1.5 degrees Celsius. Forrister also called this "frivolous."

A popular climate model from 10 years ago that served as much of the basis for the infamous U.N. Climate Treaty and the subsequent Kyoto Protocol (currently 0 for 95 in the Senate) said that, during the last decade, the globe should have warmed about 0.45 degrees Celsius. The observed temperature as measured at the surface, inflated by an urban (warming) bias, shows warming of just 0.11 degrees Celsius. Weather-balloon thermistors and barometers, two independent instruments, showed cooling, as do the satellites, even after correction for recently discovered orbital drift. Forrister shouted "frivolous!"

NASA scientist James Hansen recently has argued that the reason dramatic warming didn't show up as he had forecast was because the soil and vegetation are absorbing carbon dioxide at an increasing rate. That makes the planet greener, not browner (sorry, Carol!). Accounting for Hansen's work published in the *Proceedings of the National Academy of Sciences,* this lowers 21st-century warming to about 1.25 degree. Forrister called this frivolous as well.

Tom Wigley of the National Science Foundation has just published a paper in *Geophysical Research Letters* showing that if every nation met its commitments under the Kyoto Protocol, planetary cooling would be an undetectable 0.07 degrees Celsius by 2050, compared to what the temperature would be if we did nothing. My own research, recently published in *Climate Research,* shows that the largest warmings occur in the coldest winter-air masses rather than in the summer. "These all are frivolous arguments," Forrister said.

En coda, Forrister was asked if there would even be a Kyoto Protocol if the climate modelers had told us 10 years ago that it would only warm 1.0 to 1.5 degrees during the next century. After a long pause, he said (as best as I can recall), "I don't know. Maybe yes, maybe no."

Having thus opened the floodgates, Forrister was asked if the new findings might not make it appropriate for the Senate to pass a resolution forcing the president to withdraw the United States from the U.N. climate treaty, which allows such an option. "Frivolous!" he shouted.

"You just can't go making frivolous arguments like that!" Thus the new White House policy: Those who do not agree with their (now thoroughly discredited) view of global warming are evil and will scorch the Earth. Science is frivolous, to be dismissed quite casually when it turns out to be inconvenient. Stay tuned. Things can only get worse.

Issue 17
Social Policy: Welfare

INTRODUCTION

President Clinton's signing of the Personal Responsibility and Work Opportunity Reconciliation Act in 1996 marked a watershed for both the Democratic
Party and the nation as a whole. For the Democrats, Clinton's signature committed his party, however reluctantly, to an approach to welfare reform that
was essentially Republican in inspiration. For the nation at large, welfare reform has represented a turning away from a model of social assistance whose
roots lay in the Great Depression of nearly seventy years ago. The poor, Jesus
observed, are always with us. But our understanding of what makes people
poor and of how society ought to respond to poverty changes over time. In
broad terms, people can be poor for three reasons: bad luck, bad choices, and
bad societies. The meaning of bad luck—the death of a breadwinner—lies in
the consolations of philosophy. Organized charity under these circumstances
reflects, at its best, public compassion for the unfortunate. Bad choices highlight the fallibility or depravity of individuals. Here, the problem of poverty
arises from correctable behavior, and public compassion may be tinged with
the moral censure implied by the quid pro quo of charity in exchange for self-
improvement. Bad societies imply that the poor are with us because of defects
in the economy or of other features of the social and political life. In this last
instance, poverty represents not evidence of moral failure but of a lack of social justice. Poverty on these terms is not about luck or punishment. Rather, it
is about the order of things itself being wrong.

As a nation that takes individualism seriously, America has long resisted
the implications of the third possibility. Before the advent of the welfare state
in the 1930s, the poor were the responsibility of private charity and local government (with the disguised exception of Civil War pensions). The premise
was clear: Since poverty arose from an individual's bad luck or bad choices,

its amelioration lay in the tempered compassion of the individual's community. The Great Depression gave the lie to this premise, at a time when millions of people found themselves out of work through no fault of their own.
And short of accepting the malignancy of fate itself, the national public henceforth accepted that the problem of poverty was of a piece with regulating the
broader economy.

The Great Depression gave birth to a public commitment to social security
and welfare as "entitlements"—that is, as benefits that individuals would receive
automatically if and when they became old or poor. Yet our belief in individualism kept these commitments distinct. Social security—or old age "insurance"—was shrouded in the actuarial fiction that people earned support in their
old age through their earlier contributions. In contrast, welfare never enjoyed
the same middle-class legitimacy and support. Much as the 1960s saw a vast expansion in public resources devoted to the poor, welfare programs in America
could never shake off the taint of irresponsibility. Unlike social security, welfare
to its critics seemed either to reflect depravity or to encourage it.

The reform of 1996 revoked welfare's entitlement status and turned the nation back towards older understandings of poverty. Now, welfare recipients
enjoy benefits for a maximum of five years in exchange for a sustained effort to
find work. While the details of reform require the states to assume new responsibilities for the training, transportation, and child care of welfare recipients
seeking work, the weight of reform rests on the recipients themselves. This
weight has also altered the very meaning of modern welfare in America. No
longer an automatic and indefinite benefit, welfare has been recast as temporary
assistance that enables a recipient to return to the workforce—or else. For good
or for bad, the problem of poverty reverts to the luck and pluck of individuals.

So far, a booming economy has eased the transition of many former welfare recipients to the workforce. The drop in welfare rolls throughout the
country has been far larger than even reform enthusiasts expected. The causes
of this are as yet unclear. As much as William Miller may celebrate the efforts
of corporations to train and hire previously marginal employees, the overall
success of welfare reforms ultimately depends on the extent to which the
economy continues to generate sufficient entry-level jobs to give the poor real
alternatives to public assistance. As Miller recognizes, corporate successes in
recruiting and training former welfare recipients reflect the tight conditions of
a booming job market. It is not at all certain that the next economic downturn
might not simply create new masses of unemployed. Ruth Conniff sees a more
insidious agenda in welfare reform. In her eyes, reform has not been about
empowering the poor but about jettisoning public responsibility for them. The
poor will remain with us; they have simply become invisible. The rapid decline in welfare rolls simply means that many more poor have slipped through
the fraying strands of the social safety net. Indeed, Conniff argues, the un-
sightly rush by private companies to bid for the management of welfare services formerly administered by state governments practically guarantees that

this slippage will become a free fall. In a remarkable reversal, programs once meant to assist the poor will now benefit the rich. This remains welfare, but for a very different sort of clientele.

As you read the articles, consider the following questions.

Discussion Questions

1. Should citizens be entitled to welfare as a right?
2. If welfare means that the government gives people resources without asking for anything in return, then many other sorts of government transfers would seem to qualify as welfare—medicare, social security, corporate subsidies, etc. Why do we distinguish between welfare and these other things? Should we?
3. The traditional disapproval of welfare comes in two forms. On the one hand, its opponents argue that welfare is corrupting; on the other hand, they argue that welfare payments are liable to be abused. Can you imagine ways of answering these objections while still preserving welfare in its traditional (entitlement) form?
4. If, as some welfare-rights advocates fear, an economic downturn greatly increases the number of destitute people, should the nation reverse its recent welfare reforms?

> For more on this topic, visit the following websites:
>
> **http://www.acf.dhhs.gov**
> The U.S. Department and Human Services—Administration for Children and Families
>
> **http://www.welfarereform.org**
> The Welfare Reform Resource Project
>
> **http://www.nga.org**
> The National Governors' Association
>
> **http://www.urban.org**
> The Urban Institute

Suprise! Welfare Reform Is Working

WILLIAM H. MILLER

At least, once-leery companies find the new laws help them find workers. But will welfare-to-work success continue when the labor shortage ends?

When President Clinton signed the Personal Responsibility & Work Opportunity Reconciliation Act—a k a the welfare-reform bill—in a White House rose-garden ceremony in August 1996, it was a cause for celebration in political Washington. Enactment of the landmark law enabled the President to fulfill his ballyhooed campaign pledge to "end welfare as we know it." And it gave Republicans a substantive legislative achievement to tout in their bid to retain control of Congress in that fall's election.

But in American industry, the reaction was considerably more restrained. It was a collective shudder.

"Here the politicians go again," went the thinking of many executives. "They're winning political points for reforming welfare, but all they're doing is palming off the problem onto the shoulders of employers." Indeed, in its most notable feature, the new law for the first time clamped a work requirement upon welfare recipients. And where would the jobs come from? The private sector, of course.

Clinton even admitted as much. "If welfare reform is going to work," he declared later, "it will have to have the leadership of the private sector in turning welfare checks into paychecks." Nineteen months after the rose-garden ceremony, however, it turns out the private sector is doing exactly that. Although liberal critics accurately point out that welfare reform hasn't yet produced jobs for most of the hardest-to-hire welfare recipients, results of the new law so far have been a pleasant, unexpected surprise. Some 1.6 million Americans have left the welfare rolls since enactment of the legislation, lowering the caseload to fewer than 10 million (two-thirds of whom are children), estimates the Welfare to Work Partnership, a business-sponsored Washington group organized by the White House last spring to help companies find jobs for people on public assistance.

In some states, caseloads have dropped spectacularly. In Wisconsin, a state whose welfare-to-work initiative is considered a model, they're down 54%; in Wyoming, the decline is an eye-popping 68%. Altogether, 49 states are launching specific programs to make welfare-to-work a permanent reality. Little wonder that last summer Clinton was moved to

Reprinted by permission. *Industry Week*, March 16, 1998. Vol. 24, Issue 6, p. 27.

proclaim that "the debate is over. We now know that welfare reform works."

And, remarkably, the worst fears of employers have proved to be ill-founded. Unlike many products of Washington, the statute has no employer mandates—something many executives had feared. Instead, it seems to be benefiting companies.

Not only has the law "changed the outlook for the welfare population" by instilling in them an expectation of work, but it also "has been a boon for business," declares James D. VanErden, senior vice president for workforce development at the National Alliance of Business (NAB), a Washington-based group that coordinates private-sector efforts to improve workforce quality. "It provides a positive way for employers to expand their labor force in a tight labor market."

One company testifying to that is Gateway 2000 Inc., the giant North Sioux City, S. Dak.-based computer manufacturer. In hiring employees for its Hampton, Va., desktop-computer plant that opened in June 1996, the firm recruited heavily among former welfare recipients and now is doing so again during a major expansion of the facility. The plant has hired between 400 and 500 workers formerly on welfare rolls—up to 40% of its workforce. (The number varies by seasonal employment.) Welfare reform, says human-resources manager Bill Shugrue, "has been very successful as a recruiting tool for us."

In summing up the national success of the effort to move impoverished Americans off welfare, Welfare to Work Partnership President Eli J. Segal explains simply: "It's not rocket science. Companies need workers, and people on welfare need jobs."

The partnership has signed up more than 3,000 corporate "partners" who have committed formally to hiring welfare recipients. NAB has identified 5,000 firms that are doing such hiring. And a survey by Coopers & Lybrand LLP shows that 26% of U.S. companies have joined the trend, with another 4% expecting to do so soon.

These high numbers have raised eyebrows among welfare-policy observers. "People have been surprised by how many companies have come to the table," asserts LaDonna Pavetti, senior researcher at Mathematica Policy Research Inc., a Washington think tank, and formerly a welfare analyst at the Urban Institute. "Welfare reform has gone much better than anyone thought possible. But it isn't altruism on the companies' part to hire workers off welfare; it's in their self-interest. Employers are crying for workers, and the new law has opened up a new pool of potential employees for them. This is a perfect time for the nation to 'do' welfare reform—at a time when there's a worker shortage."

Thus, it's fair to argue that encouraging early success of welfare reform hasn't resulted from the wisdom of Congress and the White House in enacting the 1996 legislation. Instead, the bulk of the credit may be a byproduct of the booming economy—which, after all, has created the worker shortage. And that raises an inevitable concern: What will happen when the economy turns down, as it surely will eventually?

Good question. Although states now have the flexibility to set time limits, benefit levels, and other aspects of welfare previously directed out of Washington, the new law nevertheless stipulates that welfare benefits can't be paid to most recipients for more than five years; many beneficiaries are required to begin working within two years. If the economy sours, these deadlines obviously would pinch. Nor would Washington likely come to the rescue; federal funds now going to the states in the form of block grants probably wouldn't increase. Welfare experts acknowledge that when tougher times arrive, states may have to loosen their work requirements. Yet these experts are optimistic that the reforms underway now will considerably ease the welfare burden. "We recognize that companies adopt a 'last-hired' 'first-fired' philosophy in laying off workers during downturns," says Segal. "But if enough people move from welfare into the 'other' system [of work]—and learn skills and earn promotions—they'll be better positioned to survive."

Further comfort is offered by NAB's VanErden, who points out that an aging workforce likely will keep the demand for workers at a high level as current workers retire. He also notes that victims of recent corporate downsizings largely have been among mid- and top-level managers—not in lower-level jobs that tend to be filled by former welfare recipients. "And," he adds, "by getting people work-ready now, even if a downturn comes and they're laid off, they'll be more likely to be hired in the next upswing."

The experience so far of companies that have hired off the welfare rolls provides evidence that Segal and VanErden are correct in their optimism. In many, if not most, cases, former welfare recipients seem to be integrating surprisingly well into the firms' workforces. That's certainly the case at Gateway's Hampton facility. Although he won't reveal specific percentages, Shugrue indicates that, contrary to what might be expected, the plant's retention rate among employees previously on welfare is higher than the rate among other employees. "The promotion rate is better, too," he adds.

Reporting a similar experience is Marriott International Inc. One of the first companies to launch a broad-scale welfare-to-work program, the Bethesda, Md.–based hotel firm has hired some 900 former welfare recipients during the last six years after putting them through a six-week pre-hire training course at 20 U.S. locations; 800 more are expected to be hired within the next 18 months in 12 additional cities. To date, says Marriott, more than 90% of these employees have stayed on the job for at least 90 days; 65% have stayed at least a year.

Other companies have experienced like numbers, indicates Segal. Among those he cites with particularly outstanding retention records are Cessna Aircraft Co., BorgWarner Security Corp., United Air Lines Inc. (a subsidiary of UAL Corp.), and Smith Barney Inc. To be sure, skeptics argue that these promising trends are possible only because companies have been recruiting selectively off the welfare rolls, skimming off only those welfare recipients most willing—and able—to work. These firms, most analysts admit, are focusing on the first of three "tiers" of the welfare population identified by Mathematica Research's Pavetti while at the Urban Institute. The first tier consists of individuals who have some work skills and have been in and out of the workforce; the second (and largest), those willing to work but in need of training or "intervention"; and the third, substance abusers, severely disabled, and others traditionally not considered employable.

"Employers have pretty much exhausted the top tier," assesses NAB's VanErden. The challenge now, as he sees it, is to move more of the second and third tiers into the workforce. Aided by the booming economy, many companies are reaching into at least the second tier, he says.

Some firms even are sticking their toes into the third tier. One, Cessna, is working with its headquarters city of Wichita and various community partners to provide a training course for hard-core unemployed individuals in the city's impoverished 21st St. Corridor. The firm guarantees jobs to successful graduates. John Moore, senior vice president of human resources, reports "a 60% to 70% success rate" in the program. Cessna has hired some 200 program graduates, he says, while about 50 others are working for other companies.

Similarly, Walgreen Co., Deerfield, Ill., with the aid of a federal grant has trained 50 third-tier welfare recipients during the last two years. Twenty have been placed in jobs, of whom 12 are still working. "It takes a lot of work for a low placement/retention ratio," admits Jim Shultz, director of performance development. "But it's a start."

Indeed, "There are long-term, hardcore welfare people going to work now," confirms Amy Brown, operations associate at the Manpower Demonstration Research Corp. (MDRC), a New York-based firm that designs and studies welfare-to-work programs. But, echoing Shultz, she acknowledges that "it takes a lot more effort to get these people into productive jobs." Fortunately, she says, many programs are underway in states and local governments aimed at that objective; most of them involve the private sector.

For one, she cites Utah. The state exempts absolutely no welfare recipients from its work requirement; to reach out to these individuals, it has launched ambitious, state-sponsored drug-abuse services, counseling, and other programs. For another, she cites San Jose, whose private, nonprofit Center for Employment Training is aimed at the hard-core unemployed and features extensive employer participation. For a third, she points to Los Angeles County, which has redesigned its adult-education program to stress work-readiness. Welfare recipients used to go to the county's adult-education classes "to learn to read," she says. "Now they go to get a job." To employers, the phrase "work readiness" is critically important; it lies at the root of opposing philosophies on the best way to achieve the welfare-to-work transition. One philosophy, historically adopted by most states holds that welfare recipients need to get education and skills as a prelude to finding a job. The other, referred to as the "work-first" approach, calls for individuals to get a job first—any kind of job—and then move up the ladder; they develop work habits and skills on the job rather than in the classroom.

Which approach works better? "The jury is still out," answers Brown. "But in our [MDRC] research, we've come to conclude that the most successful approach is a 'mixed approach' that leans toward the work-first side. Instead of sending people to four years of college, for example, you give them instead perhaps six months of training that will help get them into the labor market as quickly as possible."

Although companies would prefer the historical emphasis on basic education, they're nevertheless pleased that many of these state training programs are stressing so-called soft skills—for example, the importance of coming to work on time and how to interact with supervisors and coworkers.

Increasingly, state and local programs also are attacking two of the biggest barriers that impede welfare recipients from getting jobs—child care and transportation. VanErden points out that Wisconsin, for example, recently enacted a huge appropriation for child-care services and that some other states are experimenting with child-care vouchers; Atlanta and Philadelphia have altered their city bus systems to accommodate late-shift workers at United Parcel Service sorting facilities in those cities; and Gary, Ind., has launched a van-pool service to transport inner-city residents to jobs in outlying areas not served by bus routes.

Companies, often in cooperation with public and community partners, increasingly are undertaking such initiatives in-house. Cessna, for one, recently built a day-care center as part of its 21st St. Corridor project. Gateway 2000 has worked with the city to change bus routes to serve its plant in Hampton, Va., and now is preparing to launch a day-care program. And Marriott has focused its prehire training program on soft skills—even including instruction on personal finance.

"A lot of these [welfare recipients] don't know how to open a checking account, how to budget, or how to figure the amount of money they'll need for transportation," says Janet Tully, Marriott's director of community development and training.

The key thing to remember, she says, is that most welfare recipients are willing, even eager, to work. "They don't fit the stereotype that these are people who want to sit at home on the couch and collect welfare. . . . But they are afraid of coming out of a system that has nurtured and supported them."

Gateway 2000's Shugrue agrees. "Companies have to get over the idea that welfare workers are lazy," he emphasizes. "They're not lazy. They have a very strong work ethic. All they need is encouragement."

By setting in motion a flurry of programs by state and local governments and by an increasing number of employers who recognize the benefits of hiring off the welfare rolls, the 1996 welfare-reform law is providing that encouragement.

LABOR DEMURS

"The jobs aren't there," unions say. Not everybody agrees that welfare reform is working. One vocal critic is organized labor. More than 80 labor organizations joined in nationwide demonstrations in December to call attention to a study, Welfare Reform: The Jobs Aren't There, which claimed that the odds are 97–1 against a typical welfare recipient finding a job that pays "a living wage." (IW, Jan. 5, Page 14). Released by Jobs With Justice, a Washington-based workers' rights group, the report includes a state-by-state breakdown detailing the lack of jobs for the "working poor."

In what may be the biggest concern of labor, the study also maintains that the influx of welfare recipients into the low-wage labor market will reduce wages in the sector by 12%. The study was conducted by the Preamble Center for Public Policy, a nonpartisan Washington research group.

Welfare Profiteers

RUTH CONNIFF

Now that the federal government has scrapped the old welfare system, corporations are getting ready to cash in. Arms contractors and other big businesses are speculating that there's money to be made in the new welfare-reform law, if they play their cards right.

In late March, representatives from Lockheed Martin, Andersen Consulting, Electronic Data Systems, and a few smaller firms came to Washington, D.C., for a conference entitled "Welfare Privatization: Government Savings & Private Earnings," at the Park Hyatt Hotel. "Capitalize on the massive growth potential of the new world of welfare reform," a promotional flier for the conference proclaimed. "Gain a leading edge in the market while it is in its early stage."

About 100 participants paid $895 a head to attend. Many were state and local government officials. They got to hear private companies market their wares—the newest methods to streamline bureaucratic systems, and "job-readiness" seminars guaranteed to get people off welfare and into work.

Company reps circulated among the public officials, handing out cards, while speakers from the Cato Institute and the Heritage Foundation extolled the virtues of a free-market approach to welfare reform.

Welcome to the post-welfare state, where military contractors, consulting firms, and eager entrepreneurs are competing for the revenue generated as federal and state governments slash aid to the poor.

William Eggers, director of privatization and government reform for the Reason Foundation, kicked off the conference, which was sponsored by the World Research Group of New York City. "I know the conference fee was not cheap," the tan, boyish-looking Eggers told us. "But as a government watchdog, I can tell you it is an efficient use of resources." When the conference is over, Eggers said, "you can translate all your new-found knowledge into millions of dollars of savings, if you're a public entity, or, if you're a private firm, into business opportunities." Welfare, Eggers explained, is "the hottest area in the country for privatization."

The new welfare law may spell economic disaster for poor families: The Urban Institute estimates that the law will push some 2.6 million Americans below the poverty line over the next six years. The law will take an especially painful toll on immigrants, disabled children, and

Ruth Conniff is the Washington Editor of *The Progressive*.
Reprinted by permission. *The Progressive*, May 1997. Vol. 61, Issue 5, p. 32.

poor working parents, who will be the first to feel the effects of cuts in food stamps, disability insurance, and cash assistance. But corporations may be the big winners. Lockheed Martin, Electronic Data Systems (EDS), and Andersen are currently competing for a government contract in Texas worth an estimated $2 billion over five years to administer the state's welfare-to-work program, as well as parts of the food-stamp, Medicaid, and unemployment-compensation programs.

How can the welfare law, which limits public assistance for the poor, translate into corporate profits?

By ending the federal entitlement to welfare, and giving states a fixed amount of funding to administer public-assistance programs, the new system offers a unique opportunity for welfare agencies to "save" money, Robert Rector, a welfare specialist from the Heritage Foundation, explained.

"If you're incompetent and you balloon your caseload upward, you don't get any more money," Rector said. "But a state that cuts its welfare caseload is going to be rolling in the dough."

Here's where the profit motive comes in. Under the new federal law, states get to keep the portion of their federal welfare money that they don't spend. The fewer clients they have, the larger the savings. Some states are passing along that savings to private contractors, who can make a lot of money by not serving the poor.

Rector used the example of Wisconsin, which has experienced a large drop in its welfare caseload over the last two years. The number of people collecting benefits in Milwaukee has dropped by one-third since 1995. "As we speak, in Milwaukee the caseload is dropping 2 percent a month," Rector said. He showed a chart, illustrating the number of people on welfare in Wisconsin with a steeply declining line. "It is far, far easier to reduce welfare-dependency than anyone imagined," he said.

How did Wisconsin do it? The state made county welfare agencies compete with private firms. If county agencies didn't cut caseloads by 25 percent in the first year, they lost their contracts. Because each agency gets a fixed sum of money from the state, "the organization now has a financial stake in the outcome," explained Jason Turner, a state welfare official from Wisconsin who followed Rector to the podium. Agencies know that to save money, they have to "get people into unsubsidized employment as quickly as possible," Turner said.

But if Wisconsin proves that it is easy—and profitable—to cut people off welfare, the state also points to the potentially disastrous results for the poor in the drive to save money by reducing the welfare rolls.

No one really knows what has happened to all those people who left the welfare rolls in Wisconsin. The state has no system for tracking them. But a recent article in the *Los Angeles Times* points out that there has been a sudden jump in homelessness in Milwaukee. There are 900 people currently crammed into the city's shelters—a 30 percent increase from last year. Advocates attribute the rise in homelessness to welfare reform. A reporter for the *L.A. Times* spoke with several mothers who showed up in Milwaukee's homeless shelters after being evicted when they lost their AFDC checks. "What we're starting to see is the erosion of the social safety net," Joseph Volk, chairman of the Milwaukee Emergency Shelter Task Force, told the newspaper.

Welfare reform may also exacerbate child poverty. At 51 percent, the poverty rate for African-American kids in Wisconsin is among the highest in the nation, second only to that of Louisiana. But this does not worry Robert Rector.

"There is a liberal myth that poverty is bad for kids," he declared at the privatization conference. Welfare dependency and illegitimacy, not poverty, are the real problems, he said. If poverty is not a concern, ending welfare is just a matter of kicking people off the rolls. It's an easy business.

Companies like Lockheed Martin are not interested in looking after poor people who slip through the cracks in the new welfare system. As businesspeople, they are interested in welfare to make a buck.

Holli Ploog, senior vice-president for business development at Lockheed Martin, spelled out the difference between altruism and good business sense at the conference. Ploog gave a presentation on setting up competitive bids for private firms hoping to get a piece of the welfare action. In a quiet, monotonous voice, Ploog explained that some states are more attractive to "vendors" like Lockheed Martin than others. States that want contractors to take too much responsibility for the poor are not going to attract many vendors, she warned.

"One state had unlimited liability for damages for the vendor," Ploog said. "So, for example, if someone fails to get support, therefore the children get sick, therefore they have to go to the hospital, and they end up having permanent damage, the vendor would be fully responsible."

The state in question couldn't drum up any interest, Ploog said. So it revised its criteria and set a cap on liability. "They brought it down to $150 million," Ploog said. There was laughter from the audience at that outrageous sum. Ploog smiled. But, she said, "they did get a bid."

In the frenzied, highly politicized climate of welfare reform, private-sector promises to overhaul the welfare system look alluring to state officials. As the new block-grant system goes into effect, state governments are under pressure to place people in jobs, and meet deadlines for reducing welfare caseloads.

The latest issue of *Governing* magazine, which everyone at the conference in Washington received, was full of advertisements for private firms promising to help welfare bureaucrats deal with rapidly changing policy and limited funds.

An ad for Unisys showed a full-page photograph of a vise, with the words "YOU ARE HERE" stamped over it. "You're caught in the middle of a welfare revolution. And the pressure is on you to make clients self-sufficient while holding the line on costs," the ad declared. "It's a tough spot to be in. But Unisys EIS (Efficiency, Integrity, and Self-Sufficiency) offers a way out." Then came a pitch for computer systems to help with fingerprinting, fraud detection, and job searches.

Companies have good reason to court state officials. Under the new block-grant system, many states are predicting budget surpluses. That's because welfare rolls have decreased in recent years, and the feds are handing out block grants set at the level of spending that was accurate a few years ago.

"Many governors are currently crowing about this 'windfall' of new federal money," Peter Edelman, who resigned in protest from the Clinton Administration over the welfare law, pointed out recently in *The Atlantic Monthly*. "But what they are not telling their voters is that the federal funding will stay the same for the next six years, with no adjustment for inflation or population growth."

In other words, making money from welfare reform is a short-term proposition. When a recession hits, and the demand for government services rises, budget surpluses will evaporate. Unless, of course, states and private welfare contractors simply decide to turn a blind eye to escalating need.

Some government officials are sensitive to the charge that they are letting corporate wolves in the door to make a profit by eviscerating benefits for the poor.

In Texas, "it's not about turning over who gets welfare to the private companies and then lowering the caseload so they profit," said Terry Trimble, the interim commissioner of the Texas Department of Human Services. "The state government decides who is eligible. The vendor does everything else." Companies will have to make their money in Texas by streamlining programs, eliminating paperwork, firing people, and closing offices, Trimble said.

Competition for the Texas welfare contract has the whole state in an uproar. Public employees are worried about losing their jobs. And government agencies that usually work together are divided against each other as they compete for a contract that might spell the end of whole departments.

The future of a $2 billion bureaucracy, with some 13,000 employees, hangs in the balance. Private firms and public agencies are forming alliances, trying to beat each other out to run the welfare system. Lockheed Martin, along with IBM, has joined with the Texas Workforce Commission, which oversees job-training programs, to make a bid. EDS has forged a partnership with Unisys and the Department of Human Services, to submit a competing bid.

The situation in Texas is further complicated by allegations of corruption, as high-ranking state officials move rapidly through a revolving door between the government and the corporations that are bidding to take over the new welfare system.

This should raise a red flag: Privatizing the welfare system opens the door for major financial scandals.

The Texas State Employees Union has filed a complaint, calling for an ethics inquiry into cozy relationships between corporate giants and state welfare officials. Dan Shelley, Governor Bush's legislative liaison, who worked to get privatization legislation passed in Texas, now works for Lockheed Martin, as do three other high-ranking state welfare officials. Greg Hartman, who helped design the initial plan for privatization, is helping Lockheed Martin and IBM prepare privatization bids.

If government officials and corporations are working together to design a welfare system for maximum corporate profit, who is looking out for the poor?

Robert Stauffer, a vice president for human services at EDS, raised this very question during the conference in Washington. "What's going to happen to children?" Stauffer asked. "That's something that hasn't been focused on much in the last couple of days." Stauffer had just returned from a welfare conference in New Zealand, he said, where "people are very worried about the social and income gap. In the United States, we don't seem to be. I'm not saying we should be. But internationally, they're worried about creating a minimum-wage culture where people are making $6 or $7 an hour, and are not able to move ahead. What I was hearing was, how do we get people beyond where they are today? There's much more of a social conscience in these countries."

Rex Davidson, executive director of Goodwill Industries of Greater New York, also raised concerns about for-profit firms taking charge of the welfare system.

"I had this crazy feeling throughout the conference that there was this underlying theme of, 'Show me the money,'" Davidson said.

Companies are scrambling to get a piece of the action as states discuss putting multibillion-dollar government contracts on the market. But corporations may not be the best people to provide services to the poor. And under the new system, nonprofits like Goodwill can't compete to provide these services.

"We don't have the resources to handle a billion-dollar contract," Davidson said. Likewise, he pointed out, "for-profits can legally make political contributions. Nonprofits can't. For-profits often hire high-level public officials. Nonprofits can't."

What nonprofits like Goodwill have to offer, however, is a different perspective on their poor clients.

"We are mission-driven, and we have a relationship with the community in good times and bad," Davidson said. For example, he said, in New York, Goodwill had a contract that wasn't paid for nine months. "But we felt the kids ought to be served in Queens, so we didn't drop it." Davidson's point—that turning a profit isn't always consistent with good public policy—seemed wildly out of place at the conference. The other speakers listened politely, then continued expounding on the pro-privatization theme.

There is something unseemly, if not downright corrupt, about a system that takes money "saved" by cutting the welfare rolls and redistributes it to corporations. But in a way, the privatization scramble is the logical outcome of a policy shift that has been taking place for many years.

As a nation, our goal has changed from reducing poverty to simply eliminating welfare. Cutting the welfare rolls will most likely make poverty a lot worse. But at least in the short term, it looks good for big business.

Issue 18
Social Policy: Bilingual Education

INTRODUCTION

In a country as ethnically diverse as the United States, language is not merely a means of communication, a lingua franca of convenience. Mastery of English, and the larger question of language instruction, raises emotional issues about prosperity, power, and the very essence of what it means to be an American. Learning English remains the traditional gateway to success in a country where economic expansion has been almost synonymous with the assimilation of millions of immigrants into a common, if ever-evolving, American culture.

In a country as vast and populous as the United States, a common language serves as the ultimate thread that binds together its diverse groups. At the same time, the contemporary dominance of the English language reflects the historical triumph of an Anglo-American heritage over its rivals. Throughout the course of the history of this country, English speakers routed and largely eliminated the speakers of Native American languages; they subjugated Spanish speakers from an annexed Mexican empire; and they showed scant regard for the linguistic traditions of immigrants from around the world. Finally, the westward expansion of the United States, fueled by successive waves of migration, in itself transformed the problem of American identity. The further away the nation drew from its Anglo-Protestant, Yankee origins, the more urgent the task of assimilation appeared. E Pluribus Unum—out of many, one—was no longer merely the rallying cry of thirteen isolated colonies. Rather, it became the formula for amalgamating disparate ethnic groups into a single American identity. According to this formula, ethnic heritages were to be suppressed rather than preserved. A common language served as a crucial ingredient for this transformation of many into one.

Perhaps because of the brute success of this process of creating an American type, the American people have proven singularly bad at learning other languages. Given the vastness, isolation, and relative self-sufficiency of the country, knowing languages other than English has been generally seen as a pointless indulgence that contributes nothing to the task of getting ahead. It is the foreigner who learns English, not the American who learns a foreign language. Yet, thanks to America's increasing dependence on a global economy, familiarity with other languages and cultures has become a necessity for doing business. Beyond that, the controversy over bilingual education has reopened the debate about the connections between language and power. In contrast to traditional techniques of immersion, whereby non-English-speaking students were placed in an entirely English curriculum, proponents of bilingual education contend that recent immigrants are most effectively integrated into the American mainstream by dual use of English and their native language. In this ideal, immigrant students acquire English language skills at the same time that they keep up with other subjects by instruction in their original tongue.

What ought to be a scientific debate about proper pedagogy (are students indeed best educated in this fashion?) has taken on overtones of cultural conflict. This conflict has centered on the educational experiences of Spanish-speaking students, particularly those of Mexican extraction in the school systems of Western states. Opponents of bilingual education, who achieved their most recent success in the passage of California's Proposition 227 abolishing bilingual programs, allege that such programs do not contribute to linguistic assimilation to the norm of English. Rather, these programs further the agenda of multicultural advocates who see a greater good in preserving linguistic heritages for the sake of diversity. Indeed, opponents contend, bilingual education actually harms students by delaying their mastery of English. At their worst, such programs perpetuate an underclass of underachievers whose inability to use English consigns them to poverty and ignorance.

In the first of the selections that follow, Rosalie Porter argues that, from their modest beginnings in federal legislation of the 1960s, bilingual programs have grown to embrace a multicultural justification for bilingualism that places greater importance on preserving language-based ethnic identities than on actually teaching children English. Such programs have also created a large constituency of bilingual teachers and other multicultural specialists with a vested interest in the perpetuation of their programs, even if they do not work. Given the choice of educational possibilities that stress either English or their ethnic heritage, California parents of schoolchildren overwhelmingly vote for English. Alas, according to Porter, the popular will is being frustrated by a state educational bureaucracy that has resorted to the court system to protect what they could not preserve at the ballot box.

Lourdes Rovira, who draws from her experiences among the Cuban population of Miami–Dade County, Florida, insists that "good bilingual programs are not remedial, but enrichment programs." Although there may have been problems in the implementation of California's programs, the promise of bilingual education is alive and well. Simply getting rid of bilingual education "is a simplistic solution to a complex educational issue." More than ever, Americans need bilingual skills to navigate the global economy. Far from disadvantaging poor students, bilingual instruction actually provides them with language abilities that had hitherto been available only through an elite education. Moreover, preserving ethnic heritages by means of language instruction not only contributes to students' self-realization through cultural empowerment but even promotes "gospel values."

As you read the articles, consider the following questions.

Discussion Questions

1. Do the opponents of bilingual education think that the idea itself is bad, or do they think that it is a good idea that is merely being implemented in a bad way?
2. Foes of bilingual education also tend to support the idea that English should be our official language. This would mean, for example, that all public documents would have to be written in English; it might also mean that certain public standards would be taught, and even enforced, regarding the usage and spelling of English. Should English be made the official tongue of the country?
3. All things being equal, if knowing another language made a person more tolerant of people from different cultures, then wouldn't it be a good idea to require all Americans to learn at least one foreign language?
4. The language debate isn't merely about convenient communication. It's also about cultural identity. What is an "American" identity, anyway, and how does speaking English reinforce it?

For more on this topic, visit the following websites:

http://www.ncbe.gwu.edu
The National Council for Bilingual Education

http://www.englishfirst.org
English First

http://www.ed.gov/offices/OBEMLA/
U.S. Department of Education's Office of Bilingual Education and Minority Language Affairs

http://www.read-institute.org
The READ Institute

The Case against Bilingual Education

ROSALIE PEDALINO PORTER

Bilingual education is a classic example of an experiment that was begun with the best of humanitarian intentions but has turned out to be terribly wrong-headed. To understand this experiment, we need to look back to the mid-1960s, when the civil-rights movement for African-Americans was at its height and Latino activists began to protest the damaging circumstances that led to unacceptably high proportions of school dropouts among Spanish-speaking children—more than 50 percent nationwide. Latino leaders borrowed the strategies of the civil-rights movement, calling for legislation to address the needs of Spanish-speaking children— Cubans in Florida, Mexicans along the southern border, Puerto Ricans in the Northeast. In 1968 Congress approved a bill filed by Senator Ralph Yarborough, of Texas, aimed at removing the language barrier to an equal education. The Bilingual Education Act was a modestly funded ($7.5 million for the first year) amendment to the Elementary and Secondary Education Act of 1965, intended to help poor Mexican-American children learn English. At the time, the goal was "not to keep any specific language alive," Yarborough said. "It is not the purpose of the bill to create pockets of different languages through the country . . . but just to try to make those children fully literate in English."

English was not always the language of instruction in American schools. During the eighteenth century classes were conducted in German, Dutch, French, and Swedish in some schools in Pennsylvania, Maryland, and Virginia. From the mid nineteenth to the early twentieth century, classes were taught in German in several cities across the Midwest. For many years French was taught and spoken in Louisiana schools, Greek in Pittsburgh. Only after the First World War, when German was proscribed, did public sentiment swing against teaching in any language but English.

These earlier decisions on education policy were made in school, church, city, or state. Local conditions determined local school policy. But in 1968, for the first time, the federal government essentially dictated how non-English-speaking children should be educated. That action spawned state laws and legal decisions in venues all the way up to

Rosalie Pedalino Porter is the director of the Institute for Research in English Acquisition and Development (READ), in Amherst, Massachusetts, and the editor of *READ Perspectives.*

Reprinted by permission of Rosalie Pedalino Porter. Appeared in *The Atlantic Monthly,* May 1998, Vol. 281, No. 5, p. 28.

the Supreme Court. No end of money and effort was poured into a program that has since become the most controversial arena in public education.

In simplest terms, bilingual education is a special effort to help immigrant children learn English so that they can do regular schoolwork with their English-speaking classmates and receive an equal educational opportunity. But what it is in the letter and the spirit of the law is not what it has become in practice. Some experts decided early on that children should be taught for a time in their native languages, so that they would continue to learn other subjects while learning English. It was expected that the transition would take a child three years.

From this untried experimental idea grew an education industry that expanded far beyond its original mission to teach English and resulted in the extended segregation of non-English-speaking students. In practice, many bilingual programs became more concerned with teaching in the native language and maintaining the ethnic culture of the family than with teaching children English in three years.

Beginning in the 1970s several notions were put forward to provide a rationale, after the fact, for the bilingual-teaching experiment. Jose Cardenas, the director emeritus of the Intercultural Development Research Association, in San Antonio, and Blandina Cardenas (no relation), an associate professor of educational administration at the University of Texas at San Antonio, published their "theory of incompatibilities." According to this theory, Mexican-American children in the United States are so different from "majority" children that they must be given bilingual and bicultural instruction in order to achieve academic success. Educators were convinced of the soundness of the idea—an urgent need for special teaching for non-English-speaking children—and judges handed down court decisions on the basis of it.

Jim Cummins, a bilingual-education theorist and a professor of education at the University of Toronto, contributed two hypotheses. His "developmental interdependence" hypothesis suggests that learning to read in one's native language facilitates reading in a second language. His "threshold" hypothesis suggests that children's achievement in the second language depends on the level of their mastery of their native language and that the most-positive cognitive effects occur when both languages are highly developed. Cummins's hypotheses were interpreted to mean that a solid foundation in native-language literacy and subject-matter learning would best prepare students for learning in English. In practice these notions work against the goals of bilingual education—English-language mastery and academic achievement in English in mainstream classrooms.

Bilingual education has heightened awareness of the needs of immigrant, migrant, and refugee children. The public accepts that these children are entitled to special help; we know that the economic well-being of our society depends on maintaining a literate population with the academic competence for higher education and skilled jobs. The typical complaint heard years ago, "My grandfather came from Greece [or Sicily or Poland] and they didn't do anything special for him, and he did okay," no longer figures in the public discussion.

Bilingual education has brought in extra funding to hire and train paraprofessionals, often the parents of bilingual children, as classroom aides. Career programs in several school districts, among them an excellent one in Seattle that was in operation through early 1996, pay college tuition for paraprofessionals so that they may qualify as teachers, thus attracting more teachers from immigrant communities to the schools. Large school districts such as those in New York and Los Angeles have long had bilingual professionals on their staffs of psychologists, speech therapists, social workers, and other specialists.

Promoting parental understanding of American schools and encouraging parental involvement in school activities are also by-products of bilingual education. Workshops and training sessions for all educators on the historical and cultural backgrounds of the rapidly growing and varied ethnic communities in their districts result in greater understanding of and respect for non-English-speaking children and their families. These days teachers and school administrators make an effort to communicate with parents who have a limited command of English, by sending letters and school information to them at home in their native languages and by employing interpreters when necessary for parent-teacher conferences. In all these ways bilingual education has done some good.

But has it produced the desired results in the classroom? The accumulated research of the past thirty years reveals almost no justification for teaching children in their native languages to help them learn either English or other subjects—and these are the chief objectives of all legislation and judicial decisions in this field. Self-esteem is not higher among limited-English students who are taught in their native languages, and stress is not higher among children who are introduced to English from the first day of school—though self-esteem and stress are the factors most often cited by advocates of bilingual teaching.

The final report of the Hispanic Dropout Project (issued in February) states,

> While the dropout rate for other school-aged populations has declined, more or less steadily, over the last 25 years, the overall Hispanic dropout rate started higher and has remained between 30 and 35 percent during that same time period . . . 2.5 times the rate for blacks and 3.5 times the rate for white non-Hispanics.

About one out of every five Latino children never enters a U.S. school, which inflates the Latino dropout rate. According to a 1995 report on the dropout situation from the National Center on Education Statistics, speaking Spanish at home does not correlate strongly with dropping out of high school; what does correlate is having failed to acquire English-language ability. The NCES report states,

> For those youths that spoke Spanish at home, English speaking ability was related to their success in school. . . . The status dropout rate for young Hispanics reported to speak English 'well' or 'very well' was . . . 19.2 percent, a rate similar to the 17.5 percent status dropout rate observed for enrolled Hispanic youths that spoke only English at home.

In the past ten years several national surveys of the parents of limited-English schoolchildren have shown that a large majority consider learning English and having other subjects taught in English to be of much greater importance than receiving instruction in the native language or about the native culture. In 1988 the Educational Testing Service conducted a national Parent Preference Study among 2,900 Cuban, Mexican, Puerto Rican, and Asian parents with children in U.S. public schools. Although most of the parents said they wanted special help for their children in learning English and other subjects, they differed on whether their children should be taught in their native languages. Asian parents were the most heavily opposed to the use of native languages in the schools. Among Latino groups, the Puerto Rican parents were most in favor, the Mexicans somewhat less, and the Cubans least of all. A large majority of the parents felt that it is the family's duty, not the school's, to teach children about the history and traditions of their ancestors. When Mexican parents were asked if they wanted the school to teach reading and writing in Spanish and English, 70 percent answered yes. But when they were asked if they wanted Spanish taught in school if it meant less time for teaching English, only 12 percent were in favor.

In the most recent national survey of Latino parents, published by the Center for Equal Opportunity, in Washington, D.C., 600 Latino parents of school-age children were interviewed (in Spanish or English) in five U.S. cities—Houston, Los Angeles, Miami, New York, and San Antonio. A strong majority favored learning English as the first order of business for their children, considering it more important than learning other subjects, and much more important than reading and writing in Spanish.

Having begun quietly in the 1980s and gained momentum in the 1990s, Latino opposition to native-language teaching programs is now publicly apparent. Two actions by communities of Latino parents demonstrate this turn of events.

A hundred and fifty parents with children in Brooklyn public schools filed a lawsuit in September of 1995, charging that because their children routinely remained segregated in bilingual programs in excess of three years, and in some cases in excess of six years, contrary to section 3204 (2) of the State Education Law, these children were not receiving adequate instruction in English, "the crucial skill that leads to equal opportunity in schooling, jobs, and public life in the United States."

New York State law limits participation in a bilingual program to three years, but an extension can be granted for up to three years more if an individual review of the student's progress seems to warrant it. And here is the nub of the lawsuit: thousands of students are routinely kept in native-language classrooms for six years or longer without even the pretense of individual progress reviews.

Unfortunately, even with the help of a strong champion of their cause, Sister Kathy Maire, and the pro bono services of a prestigious New York law firm, Paul, Weiss, Rifkind, Wharton & Garrison, the parents lost their case. Under New York law these parents in fact have the right not to enroll their children in bilingual classes, or to remove them from bilingual classes, but in practice pressure from school personnel is almost impossible to overcome. Teachers and principals tell parents that their children will fail in English-language classrooms. They play on ethnic pride, asserting that children of a Latino background need to be taught in Spanish to improve their self-esteem.

In May of last year the Court of Appeals of the State of New York ruled that there could be no further appeals. But the publicity attracted by the case may encourage other Latino parents to take action on behalf of their children. And one concrete improvement has already occurred: the New York City Board of Education announced an end in 1996 to the automatic testing for English-language skills that children with Spanish surnames had undergone when they started school.

On the other coast an equally irate group of Latino parents moved against the Ninth Street School in Los Angeles. Seventy families of mostly Mexican garment workers planned the protest through Las Familias del Pueblo, a community organization that provides after-school child care. Typical of the protesters are Selena and Carlos (I have changed their names, because they are undocumented immigrants), who left the poverty of a rural Mexican village in 1985 to come to work in Los Angeles. Their children were born in Los Angeles, but the school insisted that they not be taught in English until they had learned to read and write in Spanish, by the fourth or fifth grade. The parents complained to the school for years that children who lived in Spanish-speaking homes and neighborhoods needed to study in English in the primary grades, when children find it easier to learn a language than they will later on.

Persistent stonewalling by administrators finally moved the parents to keep their children out of school for nearly two weeks in February of 1996, a boycott that made national news. The parents demanded that their children be placed in English-language classes, a demand that has since been met. The school administrators waited too long to make this change: the previous spring only six students (about one percent of enrollment) had been deemed sufficiently fluent in English to "graduate" to regular classrooms in the next school year.

In the early 1970s almost all the students in bilingual classes spoke Spanish. Today, of the three million limited-English students in U.S. public schools, more than 70 percent speak Spanish at home; the rest speak any of 327 other languages. California alone enrolls 1.4 million limited-English children in its schools—one of every four students in the state. According to the 1990 U.S. census, 70 percent of limited-English students are concentrated in California, Florida, Illinois, New Jersey, New York, and Texas.

Controversy over native-language education is at the boil in California. In our most multicultural state, where minorities now constitute 46 percent of the population, a revolution is brewing. In 1987 the California legislature failed to reauthorize the Bilingual-Bicultural Education Act, allowing it to expire. However, the California Department of Education immediately notified all school districts that even without the state law the same requirements would be enforced and bilingual programs continued. In July of 1995 the state Board of Education announced two major policy changes: the "preference" for native-language programs would henceforth be revoked and school districts would be given as much flexibility as possible in choosing their own programs; and school districts were ordered to be more diligent in recording evidence of student achievement than in describing the teaching methods used.

Yet in two years only four school districts have succeeded in obtaining waivers from the department, permitting them to initiate English-language programs for limited-English students. Why should schools have to seek waivers when no state or federal law, no court decision, no state policy, bars them from teaching in English? The most important case to date is that of the Orange Unified School District, with 7,000 limited-English students.

Orange Unified applied in early May of last year for permission to focus on English-language teaching in kindergarten through sixth grade while using a small amount of Spanish. The Department of Education strongly opposed the district, as did the California Association for Bilingual Education, California Rural Legal Assistance, and the organization Multicultural Education, Training, and Advocacy (META). Local Latino activists publicly criticized the district's change of plan, and some bilingual teachers resigned.

Nevertheless, the Board of Education last July granted Orange permission to try an English-language program for one year. A lawsuit was filed, and a temporary restraining order granted. But last September, U.S. District Court Judge William B. Shubb lifted the restraining order. In his seventeen-page decision the judge wrote, "The court will not second-guess the educational policy choices made by educational authorities." And he added a ruling with much broader application:

> It is clear that "appropriate action" does not require "bilingual education." . . . The alleged difference between two sound LEP [Limited-English Proficient] educational theories—ESL [English as a Second Language] and bilingual instruction—is inadequate to demonstrate irreparable harm.

The federal court ruling allowed Orange to proceed with its English-language program. But the case was returned to Sacramento County Superior Court, where Judge Ronald B. Robie ruled that nothing in California state law requires primary-language instruction, and therefore no waiver is needed for a district to provide an English-language program; and that federal law permits educational programs not to include native-language instruction. Soon after Robie's ruling the Board of Education rescinded the policy that schools must obtain waivers in order to eliminate bilingual programs. Although the court decision may be appealed, these two actions signal a victory for Orange Unified and have implications for other California districts as well. The legal battle has already cost the Orange district $300,000, which no doubt would have been better spent on students. It is estimated that the new program will cost an additional $60,000 the first year, but the superintendent of Orange Unified schools, Robert French, says, "We're not doing this to save money. We're doing this to save kids."

Ron Unz, a Silicon Valley entrepreneur, has long been concerned about the California education system's failures, especially as they affect its 1.4 million limited-English students. He has decided to put his time, energy, and money into an initiative—"English for the Children"— meant to give all California voters a say on the language of public education. If the initiative passes, in elections to be held on June 2, it will give "preference" to English-language programs for immigrant children, reduce the length of time children may remain in special programs, and make the state spend $50 million a year to teach English to adults. Bilingual programs will be allowed only in localities where parents actually request native-language teaching for their children.

Last November, Unz and the co-chairman of the drive, Gloria Matta Tuchman, submitted more than 700,000 signatures to put the petition on the California ballot. The drive has the support of several Latino leaders in California, most notably Jaime Escalante, who is its honorary chairman. Escalante is the Los Angeles high school teacher whose success in teaching his Latino students advanced calculus gained him national fame in the film *Stand and Deliver.*

Though some opponents characterize the petition as "anti-immigrant," Unz and Matta Tuchman have strong pro-immigrant credentials. In 1994 Unz ran against the incumbent Pete Wilson in the Republican primary for governor and forcefully opposed the referendum to deny schooling and health benefits to illegal immigrants—a referendum that passed with Wilson's support. Matta Tuchman is a recognized Latina advocate for improved schooling for all immigrant children, but especially Spanish-speakers. The measure is likely to pass, some believe with strong ethnic support. A *Los Angeles Times* poll last October found Latino voters backing the initiative by 84 percent, and Anglos by 80 percent. A more recent survey showed a reduced amount of support—66 percent of respondents, and 46 percent of Latinos, in favor. But whether or not the initiative passes, bilingual education has had a sufficient trial period to be pronounced a failure. It is time finally to welcome immigrant children into our society by adding to the language they already know a full degree of competency in the common language of their new country—to give these children the very best educational opportunity for inclusion.

Let's Not Say Adios to Bilingual Education

LOURDES ROVIRA

A great travesty occurred in California on June 2, 1998. By passing Proposition 227, California's voters elected to terminate bilingual education in their state. It was a sad day for our country because we allowed ill-informed politicians and xenophobic voters to dictate educational policy.

The United States is a country of immigrants—immigrants who have come seeking freedom and the pursuit of the American dream. Throughout history, English has been the common language that has united these immigrants from all over the world. English is the language of this great country. None of us who support bilingual education ques-

Lourdes Rovira is executive director for bilingual education and foreign languages for the Miami–Dade County Public Schools.

Reprinted by permission. *US Catholic*, Nov. 1998. Vol. 63, Issue 11, p. 22.

tion the validity or the importance of the English language, as some would like the public to believe. Quality bilingual programs emphasize the acquisition of English. English is taught to all immigrant students; it is required, and we aim to perfect it in the school setting.

Yet to learn English, students need not forget the language they bring to school with them—be it Spanish, Vietnamese, or Urdu. Bilingual education is not like an antibiotic that we give to children who are sick, their illness being lack of English. As soon as the children are well, that is, as soon as they know English, the antibiotic—bilingual education—is removed. Good bilingual programs are not remedial but enrichment programs.

One common misunderstanding is that bilingual education is the exclusive domain of immigrant students. No, studying a second language is a right that belongs to all students—recently arrived refugees, African Americans, and, yes, white Americans. Languages expand a child's cognitive development. Knowing more than one language is not an impediment to intellectual capacity. If it were, the rest of the world's children outside of the United States would be intellectually inferior to ours. After all, the majority of them are bilingual.

Years ago, being bilingual was a privilege reserved for those who could afford to send their children to private tutors or to a finishing school in Europe. It was a privilege reserved for those who traveled and went to the opera. In today's global economy, being bilingual can no longer remain a privilege reserved for the elite. Today, being bilingual is a right that must transcend all socioeconomic strata. Denying all students that right is not only a mistake, it is an injustice.

Students are enabled—not disabled—by being bilingual; they are empowered by knowing more than one language. The American experience is strengthened, not weakened, by citizens who can cross languages and cultures. The United States can no longer afford to remain a monolingual country in a multilingual world. Being bilingual and biliterate not only gives people a political and economic advantage, it also allows them to be bridges between people of different cultures.

For immigrant students, being bilingual means having the best of two worlds—their home culture and language and our nation's culture and English language. For native speakers of English, knowing a second language means opening up their horizons to the richness of cultural diversity and becoming active participants in—and not merely spectators of—today's global society. In no way does it require supplanting one language and culture with another.

This may come as a surprise to many, but bilingual education is not a recent phenomenon in this country. Its history in the U.S. falls into two distinct periods, the first from 1840 to 1920 and the second beginning in the early 1960s.

In 1840 a form of bilingual education originated in Cincinnati with a state law designed to draw German children into the American schools. Several other similar initiatives, which provided instruction in Dutch, Italian, and Polish, among others, took place during the latter part of the 19th century and the beginning of the 20th. During World War I, strong anti-German sentiments increased, and by the end of the war bilingual programs were terminated and "Americanism" and English-only instruction were promoted. Some states went so far as to impose restrictions on the instruction of foreign languages.

Instruction in and through two languages disappeared in the U.S. from 1920 until 1963, when thousands of Cuban refugees poured into the Miami area, opening up a second phase of bilingual schooling in this country. In an effort to meet the needs of the Cuban refugee children, the Miami–Dade County Public Schools organized a dual-language instructional program at Coral Way Elementary with a student population evenly divided between Spanish speakers and English speakers. Both groups spent half of their day being instructed in English and the other half in Spanish, thus immersing themselves in two languages and cultures.

Since then, federal and state laws and court decisions have not only allowed but directed local school districts to create special programs to meet the academic needs of non-English-speaking students. But almost 30 years after the passing of the Bilingual Education Act, the debate over the benefits of bilingual education continues to be politically and emotionally charged. Also lingering after 30 years seems to be a dreadful ignorance over the definition of bilingual education and its goals and practices. Those who make for themselves a political agenda over the issue attack bilingual education as a failure based on a very limited knowledge of one specific bilingual-education model while ignoring others that have been extremely successful, not only in this country but throughout the world.

Critics of bilingual education who regard it as a dismal failure claim that children enrolled in bilingual programs do not learn English and that the research regarding the benefits of bilingual programs is contradictory and inconsistent. They assert that immersion programs are superior to bilingual programs and believe that after one year of English immersion, non-English-speaking students will be ready to be mainstreamed into regular, English-speaking classes.

Much of educational policy, whether it is bilingual education or reading, stems from pendulum swings from one extreme to another. Unfortunately, immersion programs have failed to prove a successful track record. To wipe out bilingual programs in favor of a sink-or-swim curriculum is a simplistic political solution to a complex educational issue. Moreover, it hardly seems fair to blame bilingual education for all the ills of California's 1.4 million limited-English-proficient students when less than 30 percent of them are enrolled in bilingual programs. Those of us who have dedicated our professional lives to the promotion of bilingual education can assert that properly organized and executed bilingual programs not only work, they work extremely well. This does not mean that some bilingual models cannot be improved. However, there is ample research that demonstrates without a doubt that good bilingual programs are successful—and none that could claim such success for one-year immersion programs.

The school district I work for, Miami–Dade County Public Schools, the fourth largest in the country, has been in the forefront of bilingual education since the establishment of Coral Way Elementary in 1963. Our programs are recognized nationally and internationally as programs that promote excellence in English and another language for all students who want to avail themselves of that opportunity.

Bilingual programs in our district provide instruction in English for Speakers of Other Languages (ESOL) to students with limited English proficiency as soon as they enroll in school. Students are provided instruction in their home language for approximately 20 percent of the instructional time, but the primary goal is the rapid acquisition of English. At the same time, Miami–Dade County Public Schools embraces diversity and offers all our students the opportunity to enroll in quality programs that promote literacy in a language other than English. We promote high standards for all of our students whether the instruction is in English, Spanish, Haitian-Creole, or French.

As the waves beat against the shore and drag everything in sight, it sometimes seems that whenever California voters make an earthshaking decision at the polls, the rest of the country wants to follow suit. How will California's decision affect bilingual education in the rest of the country? Thankfully, the Miami–Dade County Public Schools and districts in many other states (e.g., New York, New Jersey, and Connecticut) have no interest in eliminating bilingual education. Bilingual education is viewed as quintessential to living in this part of the country. In South Florida, and much of the rest of the world for that matter, being bilingual and biliterate is not a liability but an asset.

Bilingualism not only prepares students for today's increasingly global economy and promotes cognitive development and creative thinking, it also instills pride. And, as a Catholic, I would also argue that bilingualism is rooted in gospel values and based on justice. What position should Catholics, and Christians in general, take in the continuing public debate of this issue? It seems to me that we are called to be more informed and compassionate toward immigrants than the average California voter.

In 1963 Pope John XXIII addressed the treatment of minorities in his encyclical letter Pacem in terris (On Peace on Earth): "It is especially in keeping with the principles of justice that effective measures be taken by civil authorities to improve the lot of the citizens of an ethnic minority, particularly when that betterment concerns their language [and] . . . their ancestral customs." Language, notes a document of the Southeast Regional Office for Hispanic Ministry in Miami, "expresses the soul of the people."

The 1985 Vatican-sponsored World Congress on the Pastoral of Emigration observed in its final document: "Experience has shown that the inability of expression in the mother tongue and the elimination of religious traditions . . . greatly damage the conscience, impoverish the cultural surroundings, provoke separation and even schism, and reduce the numbers of the faithful."

Those who question the need for bilingual education are often the same people who question why Masses have to be said in Spanish. Perhaps the words of Pope Paul VI in his 1975 apostolic exhortation Evangelii nuntiandi can do a better job of persuading them than those of us in bilingual education have been able to do: "Evangelization loses much of its force and effectiveness if it does not take into consideration the actual people to whom it is addressed, if it does not use their language, their signs and symbols, if it does not answer the questions they ask, and if it does not have an impact on their particular lives. . . . The split between the gospel and culture is without a doubt the drama of our time, just as it was of other times."

It is unfortunate that California's Proposition 227 passed. It is revolting that bilingual education has been killed at the hands of people who do not understand its virtues. It is offensive that bilingual education continues to be solely associated with immigration. And it is shameful that we have forgotten that when this nation was founded, English was not the exclusive language of the country.

Unlike the western waves, Florida's waves are of a different nature. They embrace the shores with the linguistic plurality needed to fortify the shores, not destroy them.

Each month, advance copies of "Sounding Board" are mailed to a sample of U.S. Catholic subscribers. Their answers to questions about "Sounding Board" and a representative selection of their comments about the article as a whole appear in "Feedback."

Issue 19
Education Policy

INTRODUCTION

Freedom and equality are America's two most important values. We seek to realize these values through public policy, even as we argue about which value is
more important or whether they are at all compatible with each other. To be a
free citizen means, at times, to have the freedom to be different from others. In
important ways, the freedom to be different takes the form of human inequalities. At the same time, Americans value equality both in a formal, political sense
(one person, one vote) and as a range of substantive outcomes. America's self-
image is that of a middle-class society in which success remains open to the talented and the ambitious. Inequality is tolerated as long as most citizens feel that
the equal opportunity to succeed in life remains widely available.

In the American mind, education is the key to political and economic
success. From the early days of the country, an educated citizenry has been
regarded as crucial to the survival and health of a far-flung democracy. Peda-
gogues and thinkers like Horace Mann and John Dewey looked to a system of
universal education to forge an ideal American citizen out of the volatile
amalgam of industrialism and immigration. To this day, education has also
been identified with economic advancement. Parents sacrifice and save so
that their children may acquire the education necessary to fulfill middle-class
dreams. Yet educational policy must also grapple with the conflicts between
freedom and equality. At least at the primary level, the American educational
system is overwhelmingly public and secular, yet substantially under local
control. Education in America is funded largely through local property taxes.
Local control means that school districts in poorer neighborhoods have fewer
resources than those in richer neighborhoods. In effect, Americans have
sought to reconcile the civic ideal of universal education—a kind of education

253

into political equality—with the freedom of choosing localities to shape what and how their children learn.

Private schools have always operated in the shadow of public systems, but their impact on American education has been limited by the problem of cost. Without taxpayer funding, private schools cater either to an elite with the resources to pay for private tuition over and above their school tax burdens or to religious families whose churches subsidize faith-based alternatives to public education's secular humanist creed. Nonetheless, the attraction of private schools has been enhanced by the manifest failure of public schools to meet the needs of poorer, inner-city students. Whether the fault lies in a lack of funding, in the culture of inner-city poverty, or in the obstructionism of teachers' unions, the shortcomings of public education have encouraged a turn towards private alternatives. In particular, vouchers represent a distinctive combination of public and private resources. Under voucher programs, parents would be given the freedom to choose between public and private schools by availing themselves of educational credits (vouchers) that could be spent towards private tuition. According to their advocates, by giving families the freedom of choice, vouchers would force public schools to improve their educational experiences. Otherwise, such schools risk losing students (and their vouchers) to private competitors.

Barbara Miner, editor of *Rethinking Schools,* regards voucher experiments as an opening wedge in a concerted attempt by conservatives to undermine the civic functions of public education. Whatever its shortcomings, public schooling still embodies ideals of inclusiveness and equality that would be damaged if public systems had to compete with voucher-funded private schools. Not only would two parallel school systems drain resources from the same pool of tax dollars, but also the private system would enjoy unfair advantages. Unlike public schools, private schools could operate in secrecy and without regard to enforceable educational standards. Moreover, private schools would be able to pick selectively the smartest or most obedient students, leaving the problem cases—the learning disabled, the unruly, or those needing special accommodations—for the public system to cope with. Miner conjures up the specter of religious schools teaching intolerance towards homosexuals, opposition to abortion, or even creationism. In short, public resources would be diverted to private purposes. If public schools do have problems, Miner counsels, "the best response is to make the public schools more accountable, not to use tax dollars to subsidize private schools with minimal accountability."

Clint Bolick, of the conservative Institute for Justice, dismisses these concerns as a smoke screen concealing the professional and economic interests of educational bureaucrats and teachers' unions. Bolick declares, "The educational establishment fights every meaningful parental choice proposal as if its very survival depends on it—because it does." To Bolick, enhancing school choice through voucher programs would benefit American education in a number of ways. Market-oriented educational reform would enhance parental autonomy over their children's education. The ability to choose would improve educational standards, as public schools would be forced to compete with their private counterparts. Ideals of educational equity, so dear to public school defenders, would actually be supported by voucher programs, since low-income parents would finally enjoy the educational choices that have long been available to the rich. For these reasons, Bolick argues, libertarians should support voucher experiments. Otherwise, these experiments face the risk of sabotage by opponents who will use the public provision of voucher money as a justification for imposing the very sort of stultifying bureaucratic regulation that private schools have sought to escape.

As you read the articles, consider the following questions.

Discussion Questions

1. Supporters of vouchers believe that the success of voucher programs depends upon avoiding harmful government regulation. Yet, if private schools are willing to take public money, why should they be able to avoid the strings attached to those funds? Why should the receipt of public money not open oneself up to regulation?

2. Private schools have always played an important, if subordinate role, in American educational systems. Do those parents who pay tuition for private schools nonetheless have an interest in the success of the public school system, even if they don't send their kids to public schools?

3. The debate about vouchers isn't merely about the distribution of educational resources, but about the role that parents ought to play in their children's education. What vision does each side have of parental involvement? Which side seems to trust parents more? Do you think this trust (or lack thereof) is justified?

4. Barbara Miner worries that private schools, especially religious ones, will teach creationism and intolerance towards homosexuals. What is wrong with this sort of teaching, if it is what parents want their children to learn?

    For more on this topic, visit the following wesites:

    `http://www.schoolchoices.org`
    School Choices

    `http://www.nea.org`
    The National Education Association

    `http://www.data.fas.harvard.edu/PEPG/`
    The Harvard Program on Education Policy and Governance

    `http://www.heartland.org`
    The Heartland Institute

Why I Don't Vouch for Vouchers

BARBARA MINER

Supporters tout vouchers as the solution to school accountability problems. Yet voucher proposals raise disturbing questions about public information, equity, segregation, and the separation of church and state.

The principal was being fired, teachers were leaving, the school was in upheaval. At the time, I was a reporter for the *Milwaukee Journal*, covering a parents' meeting on the controversy.

I never made it to the meeting. Lawyers stood in my way. They said it was a private school and reporters were not welcome. End of discussion. I was angry but found out the lawyers were right. Shutting a reporter out of a parents' meeting is illegal in Milwaukee public schools. But private schools operate by different rules.

I was reminded of the incident when the Wisconsin Supreme Court ruled last June that Milwaukee's voucher program does not violate the constitutional separation of church and state. For now, low-income students in Milwaukee will be able to use public vouchers to attend private and religious schools.

End of discussion? Not this time. The court decision has not resolved the controversy over vouchers. It has merely opened up a Pandora's box of new issues.

PROBLEMATIC POLICY

Milwaukee began providing vouchers for private schools in 1990. The program initially was limited to a small number of low-income children at a handful of nonreligious schools. The court ruling allows the program to expand to as many as 15,000 children attending private and religious schools. Cleveland has a similar program.

Although still small in size, voucher programs are becoming the educational buzz of the day. On the federal level, the rhetoric of vouchers has been used to justify such initiatives as tuition tax credits. In addition, there are several privately funded voucher programs. If a voucher proposal is not yet available in your state, just wait. Vouchers are coming your way.

Barbara Miner is Managing Editor of *Rethinking Schools* newspaper and coeditor of *Selling Out Our Schools: Vouchers, Markets, and the Future of Public Education.*
Reprinted by permission. *Educational Leadership*, Oct. 1998, Vol. 56, Issue 2, p. 40.

Everyone knows there are problems with achievement and accountability in our public schools. But the best response is to make the public schools more accountable, not to use tax dollars to subsidize private schools with minimal public accountability. Do we really want to set up two separate school systems, one private and one public, yet both supported by tax dollars?

The U.S. Supreme Court must ultimately decide whether public vouchers for religious schools violate the separation of church and state. Constitutional issues aside, voucher proposals raise important questions. Here are just a few.

Just because something is legal, is it good public policy?

It's not mere coincidence that the term *private* is so often followed by the phrase *Keep Out!* Private schools, like private roads, private beaches, and private country clubs, don't have to answer to the public.

What does it mean when private schools that get public dollars don't have to follow the same rules as public schools? The answer is particularly important in Milwaukee because 100 percent of a voucher school can be funded by vouchers—the schools aren't required to have a single student who privately pays tuition—and the school still gets to call itself "private." Under Milwaukee's voucher program, participating schools

- Do not have to obey the state's open meetings and records laws.
- Do not have to hire certified teachers—or even to require a college degree.
- Do not have to release information on employee wages or benefits.
- Do not have to administer the statewide tests required of public schools.
- Do not have to publicly release data such as test scores, attendance figures, or suspension and drop-out rates. The only requirement is a "financial and performance evaluation audit" of the entire voucher program to be submitted to the legislature in the year 2000.

Will vouchers be used to further segregate our schools?

Families send their children to private schools for many reasons. But one of Milwaukee's dirty little secrets is that some white parents use private schools to get around desegregation efforts. In Milwaukee, the public schools are approximately 60 percent African American. At Divine Savior/Holy Angels and Pius XIth High Schools, only 3 percent of the students are African American. At Milwaukee's most elite religious high school, Marquette University High School, 5 percent of the students are African American. Some religious elementary schools in Milwaukee do not have any African American students. The issue also goes beyond race. Will vouchers further stratify our schools along religious lines?

Will private schools weed out "undesirable" students?

Private schools can control whom they accept and the terms upon which students stay enrolled. The Milwaukee program, which is far better than most voucher proposals, has two safeguards: The schools are to select voucher students on a random basis, and they may not discriminate on the basis of race, color, or national origin. One problem, however, is enforcement. Who ensures that the rules are followed? More important, controversy has erupted over whether the voucher schools must follow other requirements of Wisconsin public schools—for example, that they not discriminate on the basis of gender or sexual orientation. One of the most contentious issues in Milwaukee involves students with special educational needs, who account for about 15 percent of public school students. Voucher proponents argue that the private schools don't have the money for special education students, thus the Milwaukee Public Schools must serve them.

Milwaukee voucher schools have also used more subtle means to select their students. Some set parental involvement requirements, for instance. Perhaps most important, private schools can expel students, for both academic and discipline reasons, without adhering to the rights of due process. Will voucher schools be able to do likewise?

In one telling incident in Milwaukee in 1995, an African American student was asked not to return to the elite and private University School after she criticized the school as racist in a speech before her English class. She filed suit on grounds of freedom of speech. She lost. Federal Judge Terrence Evans wrote,

> It is an elementary principle of constitutional law that the protections afforded by the Bill of Rights do not apply to private actors such as the University School. Generally, restrictions on constitutional rights that would be protected at a public high school . . . , need not be honored at a private high school.

How can the public oversee religious schools without stepping on religious principles?

Under the First Amendment, the government is not to "entangle" itself in the running of religious institutions. As a result, however, religious schools can fire teachers who violate deeply held religious principles—such as a gay teacher or a teacher who supports the right to abortion. What will happen with religious schools that receive public vouchers? Will they be able to teach that homosexuality is a sin, that creationism is superior to the theory of evolution, that corporal punishment keeps children in line, that birth control violates the law of God, that the Jews killed Christ, or that there is no God but Allah?

Can the marketplace solve the problems of our public schools?

Some voucher supporters are guided by the admirable desire to provide individual opportunities for low-income children in urban areas.

The moving forces behind vouchers, however, have a more specific ideological agenda. In essence, voucher proposals assume that privatization and the marketplace—in other words, the dismantling of the institution of public education—hold the key to education reform.

But in what other social arena—whether health care, housing, food, or jobs—has the marketplace equitably and adequately provided services? We live in the bastion of free enterprise, the richest, most powerful country in the world. Yet one quarter of our nation's young children live in poverty, and millions go hungry and homeless.

Under the rules of the marketplace, some people live in cardboard boxes and some people have vacation homes on Cape Cod. Some take the bus, some drive brand new BMWs. In the marketplace, money doesn't talk. It shouts. Is that our vision for public education?

Further, the marketplace values individual choice and decision making over collective responsibility for the common good. If we look to private schools and parental choice to solve complicated problems of school reform, we distort the purpose of public education. We are "saving" a few children while giving up on the majority who will remain in public schools.

Up to 15,000 children will be allowed to use public money to attend private and religious schools in Milwaukee this year. With the voucher worth almost $5,000 a pupil, as much as $75 million in taxpayers' money will be taken from the Milwaukee Public Schools and given to private schools—with minimal public accountability. It may be legal. But is it a good idea?

Blocking the Exits

CLINT BOLICK

Libertarian opposition to school vouchers is an attack on freedom.

What do many thoughtful, committed libertarians and Sandra Feldman of the American Federation of Teachers union have in common? Almost nothing—except their opposition to school choice. Answering the concerns of these libertarians is essential to defeating the reactionary likes of Feldman and realizing the potential of school choice.

School vouchers empower parents to spend their public education funds in public, private, or religious schools. The cause of choice unites conservatives, most libertarians, and growing numbers of centrists and even liberals. It brings together disparate reformers because all at once it expands parental autonomy, increases competition, promotes educational equity, and addresses the greatest challenge facing America today: ensuring educational opportunities for low-income children in the inner cities.

Some libertarians fear, however, that school vouchers will not expand freedom, but will instead turn the private schools that serve roughly 11 percent of America's youngsters into clones of failed government schools. That price, they argue, is too high, even for the sake of expanding the private sector in education and improving opportunities for millions of youngsters who desperately need them.

I wish the school-choice naysayers could have shared my experiences with the public-school monopoly and the choice alternative. My original career aspiration was classroom teaching; remarkably, upon my graduation from college, the New Jersey education cartel conferred upon me life time teacher certification. But my experiences as a student teacher left me convinced that our system of public K-12 education desperately needed fundamental change. I concluded, first, that parents, not bureaucrats, should control essential education decisions; and second, that a system of parental choice should replace the command-and-control system of public education in America.

For a long time school choice held only academic interest for me, but I became downright militant about the issue in 1990, when I had the honor of defending the constitutionality of the nation's first school-choice program, in Milwaukee. I walked the hallways of the schools that 1,000 economically disadvantaged children were able to attend for the first time. I

Clint Bolick is the vice president and the director of litigation of the Institute for Justice, a public-interest law firm based in Washington, D. C. This article is adapted from a debate at The Heritage Foundation.

Reprinted by permission. *Policy Review*, May/June, 1998, Issue 89, p. 42.

talked to their parents, most of whom were themselves poorly educated yet keenly understood that this was a chance—perhaps the only chance—for their children to have a better life. And I saw the beaming faces of children—beacons of pride, self-discipline, and hope. That's when school choice became a matter of heart and soul as well as mind.

The nation's second school-choice program, launched in Cleveland in 1995, had an equally profound effect on me. It has permanently etched the figure "one in 14" in my memory. You see, children in the Cleveland Public Schools have a one-in-14 chance of graduating on schedule with senior-level proficiency. They also have a one-in-14 chance, each year, of being victimized by crime in their school. When a school district can offer its children no greater chance of learning the skills they need to become responsible citizens than of being victimized by crime during the school day, we are in serious jeopardy.

THE SPECTER OF REGULATION

I do not mean to diminish the ever-present specter of government regulation of private schools. When it was enacted in 1990, Milwaukee's school-choice program was not only challenged in court, but also sentenced to death by bureaucratic strangulation. The education establishment insisted that private schools meet all state and federal regulations applicable to public schools. Not surprisingly, every single private school refused to participate under those conditions. We fought these regulations in court even as we were defending the program's constitutionality.

The regulatory threat from federal school-choice proposals is even more ominous. For example, when some members of Congress proposed parental-choice legislation for the District of Columbia last year, we found ourselves battling to head off all manner of federal regulations on participating private schools.

Though we won both these skirmishes, we know the regulatory threat is serious. But these episodes suggest caution, not abandonment, of this freedom enterprise. The position of school-choice critics is akin to resisting the demise of communism because the free markets that would emerge might be subjected to government regulation. This is hardly a Hobson's choice.

Virtually all libertarian arguments against parental choice are grounded in hypothetical speculation. And the greatest antidote to speculation is reality. But even the critics' worst case does not trump the value of choice. The critics of choice point to the example of American higher education as the ultimate horror story of government control. In the 1980s, the U.S. Supreme Court ruled that postsecondary institutions that accept any federal funds—even student loan guarantees—must also submit to federal regulation. So federal regulators have now ensnared all but a handful of fiercely independent private colleges.

But from the standpoint of our current system of elementary and secondary education, this so-called nightmare looks more like a dream. Libertarian alarmists warn that vouchers will lead to a system of primary and secondary schools under monolithic government control. But that's exactly what we have already! Only 11 percent of America's children attend independent elementary and secondary schools, while 89 percent attend government schools. Moreover, private schools already are subject to regulations concerning health and safety, nondiscrimination, the length of the school year, curriculum content, and the like.

In my view, our overwhelming concern should be for those children who are already captive of the educational standards and ideological dogma of the public-school monolith. Surely any reform that diminishes the near-monopoly status of government schooling—even at the cost of greater regulation of private schools—will still yield a net increase in freedom. We should be particularly confident of that outcome when the mechanism of reform is a transfer of power over educational decisions from bureaucrats to parents.

Moreover, the regulatory threat to private-school independence is simply not illuminated by reference to higher education. In that instance, federal oversight entered an arena of vibrant competition between a vigorous and effective public sector and a vigorous and effective private sector. The horizons for elementary and secondary schools, by contrast, are limited by a dominant, overregulated, and ineffective public sector. The likely main outcome of expanding access to the highly effective, lightly regulated private sector will be to deregulate the public sector.

And that is exactly what we are seeing. The mere prospect of school choice has already sparked deregulation of public schools. In Milwaukee, efforts to increase regulation of private schools have failed, while the public sector has responded to choice by allowing more flexibility in the management of public schools and passing two charter-school statutes. In Arizona, a 1994 parental choice proposal in the state legislature failed by just a few votes, but a "compromise" produced the nation's most ambitious charter-school legislation. Today, one-sixth of public schools in Arizona are charter schools, many of which are operated by private nonprofit and for-profit entities.

THE MARKETPLACE MEETS THE CLASSROOM

Parental choice is the cornerstone of market oriented education reforms. If we liberate public education funding from the grip of school districts and let children take it wherever they go, we will create a dynamic educational marketplace. I predict that, if we expand these reforms across the nation, then public schools will quickly lose their eight-to-one advantage in enrollment. Instead we will enjoy a system of choice among government schools, quasi-public charter schools, quasi-private charter schools, and private schools; in sum, a system far more free than the command-and-control system to which the overwhelming majority of America's children are confined today.

I would remind critics of choice that other safeguards support a firewall against excessive regulation. First, private schools can decide for themselves whether to accept choice funding from the government. In Milwaukee, when choice was expanded to religious schools, they were all forced to think long and hard about participating and accepting the modest regulations imposed by the program. In the end, more than 100 of 122 private schools in the city agreed to participate. Critics worry that schools may be unwisely tempted by the prospect of funding, or that they will tolerate rising regulation after becoming dependent on the funding. For the many inner-city schools that are approaching insolvency, this may not be a bad deal. But that is a choice that the schools should be trusted to make on their own—and anti-voucher libertarians who argue otherwise are indulging in uncharacteristic paternalism.

Some schools will exercise their fundamental right not to participate. At the elementary and secondary level, many families can afford the median private tuition of $2,500 to $3,500. We always will have private schools that thrive outside of a choice system, and we should vigorously protect those schools. But that is not a sound basis for denying opportunity to children who cannot afford a private-school education but desperately need it.

A second safeguard is the U.S. Constitution itself. First Amendment precedents forbid "excessive entanglement" between the state and religious schools. If regulations supplant essential school autonomy, they will be struck down.

Perhaps most important, the power of the education establishment will diminish in exact proportion to the power gained by parents. The education establishment fights every meaningful parental choice proposal as if its very survival depends on it—because it does.

The more zealous and irresponsible libertarian critics oppose vouchers because they wish to see the system of government-run schools collapse altogether. The reality is that the public funding of education enjoys nearly unanimous public support. The most extreme libertarians are missing—indeed, helping to defeat—the chance to end the government-school monopoly and to allow public education to take place outside the public sector.

For some of the kids involved, getting out of inner-city public schools is literally a matter of life and death. Many of my libertarian opponents on this issue are people of enormous good will, but when I see them blocking the exits for these children, I cannot look upon them with affection. I understand, even share, their concerns about government's destructive power. But I do not understand why they fail to see where the interests of freedom lie in this fight.

To them I say: When you actively oppose parental choice, please know what you are doing. You are aiding and abetting the most reactionary forces in American society. They trot you out and use you to preserve the status quo. It is a perverse spectacle.

Ted Kennedy . . . Jesse Jackson . . . Kweisi Mfume . . . Eleanor Holmes Norton . . . Norman Lear . . . Bill Clinton . . . Richard Riley . . . Keith Geiger . . . Sandra Feldman . . . Bob Chase. Among those enemies of change, my fellow libertarians do not belong, for they want what I want: freedom. I believe that a system of parental choice would mark the greatest domestic expansion of freedom in this century.

Friends, come over to the freedom side.

Issue 20
Health Policy

INTRODUCTION

The tobacco wars are raging, and there is no end in sight. The articles in this section, which present the opposing views of tobacco companies and health advocates, are merely the latest voices in a centuries-long controversy.

Tobacco smoking is anything but new. Evidence exists that Native Americans smoked as early as the twelfth century. Tobacco was the New World's least benign gift to Europe. While in Cuba at the end of the fifteenth century, Spanish explorer Rodrigo de Jerez took up the native practice of smoking tobacco, but when he returned to Spain, he was imprisoned by the Spanish Inquisition for seven years for his fiery habit. Imprisonment, unfortunately, did no good, for the Spanish enthusiastically adopted the new practice.

In 1564, Jean Nicot de Villemain, the French ambassador to Portugal, recommended the drug to the French court, unknowingly attaching his name to tobacco's powerful addictive component, nicotine. In the following decades, the practice spread despite numerous condemnations by several Roman Catholic popes. John Rolfe began growing tobacco for profit in Jamestown in 1612, eight years before the Pilgrims set foot on Plymouth Rock. Commercial tobacco retailers first appeared in England in the 1850s, selling tobacco imported from hundreds of farms in Virginia and North Carolina.

By 1990 more than 260 billion cigarettes were being consumed in the United States alone, thus providing evidence that attempts to curb smoking in the previous two decades had not been successful. When the surgeon general, in a series of rulings beginning in the early 1970s, began to require warning labels on cigarette packages, the labels actually provided manufacturers with legal protection. The courts ruled that because people were warned of the dangers of smoking, producers were not liable for deaths resulting from tobacco consumption. Thus what had begun as an anticigarette move actually resulted in a great victory for cigarette manufacturers. It was not long, however, before cracks appeared in the wall of protection provided by the warning labels. In 1990 a jury in Mississippi ruled that the American Tobacco Company shared with a man named Horton the responsibility for Horton's own death, but the jury awarded no damages. When Mildred Wiley, who did not smoke, died in 1991, her husband's lawsuit established a basis for worker's compensation claims for victims of secondhand smoke. Legislation in the 1990s centered on tobacco advertising, eliminating it from radio, television, and eventually billboards.

By the end of the 1990s, American states, saddled with the health-care costs resulting from smoking, sued the tobacco companies, which pressed Congress for a final settlement. In the following articles, Steven F. Goldstone, Chairman and CEO of RJR Nabisco, one of the nation's largest cigarette producers, berates Congress on its lack of action to bring the matter to a conclusion, whereas the American Lung Association urges more forceful action against tobacco interests.

As you read the articles, consider the following questions.

Discussion Questions

1. To what extent are individuals responsible for the negative effects of smoking?
2. Is the economic benefit that the United States is receiving from the tobacco industry worth the lives of the 400,000 people who die from smoking every year?
3. What is the most effective way to reduce cigarette consumption?

   For more on this topic, visit the following websites:

   `http://www.rjrt.com`
   The R.J. Reynolds Tobacco Company

   `http://www.commoncause.org`
   Common Cause Tobacco Report

   `http://tobaccofreekids.org`
   National Center for Tobacco-Free Kids

   `http://www.fda.gov`
   The U.S. Food and Drug Administration

The Failure of the Tobacco
Legislation: *Where Is the Political Leadership?*

STEVEN F. GOLDSTONE

Thank you. I appreciate the opportunity to be here today; to give you a personal perspective on the ongoing national debate affecting one of RJR Nabisco's companies—the Reynolds Tobacco Company in Winston-Salem, North Carolina.

It is perhaps not an everyday occurrence when the future of a $60 billion industry, in this case the tobacco industry, becomes the focus of almost every single one of the nation's politicians.

And while there is no question that the issues presented by tobacco regulation in the country may be unique and difficult, I still think it edifying for all of us to step back and review the recent events in Washington.

There's an important lesson to be learned about the quality of political leadership in the White House and the Capitol, and it should not be a comforting one, for anybody.

Let me give you some of the background.

I became Chairman of RJR Nabisco two years ago. The company is the sixth largest consumer products company in the world. The companies we own have developed some of the greatest brands in history, such as Oreos, Ritz Crackers, Planters Nuts, and Winston and Camel.

As Chairman, I am accountable, in the ways familiar to you, to thousands of employees, shareholders and customers all over the world.

I came to RJR Nabisco with the firm belief that tobacco companies can and should be able to offer their products to adult customers. The most recent national polls confirm that this belief is shared by the vast majority of Americans.

At the same time, the tobacco industry and the country both share a paramount interest in a sound, advanced, national policy that educates people about all the public health issues concerning tobacco products.

In my early months as chief executive, I thought long and hard about how to balance this belief with my responsibilities to thousands of shareholders, as well as my obligations to 80,000 employees and thousands of retirees.

Steven F. Goldstone is Chairman and CEO of RJR Nabisco. He delivered this article in a speech to The City Club of Cleveland, Cleveland, OH, on July 31, 1998.

Reprinted by permission. *Vital Speeches of the Day*, Oct. 1, 1998, Vol. 64, Issue 24, p. 760.

I also had to consider the important interests of all the other participants in this business: important businesses like Hollin Oil, Fuelmart and BP and the thousands of smaller, independent neighborhood stores all of which take part in the business of distributing tobacco products in the United States today.

I believed all these interests, those of the participants in the industry and of the country in general, were not incompatible.

But when I arrived at RJR Nabisco, I realized that things were not so simple. I was confronted for the first time with the institutional anti-tobacco forces—what Myron Levin of the *Los Angeles Times* has called the "growth industry of sophisticated professionals who are supported by governmental contracts and foundation grants," and who are devoted to the absolutist advocacy of a single cause—the eradication of tobacco. I was amazed at the intensity of the emotion, the constant attacks, the charges and counter-charges, the harsh rhetoric—a general lack of civility and endless litigation.

I also found it impossible to plan for the future when one of our companies was portrayed as outside the mainstream of commerce absorbed in massive litigation, under regulatory, and political attack, with no normal working relationship with federal or state governments.

It was clear to me that the 40 years of litigation, in which the industry never lost a case, was not providing an answer. Further escalation of the war, even with more courtroom victories, would not change anything for the better—and would not address the problem that many Americans wanted addressed, that is, how to curtail the number of underage teenagers who use tobacco products in the United States today.

Forty years of successful litigation had avoided courtroom defeats, but had not prevented the industry from becoming isolated and demonized by its professional attackers.

Perhaps of even more immediate concern, the industry was also becoming the object of an unprecedented litigation assault, not by private citizens, but by state governments.

Let me remind you what happened here, because it bears remembering.

Some local and state politicians, combining forces with the powerful plaintiffs' bar, came up with a new way to target this disfavored industry. The states, which for years had approved tobacco as a legal product and taxed it to the point of no return, would now sue for the alleged health care costs caused by the use of the products by adult consumers.

The possibility of literally billions of dollars in legal fees attracted the titans of tort lawyers, and the politician plaintiffs were off to the races.

As Paul Gigot said in the *Wall Street Journal*, it was a "Trend explained by opportunity and ambition, fueled by government's political marriage with the plaintiffs' bar."

The politics of demonization, combined with the potential for a huge payday, proved irresistible. More states joined in. Some states like Florida even went so far as to rewrite their tort law, specifically to facilitate victory in the courtroom against tobacco.

Here is just one example from a state law recently introduced in the Vermont legislature, which is typical of others. It creates a new claim for money damages on behalf of the state, specifically against the targeted tobacco companies. And it goes on:

"In any [such] action, all principles of common law and equity regarding affirmative defenses normally available to a defendant are hereby abrogated to ensure full recovery." In other words, the government simply strips the targeted industry of all the legal rights and defenses afforded to every other defendant, to make sure the state wins and tobacco loses. In any event, by 1997, the industry was facing this kind of confiscatory litigation in states all across the country, with states essentially using their local courts as new tax agencies and changing the rules as they went along to make it easier to collect.

It's a disturbing trend not necessarily limited only to tobacco products, and some governments have recently expanded it to go after gun manufacturers for the health damages inflicted by their legal products. The next logical candidates are obvious. One health advocate at Yale University recently opined that Ronald McDonald was more evil (and perhaps more suable) than Joe Camel.

But for tobacco, the trend only guaranteed that the future of the industry, and the millions of people whose jobs depend on it, would be dictated by bet-your-company litigation results, not by a free and open policy debate. There would be no constructive dialog about the public health issues or how to solve them. It was hard to see, from any rational perspective, how anyone—in the industry, in government or the public health community—would really be satisfied with the prospect of decades of more litigation with no thoughtful resolution of the underlying issues in sight.

So we in the industry sat down and tried to come up with a solution that literally could reverse the course of history.

We asked, what could the world look like if we put on the table our traditional rights and freedoms as a company in a free enterprise system—many of which are protected by the Constitution—in order to address dramatically the real national concern about children's smoking?

What if we were willing to give up marketing freedoms—especially critical to Reynolds, trying as it is to reverse a long-term decline in its competitive position?

Yet, we ultimately did put these freedoms on the negotiating table in an effort to get to a comprehensive resolution of the tobacco controversy.

Even further, what would the world look like if we agreed to pay unprecedented amounts of money, forever, to end finally the years of litigation? There is no question there would be a serious negative impact on Reynolds' earnings.

Yet, we ultimately ended up putting these sums of money on the negotiating table. We sat down at a table with our adversaries to try to produce a better result for everyone. Three months of intense negotiations led to a remarkable, comprehensive agreement, tougher and more wide-ranging than any of us had expected, that would have settled the bulk of the litigation and fundamentally changed the way tobacco products are regulated, marketed and sold in this country.

In so doing, experts thought it would have done more to reduce youth smoking than anything anyone had previously proposed.

There has been a lot of water over the dam since that agreement, almost exactly one year ago. But let me remind you what a few people said at that time about the June 20th settlement last year.

The *New York Times* said: "Tobacco negotiators announced a historic settlement proposal today that, if ratified, promises to change forever the way cigarettes are marketed in the United States, to provide billions of dollars in compensation to states and to permanently alter the nation's legal, regulatory and public health landscape."

One attorney general, who had participated, said: "This is the biggest public health achievement and corporate settlement in the history of this country."

A leading anti-tobacco advocate, Matt Myers of the National Center for Tobacco free Kids, said: "This plan offers the best hope for protecting our children." He called it "the single most fundamental change in the history of tobacco control, in the history of the world."

What happened next, though, is by now painfully familiar to everyone, instead of embracing the achievement, Washington destroyed it.

Our national leaders prevaricated and played politics with it.

Leadership was nowhere to be found.

And into that vacuum of leadership rushed politicians on a political goldrush, along with activists bent on destruction of the tobacco industry.

In the end, we witnessed a sorry spectacle of politicians trying to tax a legal industry and 47 million American smokers into oblivion, all under the guise of protecting the nation's youth. When the Senate bill finally collapsed in June of its own weight, one editorial writer called it "a distressing example of Congress' finest product—an unrecognizable mess, confusing in content, plastered with special interest favors, stripped of its original intent."

You have to ask yourself, how could this happen? Why did it happen?

Well, I've been asking myself that question a lot, and I have two answers—one obvious, one perhaps more surprising.

First, the obvious one. We have today in Washington an Administration without the will, or the courage, to lead. After actively encouraging the tobacco companies and the attorneys general, at meetings in the White House, to risk an unprecedented compromise, the Administration opted for partisan positioning instead of bold political leadership.

We learned the wisdom of Churchill's comment that: "nothing is more dangerous . . . than to live in the temperamental atmosphere of a Gallup poll, always feeling one's pulse and taking one's temperature."

But that's the political dance the country got from a White House unwilling to seize ownership of a historic opportunity presented on a silver platter.

More surprising is what was revealed by this vacuum of political leadership, and that is this: We learned that the essential premise of our attempted resolution—that the public health leaders of our country, would support a comprehensive resolution if it provided for real public health advances—was simply not true.

The June 20th agreement gave them a public health advocate's dream come true, but they would not take "yes" for an answer.

Into the vacuum of political leadership marched the professional advocates of an absolutist cause.

And so it is that the public health activists became the greatest single impediment to a remarkable public health advance for the country.

The self-appointed leaders of our public health community, to whom the politicians ceded their responsibility of office, turn out to have an agenda which excludes mutual resolution, at any cost, whatever the public health consequences.

The evidence of this emerged as events played out after June 20th last year. Before the ink was dry, the anti-tobacco lobby turned on the attorneys general and other negotiators, and did everything they could think of to destroy the economic viability of the industry.

Here's what happened: The anti-tobacco lobby didn't concentrate at all on the public health provisions of the agreement. They focused instead on the money—on radically increasing the already punishing financial burdens on the companies and their consumers.

First, they claimed that financial penalties of up to billions of dollars assessed yearly against the industry if youth smoking rates did not drastically decline were not severe enough. No reason why . . . just not sufficiently harsh. This, despite the fact that no one in the history of this country had ever previously proposed, much less agreed to, a penalty on an industry for consumer conduct that it couldn't control.

How did the politicians respond? They obediently tripled the penalties, thereby assuring bankrupting fines for conduct that the companies
could not prevent.

Then, the public health advocates took on another new expertise.
They became experts on litigation against the industry, arguing that the
public health of the nation depended on class action lawsuits and punitive damage awards.

Any settlement of litigation, no matter at what price, was quote
"immunity" unquote for the industry, which could not be tolerated
under any circumstances.

How did the politicians respond? They dutifully dismantled the litigation settlement contained in the agreement.

And finally, the anti-tobacco advocates came up with the ultimate
weapon to achieve the destruction they desired. Changing their tune
after years of criticizing industry advertising and marketing practices,
they argued that to really stop kids from smoking, the only viable approach was to raise prices through the roof to all adult consumers.

There was never any real evidence to support this idea that sky-
high prices would have anything like the claimed effect on underage
smoking choices. In fact, you'll remember that just two years ago, the
Clinton Administration, and its FDA Commissioner David Kessler, announced FDA regulations which they claimed would reduce youth
smoking in half over seven years, all without a penny in new taxes or
price increases.

For some mysterious reason, now two years later, the only approach that would work was price increases that would make non-
contraband tobacco prohibitively expensive for most adult smokers, and
thereby threaten the economic viability of the industry.

Why would people who call themselves advocates for the public
health do this? Why would they make financial arguments and legal arguments one after the other—in an effort to destroy a compromise
which might resolve issues and move the country forward in a sensible,
balanced way?

David Kessler gave us the answer a few weeks ago, in an article in
the *New York Times*. He's got a different agenda: "I don't want to live in
peace with these (tobacco) guys. If they cared at all for the public health,
they wouldn't be in this business in the first place. All this talk about it
being a legal business is euphemism. There's no reason to allow them to
conduct business . . ." Dr. Koop's zeal on tobacco also allows no room
for compromise. In the same article, he called it "evil" for companies to
produce these products, despite the fact that our society has deemed
them to be legal adult products for over 200 years. "There shall be no
compromise," he decreed. "No bill is better than a compromise bill,"
proclaimed Dr. Kessler.

Don't get me wrong. I'm not quarreling with their right to hold these opinions. All Americans have a right to voice their opinions. But most Americans reject such unbending commands not to compromise— and would choose not to sail away on the Pequod under these kinds of orders.

Most Americans accept that tobacco is a legal business and want to find reasonable solutions to the issues presented by the product.

Dr. Koop has devoted much of his career to improving the nation's health, and for that I have the utmost personal respect. His anti-smoking message is worthy of respect when delivered individually and persuasively to his patients, or even publicly as part of an educational campaign. But it should become a cause of concern when he has it legislatively imposed on free people who have the right as individuals to reject even Dr. Koop's expert advice.

What's wrong here is how some of our political leaders, whose job it is to seek balanced and practical solutions to the nation's problems, can so easily be persuaded to default on their responsibility in favor of a single, absolutist and ultimately undemocratic point of view. This default guarantees no consensus will be reached.

It guarantees no balance will be struck.

It guarantees no real progress.

In this case, the anti-tobacco activists, in their effort to eradicate a legal industry, led the Senators into what one commentator called "The most purely punitive piece of legislation in history."

One whose aim was not to address youth smoking, but to control adult behavior . . . to punish the industry and the 47 million adult Americans who choose to use tobacco products and to coerce them to change their ways, for their own good.

Others are now finally realizing that this was the agenda all along, and that it doomed any cooperative effort to failure.

Senator McCain, who allowed himself to be led by them, says: "No matter what we put in this legislation, it has never been enough for them . . . Now I know why they haven't gotten anything accomplished in 40 years."

Mike Moore, the leading negotiator for the attorneys general in the June 20th agreement, says: "The public health people overreached."

Richard Kluger, noted author on tobacco said in the *New York Times:* "They should have understood that regulating tobacco, not punishing the industry, was the primary goal . . . their self-righteous view missed the larger point."

The country rightly should expect its elected leaders to protect us from the overreaching of professional, single-issue activists, and the well-meaning absolutists like Dr. Kessler and Dr. Koop, who have held progress and resolution of tobacco issues hostage to their own personal prescriptions of what is in our best interest. Instead, our leaderless politicians have let them snatch defeat from the jaws of victory.

Where does Washington's failure leave us today? It is wrong to say last month's event was a victory for tobacco companies. We tried last year, with the June 20th agreement that we signed with the attorney general, to chart a new course; and that effort has completely failed. Last month only proved that.

We are left right where we were when I began speaking out a couple of months ago. I pledged then that my company was going to take the debate out of the broken-down process in Washington, and engage the American people in a public policy discussion. I have told my shareholders that I see this as an important part of my job for them, as the future of their company and the industry in which it operates is truly at stake. That is what we have been doing these last two months, and that is what we are going to continue to do.

And we are going to do everything we can to bring reason and common sense back to the discussion, until Washington gets real on tobacco.

I believe that ultimately, the people will make the politicians lead, and force them to focus on goals the country wants to achieve:

Do we want to punish tobacco companies, or do we want to create reasonable and responsible rules for the future of 7 million American adult smokers, or do we want to do something effective at actually reducing underage use of tobacco products?

Do we want to promote another generation of litigation in the courts, or do we want to settle the controversies and move on?

Do we want government to coerce the legal behavior of adult Americans who choose to smoke, or do we want a balanced compromise that embraces free, informed choice and that values personal responsibility?

If there is any silver lining for the country, perhaps the events in Washington last month will finally make our leaders focus on the issues Americans want addressed.

I continue to think that a balanced, comprehensive approach, along the lines of the June 20th agreement, would do the most to resolve the controversies and move the country forward to a new era of responsible tobacco regulation.

But if that is not possible, we at RJR Nabisco remain committed to working and cooperating with responsible efforts to address parents' well-founded concerns about their teenagers.

We have a responsibility to do that, and we will do that. But only when our leaders provide a balance against zealotry and embrace consensus, can the real work begin.

Fact Sheet: Smoking;
and Statement of John R. Garrison

Smoking-related diseases claim an estimated 430,700 American lives each year, including those affected indirectly, such as babies born prematurely due to prenatal maternal smoking and some of the victims of "secondhand" exposure to tobacco's carcinogens. First-hand smoking alone costs the United States approximately $97.2 billion each year in health-care costs and lost productivity.

Cigarettes contain at least 43 distinct cancer-causing chemicals. Smoking is directly responsible for 87 percent of lung cancer cases and causes most cases of emphysema and chronic bronchitis. Smoking is also a major factor in coronary heart disease and stroke; may be causally related to malignancies in other parts of the body; and has been linked to a variety of other conditions and disorders, including slowed healing of wounds, infertility, and peptic ulcer disease.

Smoking in pregnancy accounts for an estimated 20 to 30 percent of low-birth weight babies, up to 14 percent of preterm deliveries, and some 10 percent of all infant deaths. Even apparently healthy, full-term babies of smokers have been found to be born with narrowed airways and curtailed lung function. Only about 30 percent of women who smoke stop smoking when they find they are pregnant; the proportion of quitters is highest among married women and women with higher levels of educational attainment. In 1995, 14 percent of women who gave birth smoked during pregnancy.

Smoking by parents is also associated with a wide range of adverse effects in their children, including exacerbation of asthma, increased frequency of colds and ear infections, and sudden infant death syndrome. An estimated 150,000 to 300,000 cases of lower respiratory tract infections in children less than 18 months of age, resulting in 7,500 to 15,000 annual hospitalizations, are caused by secondhand smoke. A 1992 study of the urine analysis of several hundred children exposed to smoke revealed significant levels of cotinine, the major metabolite of nicotine.

Secondhand smoke involuntarily inhaled by nonsmokers from other people's cigarettes is classified by the U.S. Environmental Protection Agency as a known human (Group A) carcinogen, responsible for approximately 3,000 lung cancer deaths annually in U.S. nonsmokers.

John R. Garison is the CEO of the American Lung Association. This article was delivered in a speech on November 20, 1998.

Reprinted by permission. The American Lung Association, www.lungusa.org

More than 22 million American women are smokers. Current female smokers aged 35 years or older are 12 times more likely to die prematurely from lung cancer than nonsmoking females. More American women die annually from lung cancer than any other type of cancer; for example, lung cancer will cause an estimated 67,000 female deaths in 1998, compared with 43,500 estimated female deaths caused by breast cancer.

As smoking has declined among the white non-Hispanic population, tobacco companies have targeted both African Americans and Hispanics with intensive merchandising, which includes billboards, advertising in media targeted to those communities, and sponsorship of civic groups and athletic, cultural, and entertainment events.

The prevalence of smoking is highest among Native Americans/ Alaskan Natives (36.2 percent), next highest among African Americans (25.8 percent) and whites (25.6 percent), and lowest among Asians and Pacific Islanders (16.6 percent). Hispanics (18.3 percent) are less likely to be smokers than non-Hispanic blacks and whites.

Tobacco advertising plays an important role in encouraging young people to begin a lifelong addiction to smoking before they are old enough to fully understand its long-term health risk. It is estimated that at least 4 million U.S. teenagers are cigarette smokers; 24.6 percent of high school seniors smoke on a daily basis. Approximately 90 percent of smokers begin smoking before the age of 21.

The American Lung Association coordinates the Smoke-Free Class of 2000 in response to former Surgeon General C. Everett Koop's call for a smoke-free society by the Year 2000. We are focusing on the three million children who entered the first grade in 1988, to increase students' awareness and education, to focus media attention on a tobacco-free society, and to place tobacco-use prevention education programs in school health curricula. These students are now in high school and the focus is on empowering them to become peer educators on the dangers of tobacco and tobacco control advocates in their communities.

Workplaces nationwide are going smoke-free to provide clean indoor air and protect employees from the life-threatening effects of secondhand smoke. According to a 1992 Gallup poll, 94 percent of Americans now believe companies should either ban smoking totally in the workplace or restrict it to designated areas.

Employers have a legal right to restrict smoking in the workplace, or implement a totally smoke-free workplace policy. Exceptions may arise in the case of collective bargaining agreements with unions.

Nicotine is an addictive drug, which when inhaled in cigarette smoke reaches the brain faster than drugs that enter the body intravenously. Smokers become not only physically addicted to nicotine; they also link smoking with many social activities, making smoking a difficult habit to break.

In 1995, an estimated 44.3 million adults were former smokers. Of the current 47 million smokers, more than 31 million persons reported they wanted to quit smoking completely. Currently, both nicotine patches and nicotine gum are available over-the-counter, and a nicotine nasal spray and inhaler, as well as a non-nicotine pill, are currently available by prescription; all help relieve withdrawal symptoms people experience when they quit smoking. Nicotine replacement therapies are helpful in quitting when combined with a behavior change program such as the American Lung Association's Freedom From Smoking® (FFS), which addresses psychological and behavioral addictions to smoking and strategies for coping with urges to smoke.

For more information call the American Lung Association at 1-800-LUNG-USA (1-800-586-4872), or visit our web site at http://www.lung-usa.org.

LUNG ASSOCIATION DISAPPOINTED AS STATES APPROVE TOBACCO DEAL (STATEMENT OF JOHN R. GARRISON, CEO, AMERICAN LUNG ASSOCIATION, NOVEMBER 20, 1998)

The American Lung Association is disappointed that the states have settled with the tobacco industry. The deal concedes far too much to Big Tobacco and provides far too little to protect public health.

Fortunately, the war against the disease and death caused by tobacco use is not over. Skirmishes continue on battlefields all across the nation. From state house to courthouse, from city hall to the halls of Congress, we have the tobacco industry on the run. The industry still faces lawsuits from health insurance providers, labor union health plans, class actions brought by injured smokers, and thousands of individual cases. Local ordinances to provide smoke-free environments were only dreams a decade ago but are becoming the norms today. Earlier this month, voters in Oregon and Maine reaffirmed their smoke-free laws despite an onslaught of tobacco industry cash that funded their opposition. The Minnesota settlement forced the release of thousands of documents that have detailed a decades-long trail of deceit by the tobacco industry. And, despite a multimillion-dollar misinformation campaign by the tobacco industry, California voted to increase its cigarette excise tax by 50 cents.

There also is growing recognition that Congress can no longer ignore a product that kills more than 420,000 Americans and millions more around the globe each year.

These successes energize the American Lung Association and its allies as we pursue aggressive action at the state and local levels. The American Lung Association will continue to lead this fight. We will work to ensure that the Medicaid dollars the states recover through the settlement are invested in protecting the public health and eliminating tobacco use.

It is unfortunate that the states have decided not to confront the tobacco industry in the courts. But the American Lung Association will continue its fight on the local, state and national levels to protect our children from the deadly lure of tobacco.

The American Lung Association has been fighting lung disease for more than 90 years. With the generous support of the public and the help of our volunteers, we have seen many advances against lung disease. However, our work is not finished. As we look forward to our second century, we will continue to strive to make breathing easier for everyone. Along with our medical section, the American Thoracic Society, we provide programs of education, community service, advocacy and research. The American Lung Association's activities are supported by donations to Christmas Seals® and other voluntary contributions. You may obtain additional information via our America Online site, keyword: ALA, or our web site at: http://www.lungusa.org.

Issue 21
Foreign Policy: Terrorism

INTRODUCTION

Although terrorism has been an internationally recognized problem through-out recorded history, America has paid close attention to it only recently. The Long Commission, established to discover how terrorists could so easily have blown up a marine barracks in Lebanon, reported in part as follows:

On October 23, 1983, a large truck laden with the equivalent of over 12,000 pounds of TNT crashed through the perimeter of the U.S. contingent of the Multinational Force compound at Beirut International Airport. It penetrated the Battalion Landing Team headquarters building and exploded, destroying the building and resulting in the deaths of 241 U.S. servicemen. The Commission found that the command had failed to take adequate security measures commensurate with the increasing Threat Level in Lebanon. While the Battalion Landing Team had adapted to the threat from indirect fire and sniper attack, it had created an exploitable vulnerability by concentrating troops in the headquarters building. Importantly, the Commission determined that as the mission of the U.S. contingent to the Multinational Force and the threat to that contingent changed over time, no senior U.S. commander had compared the evolving mission with previous guidance to determine whether it was adequate to protect the Marine force on the ground. This was exacerbated by a complex, unwieldy chain of command.

The Beirut bombing was America's rude awakening to the realization that terrorism is a growing menace to life at the end of the twentieth century. The Long Report was followed by the Inman Commission Report, which "developed 90 recommendations on improving the protection and hardening of U.S. Government facilities overseas."

Terrorist incidents in Nigeria and Saudi Arabia and the downing of Pan Am flight 103 over Lockerbie, Scotland, in 1988 gave impetus to Defense

Department task forces and readiness planning, and the bombing of the Murrah Federal Building in Oklahoma City on April 19, 1995, brought home both the probability and the difficulty of preventing more attacks.

What is the official U.S. policy concerning terrorism? Is it adequate?

As you read the articles, consider the following questions.

Discussion Questions

1. On what assumptions is U.S. antiterrorism policy based?
2. How much restriction of our own freedom are we willing to allow in order to provide more protection from terrorism?
3. To what extent is terrorism a political problem, as opposed to a military or a police problem?

For more on this topic, visit the following websites:

http://www.terrorism.com
The Terrorism Research Center

http://www.fema.gov
The U.S. Federal Emergency Management Agency

http://www.ict.org
Institute for Counter-Terrorism

http://www.thecourier.com/manifest.htm
The Unabomber Manifesto (from *The Courier* Electronic Edition)

Report on Terrorism

U.S. DEPARTMENT OF DEFENSE

RESPONDING TO TERRORISM

The number and lethality of international terrorist incidents directed against U.S. interests increased last year. The Riyadh and Al Khobar bombings in Saudi Arabia resulted in the largest number of U.S. fatalities at the hands of international terrorists since the December 1988 downing of Pan Am 103 over Lockerbie, Scotland. Terrorist violence represents a serious threat to U.S. personnel, facilities, and interests around the world.

Terrorism remains a complex phenomenon spawned by a mix of factors and motivations. Loosely organized groups of radical Islamics, such as those that carried out the bombing of the World Trade Center, pose a growing challenge. Established entrenched ethnic, nationalist, and religiously motivated terrorist movements continue to operate and have been joined by groups that espouse new causes and ideologies. Despite the collapse of the Soviet Union and international communism, leftist ideologically-based terrorists continue to operate. State sponsors of terrorism, particularly Iran, pose a significant continuing threat. Other state sponsors such as Syria, Libya, Iraq, and Sudan, although more cautious, provide safe haven and other forms of support to a variety of terrorist movements.

The world is in a period of transition and flux as it moves from the relative stability of the bipolar model to a new political order which has yet to be defined. The disintegration of the Soviet Union and the collapse of the East European communist regimes produced a power vacuum that has enabled nationalist, ethnic, and religious forces long thought dormant to reassert themselves and contribute to the volatility of the post–Cold War era. Violent militant Islamic elements, often with the help of state sponsors, now operate worldwide and have a demonstrated global reach.

Local and regional conflicts, famine, economic disparity, mass movements of refugees, brutal and corrupt regimes, and the increasing porosity of national borders contribute to instability—fueling a frustration and desperation that increasingly finds expression in acts of terrorism. Ready access to information and information technologies, coupled

Source: Chapter 9, Department of Defense Annual Report, 1997.

with the ability to communicate globally via the Internet, fax, and other media, provides terrorists new tools for targeting, fundraising, propaganda dissemination, and operational communication. Just as the established political order is in a state of fundamental flux and transition, so is terrorism and the challenge it presents to the United States, its friends, and its allies.

TERRORISM: A PHENOMENON IN TRANSITION

The terrorist threat has changed markedly in recent years, due primarily to five factors: the disintegration of the Soviet Union; changing terrorist motivations; the proliferation of technologies of mass destruction; increased access to information and information technologies; and the accelerated centralization of vital components of the national infrastructure, which has increased their vulnerability to terrorist attack. DoD [Department of Defense] expects that the majority of terrorism directed against U.S. targets will be tied to ethnic and religious conflicts. It will be primarily urban in nature, often occurring in capital cities. Terrorism for the foreseeable future will remain a weapon of choice for governments, groups, and other parties to conflict.

Traditionally, terrorist movements that affected U.S. security interests were politically motivated, and even the most brutal groups usually refrained from mass casualty operations for fear of alienating their political constituencies and potential recruits. Today, religiously motivated terrorism is increasingly ascendant. Religious zealots, when members of a terrorist group or cult, usually exhibit few such constraints and actively seek to maximize carnage. An additional threat comes from religious cults that view the coming millennium in apocalyptic terms and seek through violence to hasten Armageddon. DoD anticipates that as the year 2000 approaches, such movements will become increasingly prevalent, prominent, and lethal.

The proliferation of weapons of mass destruction and the availability of individuals schooled in their design and construction represent another development that impacts fundamentally on the nature of terrorism. The fragmentation of the former Soviet Union and the lack of adequate controls on biological, chemical, and nuclear technologies have resulted in a flood of buyers eager to purchase lethal material from an expanding black market or from rogue states. Added to this volatile mix are scientists and technicians prepared to sell their skills to the highest bidder.

An emerging and significant threat is represented by improvised biological, chemical, and nuclear devices that exploit technologies that once were the sole preserve of world and regional powers. The potential to decimate large population centers and wreak havoc on an unprecedented scale has devolved from nation states to groups and even individuals. The possibility of a biological Unabomber and all that implies is a fast approaching reality. Proliferation enables those who were traditionally at the margins to play a major role on the world stage. Improvised weapons of mass destruction will likely prove to be the great equalizers of tomorrow, providing the means for the disaffected and deranged to directly impact on the core interests of world powers.

FUTURE TERRORISM

Religious zealotry creates the will to carry out mass casualty terrorist attacks; proliferation provides the means. It is this nexus of will and means that has forever changed the face of terrorism. Traditional forms of terrorism like car bombs, assassinations, suicide bombers, and aircraft downings will undoubtedly continue, but their impact will diminish as the public becomes increasingly inured to such operations. In a world of competing headlines, terrorists will find it necessary to escalate the carnage in order to maintain their ability to intimidate and terrorize. As a result, increased experimentation with improvised biological, chemical, and nuclear devices may be expected as a means to rivet public attention and thereby advance the terrorist agenda.

Paradoxically, progress has made key elements of the national infrastructure increasingly vulnerable. These elements include telecommunications, energy distribution, banking and securities, transportation, military/defense, water supply, emergency services, and public health.

As countries modernize, they become increasingly dependent on sophisticated technologies, with computers both running and linking vital, once disparate systems into a national infrastructure. Because of its complexity and interdependence, infrastructure presents unique targeting opportunities to a technologically sophisticated adversary. Complex national infrastructures are vulnerable because they all have critical nodes or choke points that, if properly attacked, will result in significant disruption or destruction. The attack may be computer generated or rely on more conventional assaults employing truck bombs, dynamite, or cable cutting to unleash a chain of events in which a service grid, pipeline, or air traffic control system collapses in a cascading effect.

Major power failures that black out large parts of the country, systemic problems with the air traffic control system, and breaks in highly vulnerable gas and oil pipeline systems are covered in detail by the press, discussed on radio talk shows, and dissected and analyzed on the Internet. Terrorists, as part of the attentive public, are increasingly aware that the national infrastructure represents a high value and vulnerable target.

Technological advances may have the unintended consequence of increasing system vulnerabilities. For example, fiber optic cables enable phone companies to use a single line to carry tens of thousands of conversations that not many years ago would have required thousands of separate copper cables. The results have been greater efficiency, better service, and lower costs; however, there is a downside. Progress has heightened infrastructure efficiency, but the resultant reduction in redundancy has produced vulnerabilities that make U.S. infrastructure an increasingly attractive terrorist target. International banking and finance, transportation, the electric grid, the gas pipeline system, computer links and services, and more than 90 percent of all DoD communications are dependent on the telephone system. Major disruptions in service can be caused by an errant backhoe operator or an enterprising terrorist.

COMBATING TERRORISM: THE DOD RESPONSE

DoD divides its response to terrorism into two categories. Antiterrorism refers to defensive measures used to reduce the vulnerability of individuals and property to terrorist acts. Counterterrorism refers to offensive measures taken to prevent, deter, and respond to terrorism. Both fall under the rubric of Combating Terrorism. Force Protection is the umbrella security program involving the coordinated efforts of key U.S. departments and agencies designed to protect military and civilian personnel, their family members, and U.S. property from terrorist acts.

In response to the recent tragedies in Saudi Arabia, the Joint Staff established a Deputy Directorate for Combating Terrorism under the Director of Operations, Joint Staff. The Directorate is charged with the mission of supporting the Chairman and the Joint Chiefs of Staff in meeting the nation's security challenges as they relate to combating terrorism now and into the next century.

DoD also has been a leader in recognizing the vulnerability of the national infrastructure. To obtain a better understanding of the nature and extent of the problem, the Under Secretary of Defense for Policy on March 9, 1995, established the Infrastructure Policy Directorate. Its primary responsibilities relate to infrastructure warfare and information assurance. The Directorate has briefed senior government and cabinet officials and is conducting an in-depth examination of key infrastructure elements to determine how they interrelate and how best to protect them from attack. A series of working groups have been established to ensure continuity of effort.

To meet the challenge, the Deputy Secretary of Defense in August 1996 established the Critical Infrastructure Protection Working Group

(CIPWG) to support actions directed in Executive Order 13010, Critical Infrastructure Protection, which was signed by the President on July 15, 1996. The CIPWG addresses issues related to threats and vulnerabilities of the defense infrastructure and information systems, develops recommendations for assurance technologies and procedures, and examines roles for DoD in infrastructure protection and assurance.

Antiterrorism

In recognition of the changing nature of the terrorist threat, DoD on August 27, 1996, established the Antiterrorism Coordinating Committee (ATCC). The committee meets monthly, as well as on an as needed basis. Its purpose is to identify issues that affect force protection, exchange ideas and information, and develop policy recommendations. It also serves a valuable function by providing a synergism that enhances the effectiveness of DoD's antiterrorism planning. The Assistant Secretary of Defense for Special Operations and Low-Intensity Conflict and the Joint Staff Director for Operations co-chair the ATCC Senior Steering Group. Meetings are attended by representatives from the Services; the Joint Staff; the Office of the Assistant Secretary of Defense for Command, Control, Communications and Intelligence; the Defense Security Assistance Agency; the Defense Intelligence Agency (DIA); and other DoD elements as required.

To further the exchange of knowledge and experience, for the past seven years DoD has sponsored the Annual Worldwide Antiterrorism Conference. These conferences not only draw on the expertise of the U.S. antiterrorism community but on an international array of security, intelligence, and law enforcement specialists who offer new insights, perspectives, and recommendations for action. Each conference focuses on a particular theme and specific force protection issues. The 1996 theme was changing the terrorism mindset. Conference participants explored ways to make antiterrorism increasingly proactive rather than primarily defensive and reactive. They devoted considerable effort to the critical examination of terrorist attacks and the lessons learned. A conference report forwarded to Secretary Perry contains detailed recommendations for consideration and implementation.

To better prepare for the terrorist threats of the future and how they might impact on U.S. security interests, DoD in 1994 prepared a major study entitled, Terror-2000: The Future Face of Terrorism. The aim was to forecast the nature of the future terrorist threat, projecting significantly beyond the traditional one year timeframe. The study drew on the expertise and experience of American and foreign terrorism experts in an effort to anticipate changes in terrorist targeting, tactics, strategies, and capabilities. Many of the core predictions have come to pass and others appear increasingly likely. Central to the study were recommendations on how best to meet the future terrorist threat.

In response to the November 1995 bombing in Riyadh, Saudi Arabia, Secretary Perry established the Antiterrorism Task Force. The task force was directed to develop a plan of action to eliminate complacency and significantly enhance the security of DoD and DoD-associated facilities and personnel worldwide. The task force forwarded 22 major initiatives and recommendations to Secretary Perry, who approved an implementation plan on July 15, 1996. The more recent Downing Report, which examined the June 1996 bombing of Khobar Towers, produced a second set of recommendations. These have fundamentally changed the way DoD does business with regard to antiterrorism.

As a result of these two tragedies, a number of initiatives have been implemented. On September 16, 1996, Secretary Perry issued a revised Directive 2000.12, entitled DoD Combating Terrorism Program. This directive mandated Department-wide combating terrorism standards. In recognition that intelligence is the first line of defense, steps are being taken to improve its collection and use, and to get the intelligence product into the hands of the local commanders. DIA is engaged in an aggressive long-term collection and analytic effort designed to provide the type of information that can aid local commanders detect, deter, and prevent terrorist attack. Close working relationships between DIA and other members of the national intelligence community are being made even stronger, and intelligence exchanges with U.S. friends and allies have been increased. Other members of the national intelligence community are being made even stronger, and intelligence exchanges with U.S. friends and allies have been increased.

To better protect the public and U.S. military forces from the consequences of a chemical or biological terrorist attack, the Commandant of the Marine Corps established a Chemical/Biological Incident Response Force (CBIRF). Formed in April 1996, the CBIRF is uniquely qualified to perform consequence management in an environment contaminated by chemical or biological agents.

In addition to DoD's accelerated focus on combating terrorism activities, steps are being taken to improve overall force protection. These include giving local commanders operational control over force protection; strengthening cooperation with host nations; raising funding levels of force protection programs, particularly in the area of antiterrorism; making the Chairman of the Joint Chiefs of Staff the focal point for force protection activities, including initiatives to standardize antiterrorism and force protection training for deploying forces; and realigning certain force protection responsibilities from the Department of State to the Department of Defense. In addition, antiterrorism will be made a special interest item for inspectors general throughout the Department, and the

Defense Federal Acquisitions Regulations will be changed to ensure antiterrorism readiness of DoD contractors.

Counterterrorism

Counterterrorism refers to DoD's offensive combating terrorism capabilities. These capabilities provide means to deter, defeat, and respond vigorously to all terrorist attacks against U.S. interests, wherever they may occur. Resources allocated to these sensitive activities have been significantly increased, and efforts are underway to maximize readiness so that U.S. counterterrorism forces are trained and equipped to meet any challenge posed by future forms of terrorism. U.S. counterterrorism forces receive the most advanced and diverse training available and continually exercise to maintain proficiency and to develop new skills. They regularly train with their foreign counterparts to maximize coordination and effectiveness. They also engage with counterpart organizations in a variety of exchange programs which not only hone their skills but also contribute to the development of mutual confidence and trust.

CONCLUSION

The war against terrorism will be a protracted conflict. It is war in which there are no front lines and in which terrorism's practitioners have intentionally blurred the distinction between combatants and noncombatants. Terrorism differs from traditional combat because it specifically targets the innocent and, as a result, is particularly repugnant. Because each terrorist group and the challenge it represents are unique, DoD must work with the interagency counterterrorism community to develop a flexible response that is a mix of political, economic, military, and psycho-social capabilities, tailored to meet a broad range of challenges and threats. Terrorism is more than the bomb and the gun. It is a struggle that ultimately is fought in the political arena and, as such, is also a war of ideas and ideologies. Combating terrorism requires patience, courage, imagination, and restraint. Perspective is essential. Overreaction and bombast play into terrorist hands. Good intelligence, a professional security force, and a measured response are necessary. Most important for any democracy in its struggle against terrorism is a public that is informed and engaged, and understands the nature of the threat, its potential cost, and why the fight against terrorism is its fight too. It is how well the United States meets this challenge that will determine the winners, the losers, and the price paid by each.

The Terrorism Trap

RICHARD J. BARNET

We badly need an anti-terrorism policy that fits reality, not hyped rhetoric.

The war on terrorism was a linchpin of Bill Clinton's foreign policy rhetoric during his re-election campaign, and at his first post election press conference the President has put it high on his list of international responsibilities. In August at the Democratic convention the President thundered against so-called rogue states that were out to spread panic and destruction in the United States. A week later the Administration proclaimed U.S. missile attacks on Iraq to be a courageous blow against terrorism. At the United Nations General Assembly Clinton called upon the members to "isolate states that refuse to play by the rules we have all accepted for civilized behavior." The Leader of the Free World is recasting himself as Leader of the Civilized World.

The rhetoric is seductive. In a chaotic world for which the United States has yet to articulate clear goals, other than opening up economies everywhere to private investment, protecting access to cheap resources and staying top dog in the next century, international terrorism serves as the successor myth to international Communism. The idea that the Soviet Union was waging a relentless worldwide struggle to destroy the "American way of life" was critical for enlisting public support for almost fifty years of cold war. As easy as it was in those days to label even anti-Communist reformers as Bolsheviks (Mossadegh in Iran, for example), designating a brutal Middle Eastern or African government a rogue state is even easier because the criteria are vague and they are capriciously applied. (One would think that a state that has armed, trained and supplied torturers in other countries and published manuals for assassins would qualify, but nowhere on the State Department's list of rogue states has the United States ever appeared.) The Clinton Administration, boasting of its unique role as "sole remaining superpower," seeks to legitimize its increasingly unilateral approach to foreign policy by proclaiming the United States the global avenger of terrorism.

The war on terrorism is being used not only to unite the country behind a confused foreign policy but also to polish the President's image. Who dares speak of youthful draft-dodging when the leader of the civilized world is hurling missiles at rogues in Iraq? Who has the nerve to

Richard J. Barnet is a fellow of the Institute for Policy Studies. He is the author (with John Cavanagh) of *Global Dreams: Imperial Corporations and the New World Order* (Simon & Schuster).

Reprinted by permission. *Nation*, Dec. 2, 1996. Vol. 263, Issue 18, p. 18–21.

question why the United States maintains a military force far more powerful than that of any conceivable combination of enemies when there are more than a half-dozen certifiable rogue states threatening the fragile order of the post cold war world?

But encouraging panic about international terrorism has dangerous consequences. The most obvious is that it creates a receptive political climate for curbing civil liberties. The country has already been sufficiently alarmed to enable Clinton and the Republican Congress to push through the Terrorism Prevention Act, a legislative cocktail boosting the powers of the federal government to exact the death penalty, limit appeals of convicts on death row, deport suspect foreigners and wiretap U.S. citizens—all in the name of making us feel safe.

It is worth remembering the extreme reactions to sporadic violence that dot our history. A few anarchist bombs sent in the mail to prominent citizens triggered the Palmer Raids of 1920, when about 4,000 people were arrested in a single night, many without warrants. A spate of protests, unrest and bombings in the sixties and seventies led to a burst of domestic spying in the Kennedy, Johnson and Nixon eras, culminating in the infamous COINTELPRO, a vast illegal intelligence operation aimed at the left, the Black Panthers and those who opposed the Vietnam War. Public fear of unpredictable violence has been used by political leaders again and again to justify centralization of authority, stripping away of citizens' rights, surveillance and executions. Even as both major-party candidates condemned Big Government and promised its disappearance, politicians in both parties call for still broader government powers and increased expenditure to fight the global war on terrorism.

A second consequence of the Clinton anti-terrorism posture—it scarcely deserves to be called a policy—is that it isolates the United States. As the Administration proclaims its duty to act alone against rogue states, it is infuriating other countries whose help is needed for any serious effort to reduce the risk of terrorist attacks around the world. The unilateral decision to punish Iraq has resulted in collapse of the coalition that was supposed to guarantee the good behavior of Saddam Hussein. The heavy-handed measures recently enacted to compel unwilling allied governments and foreign corporations to enforce U.S. anti-Cuba policy is already making it harder to secure international cooperation to discourage and punish acts of terrorism.

But the most disturbing aspect of Clinton's handling of the terrorism issue is that the President is giving a hyped version of reality, one that is at odds with the Administration's own published reports. True, deliberate acts of violence designated as being "against U.S. interests" abroad rose from sixty-six to ninety-nine from 1994 to 1995, and the number of U.S. citizens killed in such attacks jumped from four to twelve. Yet according to the State Department's most recent annual report, "Patterns of Global Terrorism," published this past April, world-wide deaths due to acts of international terrorism have in recent years declined, from 314 in 1994 to 165 in 1995.

The report finds no evidence that North Korea has sponsored attacks since 1987. Syria, although it "has permitted Iranian resupply of Hezbollah via Damascus" and "provides safe haven and support" for several terrorist groups, has not been directly involved in planning or carrying out any attacks for the past ten years. Hafez Assad's regime "continues to restrain the international activities of some of these groups." Nor has Cuba been known to sponsor any international terrorist incidents in 1995. The report concludes that except for Iran, the "premier sponsor of international terrorism," the other rogue states largely refrained from planning, supporting or executing acts of terrorism. Phil Wilcox, State Department coordinator for anti-terrorist attacks, points out that the "long-term trend toward a reduction in international terrorism continues." But Cuba, Iran, Iraq, Libya, North Korea, Sudan and Syria remain on the official list of countries supporting "state terrorism."

No evidence has been produced or even alleged to exist that a foreign government was involved in the three most publicized explosions of the past two years in which U.S. civilians were killed: the Oklahoma City bombing, the downing of T.W.A. Flight 800 (if it was a deliberate act) and the bomb that went off at the Olympics in Atlanta. Saudi Arabian officials claim to have hard evidence of Iran's complicity in the June bombing of a U.S. military housing complex in Dhahran, in which nineteen members of the Air Force were killed, but according to *The Washington Post*, U.S. officials are skeptical because the Saudis have not fully shared the details of their investigation with the F.B.I. The Saudi government appears to be manipulating the information to serve its domestic political purposes. Five days before this fall's elections Defense Secretary William Perry declared, "We have reached no conclusions about who was responsible."

The State Department contends that the isolation of rogue states and increasing international cooperation to apprehend, extradite and punish perpetrators of political violence is responsible for the decline over the decade in state-sponsored terrorism against U.S. interests. There may be something to this, although the more likely explanation is that in the post–cold war world even unfriendly governments see no advantage in stirring up the United States. Iran still has a policy of supporting Hezbollah operations and of assassinating dissidents living abroad, but neither U.S. condemnation nor sanctions have deterred the regime from stepping up its efforts.

Like many other activities in the post–cold war world, terrorism is being privatized. The evidence supports the view that very few bombers of public places are now in the service of governments—fewer, certainly, than in the cold war years. They may work for a political movement, a crime ring or, as more of them are claiming, for God. Practitioners of violence increasingly work for religious sects and political movements (largely ethnic and mostly on the right). The private market in conventional weapons has greatly expanded. The Internet offers instruction in conventional bomb-making to all users. The Anarchist Cookbook explains that making "a bomb capable of blowing the walls out of a building is easy. You can find what you need in grocery stores, hardware stores and farm supplies."

President Clinton's message about terrorism is that the problem is of foreign origin. But in fact most of the acts of random violence that victimize Americans are committed not by dark-skinned foreigners in ski masks but by fellow citizens. Over the past ten years bombings and attempted bombings in the United States have nearly tripled, increasing from 1,103 in 1985 to 3,163 in 1994. The targets are political or racial. *The New York Times* reported in August that over the preceding two months "white, lower-middle class suburban people in Georgia, Arizona and Washington" were arrested as perpetrators or attempted perpetrators. The rash of bombings of black churches over the past two years sends a clear racist message. In Spokane, Washington, a Planned Parenthood office was bombed, and across the West a variety of government buildings occupied by the hated Forest Service, Bureau of Land Management and Internal Revenue Service have been attacked.

Some of our home-grown terrorists belong to militias or other gun-worshiping organizations. These groups have a variety of agendas: They don't like gun control. They don't like the federal government messing with their land, or land they think should be theirs. They don't like paying taxes. They don't like abortions. They hate black people, Jews, gays, foreigners. They are energized by violence. They have a holy mission.

The shadowy figures who set off bombs in airplanes, office buildings and shopping malls have succeeded in introducing all sorts of people to the possibility of their own sudden death. But shoppers and airline passengers face negligible dangers compared with the daily risks of living in crime-ridden, despairing neighborhoods in which there are no jobs. The President would rather talk about Qaddafi, Castro and the mullahs in Iran, however, than deal with the causes of the violence, hopelessness and fear that prevail in neighborhoods a few blocks from the White House. If he wants to revive decaying inner cities he has to acknowledge that they will not be lifted up by either the Internet or global trade.

What constitutes a reasonable strategy to discourage or prevent terrorist acts is not a technical question. It is a political question that involves the weighing of risks and interests. How much freedom and privacy should be sacrificed in the name of security? That should be a prime subject for public debate rather than a decision arrived at in secret negotiations between governments, police, airlines and makers of so-phisticated bomb-detection systems.

We need a less superficial and biased understanding of the problem we label as terrorism, a calmer assessment of how much of a threat it is and a more serious effort to understand its causes. For starters, we need a much less fuzzy definition. Guerrilla attacks, political assassinations, bombings and kidnappings are lumped together even though their causes and objectives may be very different, as are strategies for discouraging them. The United States fired missiles at Iraq for mistreating people living within its borders and for violating a U.N. resolution; at least a hundred other countries qualify under this weak justification for bombing.

Hyped rhetoric, though it may serve the President's purposes, does nothing to discourage attacks. Indeed, as *The Economist* has observed, "The whole point of the terrorist act is to provoke a reaction disproportionate to the act itself." The more panic a terrorist bomb sets off, the greater the success. Hamas's triumph in the recent Israeli election, when it provoked the downfall of Shimon Peres, is a classic example.

For a terrorist group with one consuming passion (as in Hamas's determination to derail the Middle East peace process), violence is an effective weapon because the panic it creates can change public attitudes in ways that serve the group's goals. But a state, however heavily armed, is at a disadvantage when it lashes out violently in response. Airstrikes and economic sanctions are blunt instruments that neither punish the planners and perpetrators of terrorist acts, who know how to fade into the night, nor discourage further violence. Both are far more likely to hurt innocent people and fuel murderous rage against governments reacting in such a manner. Assassination attempts invite retaliation in kind even when they do not succeed, and they expose the emptiness of claims to moral leadership. Exactly because the United States is so powerful, so wealthy and (because of our extraordinary dependence on complex technology) so vulnerable to politically inspired violence, the Administration should be promoting policies that would make the establishment of a genuine rule of law a real possibility. Of all nations, the United States has the most to gain in the long run from delegitimizing violence as an instrument of political change.

But pushing an anti-terrorist policy that seeks to break the cycle of violence would mean that the United States could no longer set its own rules or commit acts on the territory of other nations we would brand as terrorism were they to take place on our own.

Another Inauguration Day approaches, and the country badly needs a more effective policy, one that better fits reality: State-sponsored terrorism from abroad is declining. Ideologically tinged home-grown violence is growing. Our national security policy, based overwhelmingly on the threat and use of violence, not only legitimizes the violence of terrorists in their own eyes and in the eyes of their supporters, it also advertises the impotence of the United States. The overwhelming emphasis on instruments of violence as moral, acceptable, indeed inevitable, guarantors of security creates a self-perpetuating culture of violence and insecurity.

By continuing to spread weapons around the world, the United States and its competitors in the arms trade are expanding the opportunities for anyone with a grievance to bring death, destruction and terror to random victims anywhere, including here. By ignoring the opportunity to achieve significant nuclear and conventional disarmament that the end of the cold war provides, the United States is signaling that despite the weakness of military adversaries, we will continue to base our security on the greatest preponderance of military power the world has ever known.

A demonstration by the United States of a serious willingness to eliminate nuclear weapons could jolt the world into a radical reversal of the arms race. Were the next administration to make dramatic moves—not just promises—to reduce our dependency on violence in the name of security, it would have an electrifying impact around the world. The comprehensive test ban, signed in September after almost forty years of negotiation, could have been the key to a new era of disarmament had it been preceded by radical cuts in nuclear stockpiles. It still may not be too late. Would it end "terrorism" as the State Department defines it? No. But it would help create a climate for a lessening of political violence.

As for domestic terrorism, the conservatives' relentless bashing of government and the foolish decision of most Democrats to run away from the opportunity to debate what it is and what it ought to be—giving bipartisan credibility to the absurd notion that government is something to demean and to hate—create a hospitable political culture for violent, anarchist fantasies. Ever since the Oklahoma City bombing, pursuit of the militias by federal authorities is looking more and more like another exercise in investigative overkill. In its zeal to prevent terrorism it appears that the government is increasingly basing indictments on what suspects say rather than what they do, and that government informants may be encouraging them to engage in criminal conspiracy. All this strengthens the views of the militiamen that they have found the right enemy. Armed with the Terrorism Prevention Act, the Clinton Administration, in the name of national security, strikes out ineffectually abroad and at home hacks away at our historic freedoms.